Kol Kore Ba Midbar

The writings of Rabbi Roger Pavey from *The Bulletin* 1991–2007

Congregation Agudas Israel would like to thank everyone involved
for their dedication and assistance.

Janet Eklund

Steven Goluboff

Ursula Acton

Patricia Pavey

Don Ward

The Board of Trustees of Congregation Agudas Israel

and

Dr. Lou Horlick, who was the driving force behind this project.

This publication was funded by a generous gift from

the Estate of Richard, Martha and Irene Blum.

ISBN 978-0-9686315-0-8

Congregation Agudas Israel
715 McKinnon Avenue
Saskatoon, Saskatchewan
Canada S7H 2G2

FOREWORD

ROGER VICTOR PAVEY was born in 1939 in Kidderminster, a poor working class area in Worcestershire, England. His parents, Ellen and Harold, were carpet weavers. During WWII, Harold was killed when Roger was only two years old.

Roger did very well at school. His mother encouraged him, and as well as being a good student, he became a voracious reader (something he continued to be all his life). He became head boy and captain of the cricket team at King Charles Grammar School. He loved cricket as much as he loved studying.

"Postwar Britain was not an easy place to grow up in," says Karen Armstrong in her autobiography, *The Spiral Staircase*. "Young Britons... who came to maturity in this twilight confusion of austerity, repression, nostalgia, frustration, and denial wanted not only a different world but to be changed ourselves." Roger was certainly one of them. Education was enormously important to him. At 17, he left for London where he studied history at the School of Oriental and African Studies (University of London). He had intended to become a history teacher but met and fell in love with Miriam Walker, a Jewish student, and was encouraged to become a Rabbi. He attended Leo Baeck College and was ordained Rabbi in 1967. In his 70th birthday sermon, Roger said, "I survived while millions died. That is why I became a Rabbi."

After Roger was inducted into the West Central Liberal Jewish Synagogue in London in 1968, the Paveys moved to Southend on Sea where Roger worked as Rabbi at the Southend and District Reform Synagogue and teacher at the Jewish day school. Their two sons, Jonathan and Daniel, were born there.

Looking for more challenges and opportunies, the Pavey family moved to Canada in 1980. Roger was Rabbi first at Congregation Shaarei Zedek, Saint John, New Brunswick, then at Ahavas Isaac Synagogue, Sarnia, Ontario, before coming to Congregation Agudas Israel, Saskatoon, Saskatchewan, in 1988. During all his years as Rabbi, Roger also taught in Religious Studies at various universities. He also was an eager participant in multi-faith activities.

Miriam died in a car accident in 1989. Roger married Patricia Yates, a librarian, in 1991.

In 2002, Roger was presented a Golden Jubilee medal on the 50th anniversary of H.M. Queen Elizabeth II, for "outstanding achievement and contribution to Canada."

Roger retired from Congregation Agudas Israel in 2007 and in 2008 he was made a Fellow of the Leo Baeck College.

Until his untimely death in 2009, Rabbi Pavey led a weekly discussion group, Lunch and Learn, at Congregation Agudas Israel. It was through this group that Dr. Louis Horlick came to know and admire his Rabbi, and the group continues under his leadership.

Patricia Pavey

TABLE OF CONTENTS

1996

1997

2003

2004

A Full-Time Commitment

Heading into summer, a time for relaxation. Many of us are disappointed by the outcome of the Ahenakew hearings, but his career as a vicious anti-Semite has been exposed for all to see.

Summer Dominated by War

A war once unleashed has led us into a world dominated by fear and foreboding. We feel compassion for all who suffer.

Need Member Involvement

Rabbi Pavey calls for more regular involvement of our members in services. He will be curtailing his participation in our Synagogue activities because of his physical limitations, and hopes that we can find another Rabbi to fill the gap. He will remain in Saskatoon and do what he can. However the Lord helps those who help themselves. Rabbi Pavey's comment: "I am completely selfish here: I want and need a viable Synagogue where I can come and daven"

2007

Retired Life is Full

The New Year is an occasion for partying, sharing with family and friends and resolutions to improve one's behaviour. This year is the 40th Anniversary of Rabbi Pavey's Smichah from Leo Baeck College. Despite his infirmities, Rabbi Pavey still feels that he has much to give to the congregation. He will continue to be available for special occasions and for teaching at the Lunch and Learn Group, and for guiding and helping potential Jews by Choice. He says, "Ending one chapter of my life as a Rabbi and the beginning of another in January is an experience that is 'Janus like.' I have to cope with slowing down while also feeling that I have much left to give."

Our Tour Begins

Rabbi and Mrs. Pavey leave on an extended tour – a retirement present from Agudas Israel for his many years of devoted service as our Rabbi and spiritual guide.

Six Core Jewish Values

Rabbi Pavey defines six core Jewish values. They are study (Talmud Torah), social justice (Tikkun Olam), spirituality (Tefilah), ethnicity and culture (Yiddishkeit), Israel and anti-semitism, and the Shoah. "Those who hate us shall not have the last word."

The God Delusion – Part I

There has been a clutch of books recently denouncing religion and preaching the virtues of atheism. This one is the best, and Dawkins' critique of religious belief is well founded. Rabbi Pavey writes a review of Richard Dawkins' controversial book The God Delusion*. Dawkins' case against religion is hard to debate. However, the fundamental attitude of a religious person should be not belief, but faith which impels an eternal quest to discover "what is out there." The search for completeness gives richness, meaning and hope to life.*

Less Talk – More Action

Rosh Hashanah is early this year and the High Holy Days will soon be upon us. We need to prepare for the profound experience that the annual moral and spiritual audit imposes on us.

2008

2009

RABBI ROGER PAVEY'S ESSAYS FROM *THE BULLETIN*

1992

1993

1994

2002

2003

2004

2005

2006

2007

Congregation Agudas Israel Mourns Rabbi Roger Pavey

This season of the year is the most important in our calendar. It is the time of the New Year and the Day of Atonement and the ten Days of Awe. It is the time when all Jews – however far they have strayed from Jewish tradition – try to come back to the Synagogue.

These are Festivals that speak of universal themes. They move us to meditation and prayer as we contemplate our lives. We think about what has happened to us and to our community in the past year; we consider the past and the future; we ponder life itself; we assess the values by which we live. The theological words in our Prayer Book "sin" and "atonement," "repentance," "revelation," "judgement," they all boil down to that. We are not really satisfied with life and how we live, we worry about what we have done wrong, we are deeply troubled at how far we fell from what we could be. We do so many things wrong, even if for the right reason, and we do not do so many things that we should do. We are acutely aware that we are not really all that good as Jews or as human beings. We have hurt others and ourselves.

So we need to drop out of life for a while. We need to cleanse our hearts and minds and souls. We need to come together as a community and help each other, each in the silence of our own soul, to come to terms with life, and to strive sincerely to be better and to do better.

It is a process that requires great courage. While it is easy to fool others, it is foolish to fool oneself, and impossible to fool God. It is painful to be honest, to strip away all the pretences and rationalizations that make life that much easier to live, and to confront the reality of what we are as against what we should be.

These, therefore, are days of solemnity, a time to reach down into the depths of our hearts and souls, to confess what we did and where we went wrong, then to feel and know what it is to be wrong, then to determine to put it right when we can, and finally to go back into the world just that little bit better.

And we have to start with the little things that hurt the big people, the people that we love and whom we take for granted and can so easily hurt. A good start is a renewal of gentleness and kindness and patience between husband and wife and parents and children and friends. A kind word spoken gently, a harsh word left unspoken, these are the building bricks of a better world.

Jews are a small minority in the western world. Especially is this the case in Saskatoon, where 600 or so Jews live in a community of 200,000 non-Jews. There are times when this minority status is brought home to us with especial force. The month of December with the Festival of Christmas poses a particular problem to us, as families and parents, and as Jews with non-Jewish friends.

First and foremost, let is be said forcefully that Hanukkah is not and cannot be a Jewish substitute for Christmas. In any competition, Christmas has its hands down, for Hanukkah is a minor, non-Torah, occasion, *not* a *hag* but a *zman*. It is not even a holiday. Any attempt to inflate it, understandable as it may be, is doomed.

There are basic themes in common, but, whereas the Christian observance is of the very essence of Christian faith — centred on the birth of Jesus – Hanukkah is *not* an essential observance of Judaism. Quite the contrary; it is not for nothing that the Maccabees are so unpopular in the Talmud. Second, because Christmas must be so significant for a Christian, it obviously can have no place in the faith and life of a Jew. The attitude of a Jew to Christmas must be great respect for the faith of a Christian friend for whom Jesus is the incarnation of God, but a refusal to share that faith.

But the claim is often made that Christmas is a winter time of celebration and warmth, of family unity and goodwill, so not really "Christian." Indeed, it has become a sort of secular party and fantasy time that owes more to Walt Disney and Charles Dickens than to Jesus.

What an insult that is to Christianity as a major world religion! A pagan yule dedicated to greed and moneymaking is less attractive than a religious festival filled with faith.

A Jew stands outside a Christmas that celebrates the birth of Jesus, though with profound respect. The trivializing of Christmas as a marketing ploy does not deserve that respect.

How, then, shall we approach the "December dilemma" as Jews?

1) We must wish our Christian friends joy in their deeply significant Festival;
2) We must not help to debase that Festival by secularizing it by over-indulgence, over-shopping, spurious "goodwill," and the tinsel trash of Dickensian invention, even less the absurdities of Disney reindeer and fat men in red coats;
3) We must not try to create a Jewish Christmas out of Hanukkah — Jewish children must live with their differences;
4) We must not try to blur religious differences by having Minorot and Christmas trees together in an ecumenical no-man's land;
5) We must sensitize our Christian friends to their own faith, so that we are not deluged by decorations and carols that are supposedly "non-religious", and so

that our schools can not waste a whole month of the year in activities that are religious yet non-religious;

6) We must not, in respect for another faith, take part in Christmas celebrations, any more than we would wish to observe Easter, or would have Christians fasting on Yom Kippur.

If members disagree, I would welcome a reasoned response.

THE GULF WAR *Vol. 1, No. 2 - February/March 1991*

War is the ultimate tragedy. It is a symbol of the futility of human pretensions to civilization. It is the reality of human suffering.

It also creates as many problems as it solves.

I write this as war begins in the Gulf. It is my prayer that when you read it the world will be at peace again. But as I write, my heart is full of conflicting emotions: thanks that Israel appears to be safe, sorrow for the dead, anger at the sheer stupidity of humankind; most of all a numbed anguish. And as I look to the future, the pain continues. How thin is our veneer of civilization!

A world that has defeated Saddam Hussein, at a cost that will become known as time passes, will still be a dangerous world. One dictator and psychopath will have gone from the scene, many more will still arise. There will remain tasks to be done. We will have to bind up wounds; we will have to rebuild shattered lives; we will have to heal human relations; we will have to rekindle human hopes and faith. And that will be the most difficult of all.

Over the months that led inexorably to war when we ran like lemmings to the edge and over, I spoke in Services regularly about the implications, culminating on the Friday evening before the war with the question addressed to us all of the nature and depth of our own Jewish commitment. Looking forward to the task of creating peace, that surely must be the basic question.

There are, and will be and should be, legitimate differences among Jews. Not one of us can, or should, assume that any one way is the only proper way to be Jewish. As pressures grow on Israel and on Jews, as grow they will, we must be careful to retain our flexibility, our tolerance. We have seen the consequences in the suffering of ordinary people, of intransigence and pride, and nationalistic and egocentric hubris.

Our faith in our destiny as a people of God to be a blessing to all the families of humankind is being challenged. We must the more firmly base ourselves on God and on our covenant with God. In the dark days now and that lie ahead, we must return to God and walk with humility and faith that we may enrich our lives and the lives of others.

May the Shield and Guardian of Israel, guard and keep Israel and all humankind, and give us hope and courage. And may God strengthen all Jews in our devotion to our destiny and purpose.

"Shalom, Shalom, la-rahok ve la-karov, amar Adonai." Peace, peace, to the far off and to the near, says the Lord.

PASSOVER *Vol. 1, No. 3 - April/May 1991*

The Jewish religious experience is one lived in history. Time and time again we are enjoined to remember. And that is not just a matter of empty nostalgia or antiquarian interest; it is an injunction actually to relive, to re-enact the past in our own lives. The past lives on and the present is a promise for the future.

Nowhere is this more marked in Jewish life than at this time of the year. Pesah is the Festival above all when we are required to relive our history. We ourselves come out of Egyptian slavery as we re-enact the events of the Exodus at the Seder.

We become free again each year as we put away all forms of leaven from our homes. Nissan is the first month of the year and we begin a new year, a new life, as we burn and sell our hamets for Pesah, the leaven a powerful symbol of the *yetser ha ra*, the bad side of our lives that we purge with our leaven, as we begin a new springtime of freedom – spiritual as well as physical.

But freedom is not anarchy, for that would deny the rights of the poor and the weak. Nor is freedom easily or definitively won. We have to go through the desert as our forebears did and struggle to reach Sinai. And there we confirm our freedom in covenant with God as we accept Torah. In each generation, each year, we come forth again from Egypt and we discover our true freedom as a people of the covenant called to the destiny of Service to God and to humankind.

So it is that Pesah is bound to Shavuot, Exodus to Sinai, freedom to the covenant, and we count each night: the *sefirat ha omer*.

So it is too that from Nissan 27 to Iyar 4 we pass in one week from Yom ha Shoah to Yom ha Atsma'ut, from the depths to the heights, from Holocaust to Israel, from death to rebirth. "*Mima'amakim keratikha*, from the depths I call to you Lord" (Psalm 130); "*Zeh ha hom asah Adonai*, this is the day that God has made, I will rejoice and be glad" (Psalm 118). That is Jewish history. At this time of the year especially do we relive our history.

Patricia, Jonathan, Danny and I wish you all a wonderful and fulfilling Pesah blessed with joy and peace. *Meavdut le herut, miyagon le simhah* — from slavery to freedom, from sorrow to joy (Haggadah).

*Extracts from the Sermon of May 3 at the service honouring
the wedding of Rabbi and Mrs. Pavey.*

Traditionally, a Rabbi is a teacher, an expert on the halakhah. Nowadays, a Rabbi has become a clergy person and has adapted much of that role.

Within the Jewish community, that involves being a priest, that is leader and facilitator of public worship and the rituals of the life cycle; a pastor, that is counsellor and guide to members in need; a preacher/teacher/educator; an example of Jewish values lived.

To the outside community, a Rabbi is an ambassador (representative of Judaism and the Jewish people); and a minister of religion who exemplifies shared religious and moral values with other clergy, shown in the quality of personal and family life.

A Rabbi is subject, therefore, to demands that, almost by definition, are impossible to fulfill. Obviously she or he must have scholarship, a deep commitment to Judaism and the Jewish people, moral and spiritual sensitivity, a personal religious life, and a stable family background.

The community also develops a personal relationship with its Rabbi. Inevitably, the Rabbi enters the lives of members and they enter the Rabbi's life. Friendships are made. Others, partly from principle, partly from the chemistry of human relationships, come to dislike the Rabbi as a person. Criticism of the Rabbi's discharge of the role, and as a person is inevitable. Criticism can be especially devastating to a Rabbi and very dangerous to the community. The very sensitivity that makes a Rabbi a better Rabbi makes that Rabbi all the more open to hurt when misunderstood or criticized.

This community responded to my own personal pain when Miriam died. The acts of friendship will always remain with me. The many individuals who showed deep love and friendship to me then meant and mean more to me than they will ever know. So many members were and are extraordinary in their ordinariness.

When I discovered a woman who could share life with me, and who could rekindle love and hope and courage, I was overwhelmed that so many were able to thank God with me for the blessing I had been given, and to welcome her into the community and into their hearts.

Many found that hard. Not because it was hard to see in Patricia an out-going friendliness, concern and compassion, but because they were not sure about their Rabbi marrying a Jew-by-Choice. But this community, to its immense credit both as Jews and as human beings, accepted. They discovered a warm and loving woman who accepted them as they accepted her. Some, perhaps, find it hard still, but this community has been generous and caring to its Rabbi and family.

Relations between Rabbi and community are like a marriage. Even with a good *shidduch*, both partners must compromise, must accept imperfection, must have compassion for themselves and for each other.

We have learned through tragedy that a Rabbi is not just an employee, but is so important to the community that it is worth the community's being patient, accepting, healing wounds; that the community is not just an employer, but individual people who need their Rabbi as a whole person; that they both need a generous and loving spirit, so that they may nurture him, so that he may nurture them.

HIGH HOLY DAYS *Vol. 2, No. 1 - September/October 1991*

The Holy Days are a time to pause, to take stock, to consider seriously the important things in life and the values by which we live.

As we live under the pressures of the ordinary, we easily lose sight of the extraordinary. Everyday life takes its toll on our spiritual sensitivity. We need refreshment of the soul as much as we need refreshment of the body. And so we have this pause time, the *Noraim*, the Days of Awe, so that we can stand back a little from life and look at it and ourselves in the light of the real values.

But the exercise works only if we prepare ourselves. No one can seriously expect that the profound spiritual experience of the Holy Days can work in isolation. If we come to the Services "cold," we will contribute nothing more than our physical presence and take away exactly what we brought.

Our preparation is on several levels.

Obviously, when the Holy Day Services are an integral part of a life determined by the rhythms of Judaism as faith and practice — prayer, study, observances — they are most likely to work for us. But even if this optimism is unrealistic, all is not lost if we make a serious effort. And that, after all, is *teshuvah*; consideration of the value by which we want to live so as to give meaning, purpose, and added richness to life; mending our relations with each other as family and community and making ourselves better.

Perhaps we might then put aside some more time to work out the implications of those themes in terms of *tikkun olam*, healing, in relation to ourselves and others. For example, we could profitably consider our family life and determine to improve it in some small way; or we could try to work out a regimen of our own personal spiritual growth, a program of meditation or study, for instance.

Finally, at the very least, we could read parts of the Prayer Book so that we do not arrive at the Synagogue totally unprepared. After all, Jews spend a long time in Synagogue over these special days!

May we find renewal of spirit in our Services this year, and may we be granted a year of peace and joy and deepened Jewish meaning.

Patricia, Jonathan, Danny and I all wish you a good and sweet new year. May you be inscribed and sealed for good!

Kol Kore Ba Midbar   *Vol 2, No. 2 - November/December 1991*

People have asked about the heading that I use for my *Bulletin* column.

It means "a voice calling in the wilderness." Applied to the Prophets of ancient Israel, it sums up the experience of Jews throughout history. It is a fact of history that Jews have proclaimed the message of Prophetic Judaism to the world as a voice in the wilderness, calling for the return to God and justice without having political power. Little by little, and painfully, the world has responded.

The Jewish destiny is to be a *Kol Kore Ba Midbar*. It is an apt title for the Rabbi's column.

During the Holy Days there were special themes that I tried to develop in the sermons.

My major concern was to try to bring alive the possibilities of prayer as an adventure in spiritual growth. I tried to show that the words of our Prayer Book should not be taken literally as descriptions of reality, but should be seen as poetic insights into reality that enable mind and soul to take wing. They are *Midrash*, in the Rabbinic phrase "sparks from the anvil."

I also tried to correct some of the negative aspects of modern Jewish communal life.

We Jews are all too often too introverted and concerned with our own agenda rather than with the universal moral demands of our heritage, and I cited our lack of support for the Food Bank as an example.

We are often almost paralysed by an obsessive fear of anti-Semitism and allow it to influence our attitudes and acts out of all proportion. We are in danger of losing touch with reality.

We are exercised too much by the problem of out-marriage. When a Jew marries a non-Jew spouse, it can be a threat to Jewish survival. But it can also be a potential strengthening of Judaism if the non-Jew is attracted to Judaism. But do we value the positive aspects of Judaism enough to sell it in an open spiritual market? In other words, are we Jewish for negative reasons or positive ones?

I hope that the experience of the Holy Days remains with us as a force for a positive commitment of faith in Judaism.

It would seem that the hopes for a new era of democracy in Eastern Europe are increasingly becoming a disappointment as the former USSR and its satellites collapse into political and economic chaos.

The process unleashed so recently of transition from dictatorship to democracy, from a closed society to pluralism, has resulted in growing instability and a rebirth of ethnic hatreds, with implications that could be disastrous to the whole world.

This is particularly so from a Jewish perspective. Jews are concerned with events in Eastern Europe even more closely than others because so many North American Jews trace their origins back to there, and because there still exists a substantial Jewish population.

Of course, many other Canadians have roots in Eastern Europe. There is a fear that people will be tempted to play out old hostilities and become involved in the events in the old country despite their Canadian citizenship. A Canadian of Polish background was a candidate in the Presidential election in the new Poland. Our Prime Minister's wife was born in Croatia.

Jewish experience in Eastern Europe has been a disaster. Jewish life in Poland, Russia, Ukraine and Rumania, was wonderfully productive and rich, but played out against a background of violent and systematic anti-Semitism, totally different from the wounding but non-violent contempt for Jews endemic in Western Europe. The culmination of that experience was the Holocaust. Eastern Europe is a Jewish graveyard, its soil soaked with Jewish blood.

Can we, as Jews, therefore rejoice in a newly independent Ukraine, or in a Poland or Rumania already proclaiming once again many of the anti-Jewish slogans hitherto held in check by dictatorship, much as we do rejoice in the arrival of democracy?

Can we, as Jews, rejoice in an independent Croatia when we remember the last time Croatia was independent, a Nazi puppet-state that engaged in enthusiastic genocide — of Serbs, Jews, and Gypsies; and that today still rejoices in the title Ustasha — the Nazi militia of those days — and one of whose first acts was to vandalize the Jewish cemetery in Zagreb?

Our concern must be twofold: we must encourage the hope for growth of genuine pluralistic democracy; We must do everything possible to support our fellow Jews, whether they go to Israel or choose – for all sorts of reasons – to stay.

May 1992 be for us, for all Israel, and for all humankind, a year of peace when all our hopes and dreams may be fulfilled for good.

The Many Roles of a Rabbi

Vol. 2, No. 4 - March/April 1992

The roles of any Rabbi are numerous. They involve responsibilities to Judaism and the Jewish community both in general and specifically in a particular community. A Rabbi discharges them as best he or she can in relation to need and his or her own abilities. No Rabbi can possibly do all things equally well, and his or her order of priorities may differ from that of others.

A Rabbi, it seems, is concerned within the congregation with education (at all stages of life), with the conduct of services, the facilitation of life pattern rituals from birth to death, and with the pastoral care of members in need. He or she represents Judaism and Jews to the outside world, and here in Saskatoon, Conservative Judaism (not Orthodox or Reform) to the Congregation. In short, he or she is minister/preacher/pastor/ambassador as well as Rabbi.

We have to stress communication in order to enable the Rabbi to serve the needs of the community well. For example, when people are admitted to a hospital they are questioned on religion — their affiliation and whether they wish to receive a clergy visit. If they do not answer those questions, their names do not appear on the computer print-out that goes to the Chaplain's office, and their names will not be given to our secretary in her weekly phone round to the hospitals. In other words, some of our members are not visited because they are not known to be in hospital at all. Please, therefore, if you go into hospital, make sure that the Synagogue knows and the Rabbi knows. And similarly with events in life that you would like to solve.

Please also bear in mind that Rabbis are human, they make mistakes, have problems, go through crises, just like everyone else, especially so when supportive colleagues, friends or family are at a great distance. Like everyone else, Rabbis function best when they receive as well as give a little tender loving care.

This year is the 25th anniversary of my receiving *semicha*, ordination, and my family and I would like to share some of the specialness with our congregational family. Watch *The Bulletin* for announcements.

We are already looking forward to spring. Purim will shortly be upon us and a month later, Pesah. Time for renewal begins as we recover from winter and look to the future. The lessons of our Spring Festivals speak anew to us each year: the rebirth of nature and the rebirth of hope, freedom, human dignity and the covenant of God.

Patricia, Jonathan, Danny and I wish you all a happy Purim and a joyous, liberating and empowering Pesah, *hag Kasher vesameiah*.

Talmud Torah, the study of Torah, is an essential part of Judaism. It is a mitsvah incumbent on every Jew throughout life. To that end, we as a community sponsor programs of Jewish education for both children and adults. Thanks to the devotion of many of our members who teach, our programs are well received and often successful.

However, while all our community accepts unreservedly that educational programs should be available for our children, and that parents have an obligation to ensure that they are used, there is not always the same receptive attitude to adult education programs, and that, further, there is an obligation on members to take advantage of such programs. There seems at times to be a feeling that Jewish study (and, indeed, Jewish observance) is something for the children.

There may be two real fears that lie behind a reluctance to engage in Jewish study for adults.

First, there may be a fear of embarrassment that lack of knowledge will become obvious and interfere with learning. After all, those who come together to study probably are very knowledgeable already in Hebrew and Judaism. This is not necessarily so. There is a wide range of Jewish knowledge and commitment in any group. Not everyone was born a maven. We all have to start somewhere. And no one can learn unless prepared to make a start from where they are rather than some mythical point where they think everyone else already is. All it takes is courage.

The other fear is of being challenged. We become very comfortable with our knowledge and the attitudes and biases that we have grown up with. Perhaps we know that what we learned about Judaism was a little, a long time ago, and we should go further. But our ways of looking at our tradition and understanding it are fairly fixed, and we fear that new learning might challenge what we have come to be comfortable with. For instance, our study group has been considering women and Judaism. Many may feel that this is a challenge to what they believe to be traditional Judaism. However, challenges to our knowledge, faith and commitment do not go away merely because we ignore them. We need knowledge to cope with questions and to confront the changes of life. Study is not a threat, it is a resource. Again, all it takes is courage.

So, especially as we celebrate Shavuot, *Zeman matan Toretenu*, the time of the giving of Torah, I invite all members to join us in study in our Tuesday Lunch and Learn sessions, and on Saturday mornings for study in worship.

Zil gemur – come and learn!

SUMMER – A TIME FOR REST Vol. 2, No. 6 - July/August 1992

Summer is the time for rest and relaxation, the time for recharging batteries and refreshing mind, body and soul after a hard year. And this has been a hard year for our community.

We have been busy. We have celebrated the huge success of the Silver Spoon Dinner; we have shared the simhah of Bnot Mitsvah; we have maintained our religious and educational life as a congregation of Israel.

But we have also mourned too many deaths and wept too many tears with too many of our families. May this summer be a respite for the body and also the beginning of a healing for the spirit.

Let us not forget, though, as we enjoy our well-earned vacations, that Judaism continues and the Synagogue is not closed for the holidays. We have a duty to maintain a minyan at all Services. And even if we are travelling, local Jewish communities, wherever we may be, would be pleased to welcome us as visitors to their Shabbat Services. (They, too, may need a minyan!)

And whether we are at home or travelling, there are Jewish books to read, and our own spiritual life to be nourished in prayer and study.

I shall be in England from July 12 to August 3. In emergency, members can contact Rabbi Truzman in Regina.

Patricia, Jonathan, Danny and I wish all our community a relaxing summer bringing enrichment of both body and soul. May we all rest, relax and enjoy.

RABBI PAVEY VISITS LONDON Vol. 3, No. 1 - Sept/October 1992

We are beginning to turn again from thoughts of holiday rest and refreshment to the rigours of everyday living. A new year is about to start, in our work lives, in the lives of young people returning to school or beginning their advanced education in universities and colleges. It is a time to look back over the past year and to consider all that has happened to us, all that we have, hopefully, learned; and to look forward to a new year, with some trepidation as we turn a new chapter in life, but also with hope and renewed faith.

It is no accident that our tradition celebrates the New Year at this time. As the seasons change and summer gives way to autumn and the hot days shorten and cool, nature itself reminds us that it is time to take stock. Our Holy Days call upon us to change pace, but allow us to take a little time before we plunge into the hectic days ahead to make a spiritual and moral inventory, to consider what the values are on which we want to base our lives so that we may live the future perhaps a little

RABBI PAVEY ✿ 11

better than we did the past.

I am personally reminded of this. I spent part of the summer in England and had the chance to preach at the Synagogue in London where I was active as a student, and to attend the Synagogue in Birmingham that I attended in my growing-up days. There were many poignant memories, many reminders of the past, many signs of the continued changes of life. Ou sont les neiges d'antan!

At the same time, it is now 25 years since I received simicha, Rabbinic ordination. This is therefore a time in my life to pause and to look back over a long period of time in my career. It is also, though, a time to look forward to the future, to reconsider what brought me to want to be a Rabbi and what impels me to stay a Rabbi. Memory, introspection, planning, merger.

I am sure that similar thoughts are in the minds of many members as they begin to prepare themselves for the New Year after the lazy days of summer — thoughts of past, present and future.

Such thoughts are the basis of our spiritual preparation for the Holy Days. May we all use this time so that we can learn from the past and go forward into the future with renewed faith and courage. Together may we build a better life for us all.

May this New Year be for each one of us, for all Israel and for all human begins, the beginning of a life of peace and blessing. May God renew for us all a year of sweetness and hope. Patricia, Jonathan, Danny and I wish all the community a *Ketivah ve Hatimah Tovah*, a year of peace, health and happiness.

KINDLING OF LIGHT *Vol. 3, No. 2 - November/December 1992*

It would be remiss of me not to look back on the major Festivals, first to thank all who worked so hard and did so much to make them so successful, and second to pray that their influence may abide with us as a continuing force in enriching our lives and the life of our community.

It is also time to look forward. After the welcome break of Heshvan, we shall be anticipating Hanukkah with all that it means in terms of Jewish survival, and its simple but beautiful symbols. It is also a universal time, when we share with our non-Jewish friends the kindling of light in mid-winter darkness. In all the stresses and strains of life, the symbol of light, of kindling candles in the dark, is a statement of rebirth of hope and courage and of life itself.

As we follow the process of reconciliation around the world, especially here in Canada, following the Constitutional referendum, and in the peace process in Israel, our prayers are renewed at the time of Hanukkah. The events of our history that we remember then, of survival against all odds, strengthen those prayers. Miracles do happen, have happened and, with the partnership of God and humankind, will happen again.

A joyous Hanukkah to us all!

There are times to be critical of ourselves, and to look at what is going wrong and to try to put things right. But too much self-criticism is paralyzing and disempowering. There are also, therefore, times to look at what is going well. Not with any sense of complacency, for we can obviously always do better, but in order to target better our efforts for improvement.

And there are many things that we are doing in our community that really are very well done. We owe a debt of gratitude to the lay leadership that is steering the community through the waters of financial stability and prudence. The principal and teachers in the school are providing a good Jewish education for our children despite sometimes strident circumstances.

Our services are well attended and well presented. Our education program for adults is proceeding well. We are holding our own in terms of membership. We have Board members and committee members who are conscientious and committed. And as the survey has shown, many of our members are concerned and involved.

Sometimes though, it takes the outsider to see the broader picture; we who are involved from day to day often lose sight of the reality and become dispirited by problems that seem to loom so large when we should rather be encouraged by the answers that we are so often actually finding. The visits of Saranee Newman and Dr. Morton Segal were important to us, not just in themselves or in the quality of the time we spent with them, but also for the opportunity to see our community through their eyes. Their verdict was extraordinarily positive. We are a healthy congregation, well within the parameters of the Conservative Movement, and we have many areas of strength.

There is much still to be done of course; we are not complacent. These winter months when so many are away and programming is somewhat less hectic than it has been are the times when we are planning for the future. The input of those visits will be part of that process, as of course, will be the analysis of the survey. Sometime later in the year we shall be meeting together as a community in a Kallah based on the survey. Then we shall be able to look to the future and tackle our weaknesses together based upon our strengths.

To those who will be spending time away during the winter, we wish a restful vacation in the sun or on the ski slopes, and look forward to your return for Pesah. May the rest of us, condemned to the Saskatchewan winter, also find some refreshment of body and soul.

Now that we all know that I shall be remaining in Saskatoon as your Rabbi, there are three important things that I want to say to all our members.

First, I am deeply grateful for the confidence so many of you have placed in me. You have given me a vote of confidence that few people in any position are privileged to receive. President Clinton should have polled so well! It is a humbling experience and I hope that, together, we can work to strengthen our community and its commitment to Jewish life and values.

Second, to those who voted against me, let me say that I seek to serve as Rabbi of all the community. Your input into our life as a Synagogue is welcomed and valued, and your opinions are taken note of and listened to seriously. Please join with all of us to work to improve and enrich our Synagogue in an attitude of mutual respect and tolerance.

Third, I want to make clear what I see my role to be as your Rabbi in my sermons and teaching. We are a member of the Conservative Movement and our services and communal life adhere to those norms. However, it is essential that a Rabbi have freedom of the pulpit and not be only a mouthpiece for a particular point of view. Not everyone will agree with what a Rabbi says — nor should they. The Rabbi's task is to stimulate thought and discussion. Further, I see it as my role to facilitate dialogue between Jewish services and the community, and to bring to bear on our life insights from the moral and spiritual traditions of Judaism. I am, in short, a religious leader, not a political commentator or social worker or psychiatrist or institutional public relations officer. While I will use political events, for example, as illustrative, my prime concern as preacher and teacher is with the religious tradition of Judaism. I am as concerned as anyone with events in Israel and the world around us, but I have no more information about them than anyone else. I am not privy the Cabinet Room in Jerusalem. On the other hand, I do have area of expertise: our classical sources of faith, Torah. And my job as a Rabbi is to preach and teach Torah, to grapple with ultimate questions of faith, to open up possibilities of prayer and study.

I hope and pray that we shall work together to enrich Jewish life in Saskatoon, that personal rancour will give way to respect, that strong convictions will be moderated by tolerance, and that, as a result, our congregation will grow *my hayil le hayil*, from strength to strength.

Rabbis are supposed to be kind, gentle and long suffering, and when dealing with members as human beings in pain and need I am sure that we do try to be exactly that, even when dealing with people who are at time distinctly unlikable. However, when we are functioning as teachers and religious leaders of the community, to be kind, gentle and long suffering would be a betrayal of our calling.

I know all the reasons why people do not attend services, all the rationalizations and excuses. And I do try to be patient and understanding. But when a community of Jews cannot make a minyan for services at Pesah, I am no longer willing to make those excuses and understand those reasons; bluntly, this Synagogue's attendance for the Pesah morning services on the 1st and 2nd days goes well beyond pathetic; it was a *hillul ha Shem*.

Our members make every effort to prepare for the *seders*; those who religiously keep treif for the rest of the year become rigidly *kasher le Pesah*. But apparently in the eyes of the majority of Jews in Saskatoon, Pesah equals seders plus eating matsah for lunches at work; *Yom Tov Services* do not apparently exist.

And as a look to Shavuot, I come near despair about the state of Judaism here. Shavuot is not the best observed Festival of the Jewish year as it is. In the light of our Pesah attendance; it is obviously not worth opening the Synagogue for Shavuot.

Yet, Shavuot is a major Festival of our year. It is the second of the hagim, the harvest Festivals; it is the time of the giving of Torah. It encapsulates the very essence of our faith. On the eve, it is the custom to spend time in study to prepare to receive Torah, symbolized as we rise in the morning service to re-enact the giving and receiving of the Torah: *na-aseh ve nishma*, we will keep it and learn it. That is a custom that we observe in our community.

So I issue a challenge to all our members. Come to our Shavuot Services, let us pray, worship and study Torah together as a community. And, just for once, forget the cheap excuses: the office will carry on without you for a couple of hours, a couple of classes missed will not cause you to fail your exams, the warmth of community coming together to observe a Festival that expresses the very core of our identity as Jews is surely worth missing a round of golf for.

Or is it the question asked of me at Pesah by someone who travelled 2-1/2 hours to attend the service, what Saskatoon Jews really want to answer in the negative: "Don't Jews in Saskatoon think that Pesah is an important Festival?" Nu?

REDEDICATION OF LIBRARY Vol. 3, No. 6 - July/August 1993

On the weekend of May 28-30 we rededicated our community library, the Rev. David Avol Memorial Library. As part of the weekend, I made the following remarks during the Friday evening service.

We Jews are called "The People of the Book." It is interesting that the phrase actually comes for the Quoran, Sura 2, 111, 113, and is used often in other Suras. We have adopted the phrase as applicable to the Jewish people, because it really does reflect an important truth about the Jewish people and tradition.

For the very essence of Judaism is literacy and knowledge. After all, in a real sense the whole of Judaism is an attempt to answer the Prophet's question, "What does Adonai your God want from You?" So it is that the focal point of our worship is the reading of Torah, not only on Shabbatot and Yamin Tovim, but even on weekdays; as no more than three days are to pass without reading Torah, it is read on Monday and Thursday morning during the weekday Services. We know that there is no occasion when Jews come together that would not be marked by a *devar Torah*, a lesson from Torah. According to *hazal*, life should be equally divided between work, rest and study. Indeed, literacy was so important that the *Pirke Avot* says bluntly, "Lo am ha arets hasid," an illiterate cannot be religious.

There are two reasons for this emphasis on study. First, and foremost, to seek the answer to the Prophetic question, to enrich the quality of life by living as best we can as God wants us to live, both as individuals and as a community. Judaism has to demand of us an enquiring faith. It does not require of us blind faith or gullibility. Saadia Goan reminds us that Judasim does not require us to believe absurdities, and Maimonides comments that miracles weaken rather than strengthen religious faith and life.

The second reason is that study is a pleasure for its own sake, "*lishmah.*" The secular achievements of so many Jews in so many fields owe much to the fact that, for Jewish tradition, learning and study is a joy and a pleasure. It is fun to study! To exercise the mind is as important as to exercise the body.

And the scope of study is life itself. Judaism is concerned about the way we live in all its aspects, because we live in the presence of God. Religion, therefore, for Judaism is not confined to ritual or theology, or even ethics; it includes every part of life, even what we have come to call the secular. We can learn from non-Jews as well as from Jews. If the seal of God is, as our Midrash says, emet, truth, we have to remember that to come to know truth, we must have knowledge, and that knowledge may come from many sources. Therefore, a Jew should be at home in our classical sources, Bible and the Rabbinic literature, and also in philosophy, the whole range of human experience and knowledge. Nothing should be closed to the enquiring mind; as the Roman dramatist Terence puts it, "Nothing human is alien to me. Knowledge liberates the soul and nourishes the body, mind and spirit."

It is proper for us to take seriously our Synagogue library and the theme of books. It is incumbent upon us to study and to read as widely as possible, fiction as well as non-fiction, for we can learn much from the themes of Shakespeare. In learning we enrich life and we empower ourselves to grow as Jews and as people. *Talmud Torah keneged kulam*: Study is the core of everything.

TAKE STOCK OF OUR LIVES   *Vol. 4, No. 1 - Sept/October 1993*

So as will all things, the summer is coming to an end, and we begin to pick up the reins of normal life again. The office, the new academic year, the run of committees, the stress of schedules, the call of deadlines, are back with us. Holidays are over and gone, autumn is just around the corner, winter nearly upon us. If winter is here then can spring be far behind? Yet, certainly in Saskatchewan, the poet's question feels a lot more rhetorical than real.

So, thoughts are turning to a new year, for we Jews are heirs to a tradition that moves us to look back on the past and forward to the future in the autumn of the year, immediately after summer. It is now that we feel re-invigorated and re-energized for a new year. It is now, therefore, that Judaism impels us to take inventory of life.

Our tradition does not encourage navel-gazing and self-absorption. It encourages us to live life and get on with things. But it knows that there is a time to think carefully and seriously about the direction of our lives and the values by which we choose to steer. There is a time for taking stock, for thinking about what has passed, what is to come, what we have learned from experience, what we have to change, and what we must cling to more firmly.

We know that we have not been perfect: we are not expected to be perfect. But there were things that we did that we would rather not have done: they hurt others we care about, they were spiteful, cruel, and they made us poorer than we could have been. And there were things that we didn't do but should have done: there were so many missed opportunities to help others, to encourage rather than cut down, to be positive rather than negative. We could have been better than we were. Even if we stayed out of trouble and didn't actually do anything too morally horrendous, we still feel that we didn't use life fully, we weren't as good as we could have been. There is a feeling of regret, for what was done and what was not done. A regret embedded in a sense of the passage of time. We do not know how long we have on earth, but we do know that, however many years we may be granted in life, they are still too few to do all that we want to do, be all that we want to be, and to grow morally and spiritually as we want to. It is soon over and we fly away.

But mere regret for what we did and the opportunities we missed and the shortness of life is, itself, more self-indulgence and self-pity. Judaism stresses the positive. Regret must produce determination. The past is over and gone, nothing can being it back. The present gives us a chance to move on, to express regret, to come to terms with loss, and then to let it go as we go on to the future. But, with God's help, we can take with us a determination to learn from what has been so that what will be may be better, richer, nobler. We can change, life can change. It is for us to decide. It is for us make our lives. We can choose. And our tradition gives us richness of spiritual and moral weapons to use as we struggle to make those choices. As we come to the services for our New Year and for the Holy Days, it is for each one of us individually and all of us united as a community to determine to make those choices well and to use the resources of Judaism to become better, more sensitive, gentler and kinder. Hazak, hazak ve nithazek. Be strong and let us strengthen each other.

Roger and Patricia, Jonathan and Danny wish all our members a new year filled with health, happiness, fulfilment and peace: a year of renewal of hope and courage; a year of spiritual and moral growth; a year of healing and rebirth for us, all Israel, and all humankind.

A BUSY COMMUNITY   *Vol. 4, No. 2 - November/December 1993*

We were privileged to experience moving and inspiring services for the Holy Days and *Sukkot*. We owe our thanks to our members who worked so hard to that end, and especially to our Ritual Committee who organized the services; to those who read and chanted *Haftorah*; and of course, to Cliff Hendler who led our services once again with the spiritual sensitivity that he has trained us to expect.

Sukkot Services were also well attended and of high quality. This year we enjoyed a new Sukkah, and we are grateful to our hard-working House Chairman, Harold Gonick, and Adam Melnychuk who actually constructed our new Sukkah.

There is a natural tendency to relax after these strenuous three weeks, the highlight of the whole Jewish year. However, being Jewish is a full-time calling, and we have to continue to live our Judaism, day by day, Shabbat to Shabbat, even after the peak experience of the Holy Days recedes into the past. Our congregational calendar is full. We are a busy community.

There is our Kallah. Every member is needed to help build a richer community. Judaism in Saskatoon will survive only if we all want it to and work for it.

There is our library. Without study, Judaism will stagnate. We need our informed, knowledgeable and Jewishly literate membership.

There is our study program. This year's Lunch and Learn sessions will meet on

Mondays at noon, starting on November 1st. Come, bring your non-meat lunch, and let us learn together. There is also a study session on Thursday evenings at 7:30, starting that week if you can't make it during the day. If you can't make either time, but still want to study, contact me and we'll see what we can do!

Still on the theme of learning, note that there will be two Friday evening services in November and December when the sermon will be replaced by a Question and Answer session. Ask questions, for unless we question we cannot learn.

And there are our services. Regularly, each Shabbat we come together to worship, to do what any Synagogue is all about — pray and study. Come and join us. We are sensitive to the needs of all our members, but we cannot know what you want nor can we be expected to take note of your Jewish needs unless you let us know directly and are involved in the ongoing dialogue of our Jewish life. No taxation without representation is a fine slogan; the reverse is perhaps even truer.

By the time this is published, we shall have elected our new government. Let us pray for God's blessing and guidance on our leaders, whomever we have chosen, in these difficult times for our country.

REFRESHMENT OF THE SOUL *Vol. 4, No. 3 - Jan/Feb 1994*

For many people, this time of the year is when they are at their lowest ebb, physically and emotionally, and perhaps also spiritually. Though it is true that the days are beginning to lengthen, the effect is not really yet obvious; and it is also true that we are now in the depths of winter, a winter that seems to stretch out into eternity.

All of us need a refreshment of the soul as well as the body at this time. And the brave little candles of Hanukah, with their wonderful message of light in darkness and renewal of hope and courage, seem to get easily lost in the gloom of January and February.

We can however, find some of the renewal that we are looking for at this time of the year in the wonder of books. Now is the time, more than any perhaps, when books can weave their magic most forcefully for us and we are most open to their message.

And while we are discovering the joys of imagination through books — the voyages of discovery as we travel the world and especially of course the hot beaches and warm seas of summer or reliving stirring events in history — while we do these things, let us not forget our own heritage and tradition. This is the time, too, to find our way to our Synagogue library, and discover the joys and riches of Judaism and Jewish history and faith.

And not merely because there is delight in reading Jewish books and discovering

Jewish faith, culture, history and tradition, the wide wonders of the creativity of our people. But also because there is a wondrous and never-ending source of inspiration and of spiritual growth. There is food for the soul in learning from Jewish books.

But we must of course remember that Judaism is not only reading and learning, it is doing as well. The living of the Jewish life is also a refreshment of the soul and that we especially need in the dog days of winter. So, in addition to coming to the Synagogue to browse in our library, perhaps you might consider coming to the Synagogue also to attend a Shabbat Service. And, without coming to the Synagogue at all, you might like to introduce the lighting of the Shabbat candles into your home as a family, just as Jewish families have done for millennia now. Making those links with others is a wonderful boost, a bright light in the darkness of winter, a warm fuzzy in the cold, a pleasant immunization against the burned out feelings of this time of year in Saskatchewan. Anyway, try it!

PURIM, PESAH AND SHAVUOT   *Vol. 4, No. 4 - March/April 1994*

In the depths of winter it is hard to remember that spring will return. Our Jewish calendar reminds us that the cycle of the seasons does continue. So, even now, we look forward to Pesah. Already we have celebrated Purim and we have learned yet again, as we do year by year, the wonderful lesson of survival against all odds. The machinations of the Hamans of our world are always finally defeated, and we, the Jewish people, like our forebear Jacob/Israel continue to limp through history, hurt, yet surviving undefeated.

So, we look to Pesah. For this is the lesson that we learn about the reason for our survival. The Jewish survival of the attempts of the Hamans to destroy us has a purpose and a meaning: we have survived the bloody events of our history because we are in a covenant with the Living God, we are to be *an or la goyim*, a light to the peoples. And at Pesah we are given freedom, the freedom that we learn is confirmed at Sinai seven weeks later at Shavuot when we accept Torah.

These three Festivals are a unit that retell each year the lesson of our history as a special people. At Purim we experience the joy of defeating those who would seek to destroy us, and we learn the importance of our survival. At Pesah we experience the joy of becoming free — free from superstition and the barriers that prevent human moral and spiritual growth. And at Shavuot we learn that that freedom is not just for us, it is important for all humankind as well. God doesn't play favourites: God's choice of us and our choice of God is covenant that is to bring a blessing to all people. Our survival and our freedom is somehow essential to God's purpose for the world.

We symbolize our Jewish faith in our observance. And at Pesah we are able to relive the events of our history through the very special observances of the time. At this time of the year even those Jews who are remote from Judaism as a living pattern become aware of their Jewish roots through the observance of the special dietary regulations. If, therefore, any member has any question about Pesah observance, the custom of *bedikat hamets* (the search for leaven), *mekhirat hamets* (the selling of all leaven to a non-Jew), or the halakhah and minhag relating to foods, please do get in touch with me directly, and I will be delighted to help.

Patricia and I and the boys wish all the community a *hag kasher ve sameah* (yes, this one really is a *hag*!)

PEACE IN THE MIDDLE EAST   *Vol. 4, No. 5 - May/June 1994*

As I write, we are all poised expectantly awaiting the outcome of the peace process in the Middle East. We are all hoping that that process has become irreversible: that, though there is much negotiation to come and there will be setbacks, there will be a lasting and just peace and this is now inevitable.

There are obstacles, of course, real and perceived. There are psychological and emotional problems, as seemingly intransigent enemies have to come to terms with seeing each other instead as, if not friends yet, at lease potential partners. There is fear and distrust, national pride and paranoia. We need to un-demonize our perception of each other, to see each other, Israelis and Palestinians, Jews and Muslims, as human, with human ideals and hopes and the human right to live in peace and dignity.

Nothing should be allowed to derail the peace process, whether individual acts of terror, groups with a vested interest in hatred, or religious or tribal triumphalism. Compromise is the essence of the human condition. This is not the arrival of good will and mutual acceptance; but it is the beginning of a process that, with patience and prayer, can become good will and mutual acceptance.

We are responsible moral agents. This above all, is the essence of our Jewish tradition. We cannot avoid responsibility for what we do and what is done in our name. To plead "insanity" is to do exactly that, it is to destroy the very base of civilization by cutting us free from the duty of moral choice and acceptance of responsibility. If we are not morally responsible by reason of insanity, there is no morality left.

Let us all, therefore, beware, lest any word or act of ours should upset this peace process. Speculation is easy: the advancing of a point of view is tempting. Perhaps what the peace process needs is actually a prayerful silence. Certainly we need less public posturing, less violence, fewer unconsidered words; for the result of these is a continuation of misunderstanding, hatred and violence.

May real peace, the peace that flows out of justice come soon. And from that peace may there come love. *Volechein yehi ratson - Ve omar Amen.*

It is inevitable that when one returns from a visit to another country there is a need to gather together experiences, thoughts, impressions, and to build a picture that will make sense of the bewildering differences in perception of reality through which one has passed. All the more so is the case with Israel, the land throughout history so integrally intertwined with the very identity of the people.

I suspect the instant reaction. By nature I am a cautious person who needs to reflect on experience and seek to understand it in a broader and deeper context. Further, I am a Rabbi, not a political commentator, and therefore must reflect on the longer term and the moral and spiritual significance of events, rather than on the passing scene as such. Nor am I a prophet who can foretell the outcome of events. I do not know whether the peace process in Israel will be successful. I hope and pray with all my heart that it will be, but I am neither optimistic nor pessimistic. I do not know what will be. And in our world that has seen the sudden demise of Communism and apartheid the unexpected has become exactly what we should expect. The Heisenbergian universe has come to pass, and we are awash in miracles.

Therefore, I want to share a few impressions and thoughts as to the long term, based on my visit and my reading. I should add that the purpose of that visit was two-fold: a holiday, but more specifically a holiday with a Jewish focus — a pilgrimage to Israel that I have been promising myself for many years, and now had the resources actually to do. My interest was as also two-fold: the land and the people, rooted in history, but also very much a part of the Jewish present and future. And, although both are important, my personal bias is toward people rather than place, and despite my training in archaeology and ancient languages, toward future rather than past.

We began our journey in style. A few minutes out of Heathrow our El Al Jumbo was struck by lightning — the starboard wing was hit twice. The impact knocked out the pilot's instrumentation, with the result that he did not know whether the wheels would come down for landing, and if they did, whether they would lock. So we made an emergency landing in Tel Aviv. Fortunately, the landing turned out to be normal. The crew was efficient and there was no panic. However, the fire trucks and ambulances that met us were certainly an unusual welcome to Israel.

We carefully interspersed hectic touring and periods of inactivity on the beach, though even the times of seeming inactivity were often opportunities to watch the passing world and to listen in on conversations. We managed to see and do almost everything that we wanted to see and do, and not to see and do everything that we wanted not to see and do. There are great advantages to not being on a tour, and even more, despite the remarkable facility of Israelis with English, to having enough

Hebrew to read and hear what is not being translated.

We went to all three major cities. Speaking for myself — and I would not presume to speak for Patricia — I did not like Jerusalem (and I will explain later why). I liked Haifa and was quite happy with Tel Aviv. We went to Masada and the Dead Sea, through the Galil (including a boat trip on Kineret), and visited a Druze village. We were in Hadera and Jerusalem the day before or the day after terrorist incidents; so, despite the determination of guides to encapsulate tourists, reality kept breaking through. Obviously, we visited the major sites, and the only one on our list that we didn't was the Israel Museum in Jerusalem. Some were better than we expected, such as the Eretz Yisrael Museum in Tel Aviv, others a disappointment, for example, Bet ha Tetsufot; and the exhibition of a painter called David Reeb in the Tel Aviv Museum of Art was a serendipitous discovery. Our hotel was excellent. Some things were marvellous value — the outstanding beer and the shwarma, for instance; others, an outrageous restaurant in Jerusalem, for example, were not. The bus system was cheap and efficient and a model for public transport.

My first reaction was that, despite terrorist attacks, we were safe. The police and army presence was ambiguous. Of course, this is two edged: on the one hand, we were safe, but on the other, it was a symptom of an underlying and omnipresent mailaise: violence, counter violence, and the danger of an incipient militarism.

In Tel Aviv or Haifa, the police and army presence was, of course, totally acceptable. On the West Bank, particularly as the border was closed because of terrorist attacks, the military presence, however necessary, contributed to the escalation of tension and was a symptom and symbol of the major problem that confronts Israel immediately. Our time in Bethlehem was not pleasant. But the same could be said of Nazareth within the Green Line. It will take time to repair relations between Jews and Arabs, regardless of whether the Arabs are Israeli citizens or not.

This, then, was the second reaction: an atmosphere of tension. As an illustration, our hotel suggested strongly to us it might be better for us to watch the Yom ha Atsmaut parade from the hotel roof than from the beach or street. And the manager locked the doors and refused to let his own children out to celebrate. As I watched young soldiers who looked barely Bar Mitzvah age, stopping cars in Bethlehem and frisking drivers and passengers, while I was grateful for the security, I was also chilled by the corrupting influence on human beings of violence and fear. *Ein b'reira*, there is no choice, but it remains in itself a threat.

However, there remains no option but peace. The process now begun must continue. But, it is not straight forward — there are people on both sides with a vested interest in conflict and hatred. And there are interpretations of religion that teach contempt for the other and tribal hubris. Baruch Goldstein did not spring to life and death out of a vacuum. Some, not all, of the *yeshivah* world has been teaching a message of Jewish superiority that has confused the moral boundaries.

The Kahane perversion of Judaism, though a minority within that world, has put down roots. Both Hamas and Kah are teaching a hatred and violence that is vicious and ugly, and also in the long run futile and suicidal. We are groping toward the beginnings of reconciliation and healing. Beware those who proclaim peace as they prepare for war, who believe that the path to peace lies, at best, in unconditional and humiliating surrender of the enemy; at worst, the enemy's extermination. And let it be said clearly; the Kahane followers like Goldstein, who shoot Arabs at prayer, and the Hamas gangsters who bomb and axe Jews on buses, are neither of them insane for insanity is defence of the indefensible, and abdication of moral responsibility: they are evil.

But if, with God's will, there shall be peace, there is another problem that must be confronted. Everywhere in Israel there are those whose Jewish identity is expressed through ultra-orthodoxy, a fundamentalism that sees the world in black and white, right and wrong, Torah and error, Jew and non-Jew — in which category incidentally they are sorely tempted to place fellow Jews whose vision differs from theirs. They wear the black business suit or caftan, the beard, the *peyot*. I do not speak of the many who wear *kipot* and live a traditional life style but who know that compromise is necessary. There are degrees to Jewish *meshugas*, from *Dati* to *Haredi* on the right, to *Hiloni* on the left. The ultras, the *Haredim*, are determined that Israel shall be a Jewish state, not as Herzl or Ben Gurion saw it as pluralistic democracy with a Jewish majority, in which Judaism would play a role, an essential role, but a role that would include many visions of Jewishness, but as a halachic, Torah-based, theocracy. To them, Judaism and democracy are incompatible, Jews and non-Jews cannot live together, God has given to Israel the whole land, and God will give victory by miracle to Jews though opposed by the whole world. The apocalyptic vision of the Haredim is one of tribalist violence, a violence directed at all outsiders.

There is a battle for the Jewish soul. And Israel is torn by a kulturkampf of polarized extremes. While we were in Israel statistics were issued showing that Jerusalem will have a majority of Haredim by the end of the century as the secular and traditionalist Jews leave and have fewer babies. The conflict with the Jewish majority, and also with the Muslim and Christian minorities, is probably inevitable. Israel needs a modern liberal vision of Judaism to ensure tolerance among Jews and to guarantee the survival of secular Israelis as Jews. Conservative and Reform Judaism is there and growing; and in the Israeli context there is no difference between them. But whether liberal Judaism in either form will be able to mediate between Haredim and Hilori in a way that the Datism cannot is moot. A revival of the non-halakhic Jewish spirituality is perhaps the greatest challenge of all, in Israel as much as here.

An even longer term challenge will be the very question of how we define our Jewish identity. If peace comes, as come it surely must, Israel's economy will boom and her economic and psychological co-dependence with the Diaspora will lesson. Both the Israelis and non-Israelis will have to reopen the dialogue with identity. And those whose Jewishness is defined second-hand through Israel will have to give up a negative and parasitic Jewishness for a coherent identity in the post-modern world. When Israel is secure and prosperous and at peace, as surely she will be, and when she grapples successfully with fundamentalism and the *sinat hinam* that ultra-orthodoxy of all religions injects into human relations, then we can no longer be Jews, merely because we identify with Israel; we shall have to rediscover Judaism for ourselves, just as the Israelis are doing.

Thirty years ago I was seriously considering *aliyah*. Now that I have experienced Israel, would I consider *aliyah* again? I have to say, no. I went to Israel because I wanted to. I wanted to put down roots in the past. I wanted to confront the Jewish challenges of the present and future. But ultimate questions of Jewish meaning, identity and purpose, confront us everywhere and there are ultimate answers nowhere. Places are not holy in themselves, but only insofar as they confront us with what lies beyond. When I stood at the Kotel, it was not to proclaim my Jewishness, nor to petition, even less to feel some link with the past; it was to know that I am a Jew anywhere, even in Jerusalem, even in Saskatoon. I said the *Shema*.

DAYS OF AWE ARE UPON US   *Vol. 5, No. 1 - Sept/October 1994*

This year the transition from the lazy days of summer to the busyness of a new year is more abrupt than usual because *Rosh ha Shanah* comes so much earlier. We're barely back to work or school and only just after Labour Day when the *Noraim*, the Days of Awe are upon us.

Ideally, these special Holy Days should be part of the rhythm of the Jewish calendar, a heightening of the worship experience of the year. But in realistic terms, we have to accept that, for many Jews, this is not the case, and the experience of the Noraim is totally isolated from the normative Jewish context. In this case, *Rosh ha Shanah* and *Yom Kippur* have of necessity, therefore, less meaning than they should.

If we are to get the most from our coming to the Synagogue for these services, especially if they are divorced from the Jewish rhythm of living — as for many they are — we owe to it ourselves and to the community to prepare ourselves a little beforehand. That we should sit through long services bored and unmoved merely because they are there to be got through, is fair neither to ourselves nor to our fellow worshippers, especially when we could give so much and in turn receive so much with just a little preparation.

I would suggest that these steps would help:
1. Glance at our Holy Day Prayer Book and become familiar with both the general pattern and design and also with some of the detail.

2. Pick out some of the themes that are developed — God, prayer, life, sin, atonement — and meditate a little on them.

3. Prepare mentally and emotionally for the experience of contracting out of life for a little while to concentrate on the more important things. In other words, coming from a holiday mode, not directly into business mode, but into concentrated and serious-minded consideration of what things are all about and how we fit into life. That *Rosh ha Shanah* is so early this year may help.

4. Come early to services and prepare for the prayer and study experience, especially if it is not something that we normally do.

In other words we need a little spiritual toning up to get into shape for the Holy Days. We cannot seriously expect anything to happen or result from coming to these services if we are not prepared for them and not willing to put some effort into them.

I hope that together, we shall be able to create an atmosphere in the Synagogue in which each of us is impelled to invest a genuine striving for moral and spiritual improvement, for then our worship will be worthwhile.

Patricia, Jonathan, Danny and I wish every member of our Agudas Israel family a *ketivah ve hatimah tovah*, a year filled with love and beauty and ever-renewed hope, for us and for all humankind.

Yizkor: What Is It? *Vol. 5, No. 2 - November/December 1994*

Since I have been in Saskatoon, I have noticed a strange phenomenon in Jewish life. Wherever I have been throughout my career and before when growing up, the *Yizkor* Service has been well attended. Even when the last days of Festivals fell on a weekday, people took time off from work, maybe not for the whole day or even sometimes for the whole service. But the Synagogue was filled for the *Yizkor* prayers.

This is not the case here. Indeed, one year when I noted that the *Yizkor* Service would be on the last day of *Pesah* and *Sukkot*, I was asked to explain what it was. And certainly if the last day of the Festival falls on a weekday, it has been unlikely to have a minyan for the *Yizkor* prayers.

I am puzzled as to why this should be so. Is it merely ignorance of Jewish tradition? Or is it that Jews here do not want to remember the dead? Considering the importance that our community grants to *Yarhzeit* notices, I think not.

Perhaps it would be useful to consider what *Yizkor* is about and why we remember the dead on these occasions.

The tradition is that special memorial prayers, call *Yizkor* after the first word of the traditional prayers, "May God remember the soul of...", are read after the Torah

Service but while the *sefer Torah* is still out and held by the sheliah tsibbur on the last morning of the three *hagim Pesah, Shavuot* and *Sukkot*, and on *Yom Kippur*.

Our tradition teaches that the dead should not be forgotten. They are still part of us, their memory an enduring inspiration to deeds of goodness. Hence it is a wonderful custom to give to a charity in their name on the anniversary of their death. In addition, we are reminded as we remember that all Israel is linked together vertically throughout time and horizontally throughout space. Just as all Israel throughout history was already gathered at Sinai to enter the covenant, so all Israel throughout history is gathered in an eternal present. And there is yet another lesson that we can learn. Our love overcomes suffering and sorrow. When we remember, we are enriched, those we have loved are given renewed life, and our Jewish faith in the eternity of life is restated.

It is therefore important that all of us should make a particular point of attending the services that include the *Yizkor* prayers. The *Ashkenazi* custom is that those whose parents are still alive do not attend. This is pure superstition and should not be observed. And even if there should be someone who has not known a death in the family, they too should still attend, for every Jew has an obligation to say *Kaddish* for the six million.

When we attend *Yizkor* prayers, we not only say *Kaddish*, we are a *Kaddish*. The root KDSH means to be special, to make special, hence to consecrate, to sanctify. We are better people because we have shared love, and in remembering them and saying *Kaddish*, we consecrate our memories as a source of goodness in our lives, and in so doing we become partners with God in *tikkun olam*, the healing of the world.

I hope to see a reversal of the Saskatoon custom. Next Yizkor services, even if they are on a weekday morning, let us aim to have a full Synagogue.

Torah Commentary   *Vol. 5, No. 3 - January/February 1995*

During our strategic planning session, various suggestions came up to improve our services and, possibly, to increase attendance. Some of the ideas are actually already being acted on, others are under active consideration. It might be helpful to bring people up to date.

Every Saturday morning there is a discussion/study period relating to the Torah reading of the week. Obviously, this is within the context of the Service and therefore constrained by time. However, fifteen minutes or so has become the norm and appears to be appreciated by the regular attendees. The possibility arises of extending this to a session of study following the service. There are some logistical problems that present themselves, however, there is no reason for not trying it. So in January we shall be doing this. On January 14 and 28, therefore, those coming to the service should be prepared to stay on for an hour afterwards for study and discussion. Bring your concerns and questions.

Already on the *Shabbatot* preceding Festivals, I talk about the Festival and the meaning and observance. This could certainly be extended. In addition, before the Festivals we are proposing to hold a seminar relating to all aspects of the Festival. Book Sunday afternoon March 19 at 2:00 for a session on "Everything you need to know about Pesah," its meaning and observance.

Please note, too, that we are trying the early Friday evening service again. Our past experience with the early service has been ambivalent. Our community has grown accustomed to the late Friday service. However, there are some members who have persistently requested an earlier service. Speaking personally, I am strongly in favour of the early service. The last place, it seems to me, that a Jew should be on a Friday night is in the Synagogue. Friday night is for the family at the Shabbat table. So, in January, February and March, the last Friday evening service each month will be at 6:00 pm and not at our normal time of 8:00 pm. If we tap a different group of our members to attend these early services, we shall be fulfilling our mandate, to speak to the needs of the whole spectrum of our membership. Each Shabbat will "feature" a group of our community in the conduct of the services: In January the Hebrew School, in February the JSA, and in March the BBYO.

Although this is a purely secular year, nevertheless Patricia, Jonathan, Danny and I would like to wish all the members of the Agudas Israel family a happy, healthy and blessed 1995.

SEMINAR ON PESAH   *Vol. 5, No. 4 - March/April 1995*

We are looking forward to the renewal of spring marked for us by the Festival of Pesah. On Sunday, March 19th at 10:00 in the morning, we shall be holding a seminar on Pesah. Do make every effort to come along and I shall try to answer all the questions you always wanted to ask about Pesah, the Seder, *Kashrut* of foods, selling your hamets, and all the customs and halakhah relating to our observance.

Please also make an effort to attend the Festival Services and ensure that we have a minyan for all of them.

The rules and customs of observance of Pesah are not an end in themselves, nor should we be overwhelmed by the seemingly extra complications relating to the Festival. Pesah enshrines basic meaning and values that are important to us as Jews, indeed as human beings, and we should keep those values firmly in mind as we observe it in our homes and in the Synagogue.

Pesah is not worrying about food; its discipline of food is to enable us to concentrate on its meaning; the lesson of freedom within Torah, the freedom that is not a "do what you will" chaos, but disciplined by responsibility. Pesah and Shavuot are a unit. We tend all too often to make Pesah a burden, its message lost in the detail of rules and laws. It is actually quite simple, and the more we bring out that simplicity in our homes, the more we shall learn its essential teachings for us.

On an entirely different matter, I should like to suggest that we try to work toward consistency in our method of transliterating Hebrew into English letters. A good example of our inconsistency can be seen every year when we are involved in the season of Hanukkah. People tend to transliterate the Hebrew name into English using a bewildering variety — *Chanukah, Chanukkah, Hanukah, Hannukah*, being some examples. Another inconsistency is the transliteration of the Hebrew letter tsade using "tz". In these chases, "ch" will be read by an Anglophone as in "cheese", and "tz" is totally unsayable (try it!).

There are many consistent methods. The one I would suggest is that used in the *Encyclopedia Judaica*, which is used in the Library of Congress. It is in two versions, academic and general. I suggest we make a real effort to use the general version whenever we transliterate a Hebrew word into English letters. The intention is to represent as best we can a standard Sefardi pronunciation for those who do not read the Hebrew itself. There is a copy of this system available in the office for people to consult.

Patricia, Jonathan, Danny and I wish all the members of the community a happy and meaningful Pesah, with renewal of body and soul, a *hag kasher ve sameah*.

TOWARD A FEMINIST JUDAISM? *Vol. 5, No. 5 - May/June 1995*

By now, many members will know that I have completed the requirements for the degree of STM (Master of Sacred Theology) through St. Andrew's College. In addition to the course work, I wrote a thesis and it may be of interest to share something of my research with the members.

My subject title was *Beyond "Equality": Toward a Feminist Judaism?* The punctuation is important. My intention was to consider the response of Jewish women in North America to the feminist critique of traditional Judaism. I therefore considered the work of three representative Jewish feminist women.

There are three possible reactions to traditional Judaism. There is rejection of Judaism as being irredeemably patriarchal, and for this response I took Naomi Goldenberg as representative. There is affirmation of a reconstructed form of Judaism, a feminist Judaism that takes account of feminist critique. Representing this option, I considered Judith Plaskow. In addition there is what I came to call "equivocal rejection," and I chose to consider Starhawk, the famous Jewish witch, as the protagonist of this position. While both Goldenberg and Starhawk affirm their Jewish identity while rejecting Judaism, Goldenberg as an atheist, Starhawk as a wiccan, they both also attempt to relate their spirituality to Judaism, Starhawk in a more positive way.

Plaskow tries to redefine Judaism in such a way as to include the voice of Jewish women. She therefore considers what we can mean today by the traditional categories of God, Israel and Torah. She also considers what methodology would be available to Jewish women who want to affirm both their Jewishness and their personhood as women to discover a traditional form of Judaism that would be non-patriarchal. This she finds in *Midrash*, the traditional technique of story telling.

I placed these women in the context of the feminist movement in general. It was also important to relate what Jewish feminists, both women and men, are doing in the context of the place of women in the traditional Jewish sources, both halakhic and midrashic. Plaskow's critique of halakhah as both a system and as a category of thought required detailed assessment.

Before deciding whether it is indeed possible to reconstruct Judaism in Plaskow's direction so as to include women in a substantive rather than merely cosmetic sense, it was necessary to decide on definitions of Judaism that would make this possible. If Judaism were to be defined as a system of beliefs and practices whose cohering factor is basically Torah as halakhah, then it seems to me that the feminist critique would be impossible to answer: Judaism would indeed be irredeemably patriarchal, hierarchical and intrinsically subject to violence. I therefore developed a definition of Judaism as dependent on a constellation of core values that cohere into paradigms in history that are interrupted by radical disjunctures. The possibility of continuity rests not in ethnicity or halakhah, or the pattern of any particular paradigm that the Judaisms of the past have taken, but in those core values that are shaken in the kaleidoscope of Jewish experience into differing patterns. In this case, the feminist Judaism not only is possible and makes sense, it is actually the only way in which the Judaism of the future can develop into a new paradigm to replace the halakhic system of c. 200–1800 that has now broken down.

Finally, I tried to develop some ideas as to how such a new, feminist paradigm of Judaism would function. The new definitions of Israel and a non-halakhic Torah and an imaging of God that would include specifically women's spirituality, would, it seems to me, involve an on-going trialog between the Written Torah, the Oral Torah (Jewish tradition) and the present situation of Jews, that will result in change that will be radical, though disciplined by authentic Midrashic methodology.

I much enjoyed this work, hard though it often was. And I am grateful to the congregation for allowing me to work out my ideas in discussion and study groups and sermons. I am also grateful to teachers and friends at St. Andrew's, the Lutheran Seminary and St. Thomas More, for stimulating dialogue across denominational borders. Doubtless the congregation will be sharing more as my thinking develops.

Reflecting on the Year
Vol. 5, No. 6 - July/August 1995

Now that we have a chance to rest a little and enjoy the activities of summer, perhaps we might look back over the past year with some degree of satisfaction. Our community has sustained some losses as senior members have experienced ill health and the effects of advancing age. Some have unfortunately died and we mourn their passing and know that we shall miss their wisdom and contribution to our community. But new members have also joined. We have been extraordinarily active for our size. And, on balance, we can see that we have had a good year.

The morale of our community is high, and we have managed to continue to work together with tolerance and good will to maintain Jewish life in what is, after all, one of the most isolated communities in the Jewish world. That is no mean achievement.

We should also look forward to the future, to the AGM that will be coming in September and the opportunities that we have to plan for that future. Changes will occur. They are inevitable in any living organism and, thank God, ours is very much a living community. Every individual member is and will be part of that process of evolution of our community. Change will, therefore, always be thought through carefully, and put into effect responsibly. Our intention is to continue to have a broad consensus of opinion so that our community will be satisfying the needs of as broad a range of Jewish opinion and practice as possible, and every Jew, secular or religious, traditional or liberal, will feel welcome and find a place of comfort. We know that if we are to maintain a Jewish presence here it has to be through the involvement of all of us.

So we should be pleased with what we are doing, though to complacent; and we should look forward with confidence. We have a future as a Jewish community here in Saskatoon. We shall hand on a viable Judaism to our children. That will always mean that each one of us will have to make a contribution. We cannot, as in larger communities, wait for others to do it for us. But that is good. It means that the community really is ours, it belongs to all of us, and that is based on acceptance and tolerance, the genuine belief that all Jews are sisters and brothers, and our agenda is the common good and never our personal opinions.

In the meantime, let us enjoy the summer. Saskatoon in the summer is a wonderful place to be. Now is the time for rest and refreshment of the body, mind and soul. We have done well; we shall do better. So let us now take a break and enjoy!

Time passes so quickly. It is sobering to come again to the Jewish New Year and to realize that yet another year has gone by, that all the good intentions of last year have remained just that — intentions — and that we are basically not what we were then.

On the other hand of course, we do have yet another chance to make the changes that we want so much to make, and to discover deeper meaning and greater richness in our lives, a more fulfilled and loving relationship with partners, friends and families.

The details for the arrangements for the Holy Day services for the new year and Day of Atonement this year are elsewhere in *The Bulletin*. I want here to expand a little on the Services in the Synagogue.

Obviously we get more out of Synagogue services the more we are prepared to put into them, in terms of our own preparation for them and also of how we participate in them. If we just come without any preparation at all, without thinking about what *Rosh ha Shanah* and *Yom Kippur* mean and are supposed to mean, and with no intention to pray, to study, to meditate, to join with the community in worship, then we shall get nothing at all from having been present. If, on the other hand, we are determined to approach this special time seriously (which is not the same thing as lugubrious pomposity) and with every intention to join with fellow worshippers to make the services come alive and speak to our very depths, then, who knows, this may be the year when we shall actually change, really take control of our lives, really discover the presence of God and the beauty and inspiration of Judaism.

So I would suggest that we should think about this program of preparation.

1. Come to the Synagogue a little before time, and sit quietly and settle the soul.
2. Choose words from the Prayer Book that speak directly to us personally and dialogue with them, rather than just pile up prayers wholesale.
3. Read beforehand about the structure of the Prayer Book and the themes of this special time so that we can respond to the service as it develops.
4. Determine to do something as a result of the worship experience that will concretize the words, the themes, that we announce in our prayer. For example, accept the *mitzvah* of *tsedakah*, and give something to a charity specifically because of the Holy Days.
5. Make peace with another human being before praying. We hurt each other so easily, particularly ones we love, by a silly word, insensitivity to their needs, a thoughtless act. Accept responsibility and begin the healing between us.
6. Help our community to join together in worship by trying to concentrate on the services, taking part, reading or singing with a generous heart.
7. Try to go deeper than the surface of the words, prayers, rituals. For example,

if anyone fasts on *Yom Kippur* they should know that fasting is not an obstacle course, a spiritual 'one-upmanship', it is a serious attempt to grow spiritually and morally.

8. Above all, let us all know, really know, that what we are engaged in is not coming to the Synagogue for the children, in deference to what parents would have liked, attending the AGM of the Jewish people, or just for old times sake. It is a wonderful opportunity to explore spirituality, to try to change, to become better people and a better community.

Our services are basically traditional, and I am very aware that many of our members are not comfortable with Jewish tradition and do not know or understand very much about it. That is not entirely their fault. Nor is it true that we cannot use new material and have different understandings of our spirituality than our forebears had. We are not bound by tradition, however, we should be respectful of it. Therefore, both to learn about the traditional ways of understanding these Holy Days, and also how to integrate those understandings with our present day needs and aspirations, there will be a Symposium on the Holy Days at the Synagogue on Sunday morning, September 17 at 11:00. Come along and let us learn together, prepare ourselves for those special days, and also perhaps find that we can add to and enrich the tradition with our own insights.

Patricia, Jonathan, Danny and I would like to wish all our members a year of renewed health and joy, a year in which all our prayers for love and peace and justice may be fulfilled.

ARE WE PRAYED OUT? *Vol. 6, No. 2 - November/December 1995*

After the run of the major Festivals there is often a sense of being 'prayed-out', *kivyakhol*. After *Simhat Torah* there is a sort of anticlimax, a reaction to the intense exercise in spirituality in which we have been engaged, and which may be, for some of us, perhaps the use of religious muscles that we do not normally exercise.

However, we should not let our experience go. Obviously, we cannot — probably indeed, should not — maintain the intensity of a Yom Kippur throughout the year: there is a normality of life to be lived. But, even so, it is essential not to let the whole thing just go, but rather to build on it. The improvement of ourselves and our community and world that we prayed so fervently for during those days so rightly termed "Days of Awe," will be a gradual and incremental process. But we do have to continue to work at it, to build little by little on the foundations that we, hopefully, laid in the Synagogue.

We are not going to become overnight *talmide hakhamim*, Jewish scholars, totally committed to a Torah-centred life. Our tradition warns us against trusting to miracles! That may not be where we should be or even want to be. But we must not ever give up the investigation of our own spirituality in the context of the guidelines of Judaism. That is the contribution that we can make to ourselves and to others. For if we are richer people, then we have that much more to give to our fellow Jews and indeed to our fellow creatures. And our riches really are not physical, but the quality of our own personhood.

There are steps, not to perfection, but to improvement.

First, let us put aside a little time each day for prayer and meditation, for being alone with ourselves and God. Second, let us put aside a little time to study the wondrous heritage of Judaism and the blessing it can give to our lives. Consider for instance, coming to the Lunch and Learn sessions at the Synagogue this year.

At the very least, one can always read a Jewish book, and the Synagogue has a useful library available to all members.

Third, why not select a Jewish moral value and exercise it? For example, consider the concept of *lashon ha ra*, hurtful speech through gossip, and determine to become that little more careful about what we say about each other, and try to judge each other (and ourselves) a little more charitably in word. It might be that then we gradually come to be a little more charitable also in deed.

Fourth, why not consider what *tsedakeh* might mean in terms of choosing a charitable organization that works to ameliorate human suffering or to improve the human condition, and giving time and effort and money to help? There are so many. I would suggest the Jewish organization Mazon, dedicated to relieving hunger among Jews and non-Jews alike, is worthy of the support of every Jew.

If we just let these Festivals go by as merely an event in the calendar, then next year we shall be back where we were. But if we try to use them then we might, with God's help, come out of next year's Holy Days with the wonderful feeling that it has been worthwhile; that we have indeed, as individuals and community, advanced along the path to true healing.

SERVICES, RITUAL & PLURALISM Vol. 6, No. 3 - Jan/Feb 1996

In our discussions about ritual matters, the *Kashrut* of our kitchen, the status of *kohen* and *levi* in the *aliyot* on Shabbat morning, for example, we often lose sight of an important consideration: Although we are members of the United Synagogue and are therefore loyal to the guidelines of Conservative Judaism, we have to try to relate this to the actual situation of our community. As the only organized community in Saskatoon, we include a wide spectrum of Jewish commitment, and must always bear in mind that essential pluralism.

On the one hand, it may be seen as a source of weakness: the halakic guidelines of the Conservative movement are more clear cut than the situation we are trying to apply them to. On the other hand, that could also be seen as a source of strength: we do reach out to fellow Jews of all and no denominational loyalties, in on-going dialogue in which all have a contribution to make.

We do, however, sometimes get a little impatient with each other and try to impose a *halakhic* ruling, or an amended halakhic ruling, without taking full account of our pluralist membership. And we sometimes assume that, as Conservative Judaism is basically halakhic in its approach to Jewish life, we are bound to follow those guidelines without consideration of our specific circumstances, which, within reason, is not the case.

Perhaps, during this new year, we should take more notice of the essential pluralism of Judaism in general, Conservative Judaism in particular, and our own situation as a community of diverse membership. Where we represent, as we do, the commitments of a wide range of Jews, all of their concerns and needs must be considered. It is not appropriate to impose standards on our members that they are not democratically able and willing to abide by, merely because they do not have the options that would be available to them in larger Jewish communities.

Another aspect of this is that we all need to respect each other's Jewish choices, and therefore seek change by consent and consensus. Of course, we can, and should, seek to advance the knowledge and understanding of Conservative belief and practice among our members, and try to persuade them to a deeper and richer personal commitment. But this should be a process of education and informed consent.

Perhaps, too, during 1996 we should all determine to seek to understand Conservative Judaism better. There is a specific philosophy that can be called "Conservative" in Jewish terms, as well as an understanding of Jewish tradition, history and the halakhah. We should aim to make our affiliation more meaningful than perhaps it sometimes has been. But, at the same time, let us remain sensitive to the choices that each of us makes in our Judaism.

There is a hierarchy that runs I am a pious Jew, You are non-observant, he is not even Jewish at all. Not so. In Saskatoon, we are all Jews who happen to be in different spiritual spaces, some of us more or less knowledgeable, committed or observant, but all of us with a part to play in the development of Judaism on the prairies.

A useful New Year resolution I think — to be a little more tolerant, and express a little more *shavat Yisrael*.

With the arrival of Purim, the promise of Pesah and spring can't be far behind. And considering our record-breaking winter that is eagerly awaited!

In our reading from the Torah of the events that culminate in the Exodus of the people from their slavery in Egypt, we are told, almost *en passant*, this month (Nisan) shall be the first month of the year for you. (Exodus, 12,2).

This reminds us that the original Hebrew calendar began the year in the spring. How apt this is, with the rebirth and renewal of life in nature after the long, dark winter! Later, during the Exile in Babylon, the people came into contact with a culture that started its year in the autumn. Hence, we now have *Rosh ha Shanah* in the month of Tishri, the seventh of the calendar.

But there is another dimension to our understanding of our Torah text. This time of year, the spring month of Nisan, is a very real New Year for us religiously as well as physically. It is another *Rosh ha Shanah*.

For now the people leave Egypt and become free. But they immediately begin a special journey that is to lead to Sinai. There they make a Covenant with God, the God who brought them out of Egypt. That covenant is spelled out in Torah. They were slaves, they became free; but, more important, they became Jews.

This time is, therefore, a time of beginnings. In our preparation for *Pesah* we clean out our homes. But this is more than external spring cleaning: it is also a spiritual preparation. The *se'or*, the leaven, that we remove from our homes is also according to the *Midrash*, the *yetser ha ra*, the leaven in our hearts that leads us to do what is wrong. At *Pesah*, we prepare ourselves to become Jews, members of the covenant people of Sinai.

So, beginning with the Second Day we start to count the *omer*. This is more than a historical reminiscence of the bringing of an offering to the Temple: it is a real countdown until we come again, each year, to Sinai and the making of our covenant with God. It is therefore also a time of spiritual and moral accounting, just as much as are the *Noraim* in the seventh month of the year.

Of course, it is also true to say, as indeed the Midrash does, that every day is a beginning of a year for each of us and for the community.

This year, as we celebrate Pesah and meditate on its multi-dimensional layers of meaning, it might be helpful to remember this Torah verse. For ourselves, for all the people of Israel, for all humankind, may this indeed be the beginning of a year that is new and a life that is reborn.

Patricia, Jonathan, Danny and I wish all our members a *hag kasher ve sameah*, a joyous time of spiritual renewal.

On the second night of *Pesah*, we start to count the *Omer*, and we continue each night as part of the daily services until we reach the next Festival, *Shavuot*.

This custom was originally a reminiscence of the bringing of the offering of an *Omer* of grain to the Temple. But for us it serves more importantly to link the two Pilgrim Festivals of *Pesah* and *Shavuot*, and thereby to remind us that they are essentially interwoven.

Pesah and *Shavuot* are both, of course, occasions that celebrate the harvest. And reminding us of nature with its growth and decay, death and rebirth is itself important. In our urban living we can easily lose sight of our connectedness with other life forms, and we should turn aside from time to time to remake our links with nature and rediscover our mutuality and dependency on our earth.

But there is a deeper connection of the two Festivals. *Pesah* is the birthday of the Jewish people, when we celebrate coming out from Egypt and slavery and the gift of freedom. However, we misunderstand what freedom means, for it is not licence to do whatever we please, it is responsibility, a gift that we should use for others. And this is taught as we live our calendar. For Shavuot is the birthday of the Jewish religion, Judaism, as we gather again, as did our forebears, at Sinai to receive Torah. In receiving Torah and entering into the covenant with God, we fulfill the freedom of the Exodus from Egypt. *Pesah* is not finished until we reach *Shavuot*.

There is a lovely tradition to spend the eve of *Shavuot* together in preparation for *mattan Torah* (the giving of Torah) on the morning of the Festival. This is called *tikkun leyl Shavuot*. And because Torah has not yet been given, we as yet do not have the rules of *kashrut*, so we can eat only dairy foods.

So, I would invite all the members to come together on *erev Shavuot*, Thursday, May 23, at 1800 hours. Bring your contribution to a potluck dairy meal for us all to share, and we shall engage in Torah study culminating in the service welcoming the Festival.

As we come into the summer, perhaps we should remember that our Pesah freedom is confirmed by the Shavuot covenant of Torah. And this, of course, is not confined to Festivals, nor can it merely be a nostalgic genuflection to the tradition. It must become the essential way that we are to live as Jews. For so long as we really do place Pesah and Shavuot, Freedom and Torah, in the very heart of our Jewishness, for so long shall we really be as a people a source of blessing to all humankind.

Normally, in the summer the community relaxes and the calendar of events becomes a little less full. This is not the case this year.

August is a busy time for the community, and we welcome the fact that we shall have much cause to celebrate. We have a had a long and hard winter with much illness, disappointment and death. But now in compensation and sharply teaching the lesson that joy and sorrow are so intermingled in life, we shall be rejoicing with families in *semahot*.

We have two weddings which we shall celebrate with two young couples as they begin their lifetime partnership. We wish them many years of love and happiness together as they go through life, and we share as a community in their affirmation of our human right to joy in life.

Continuing that theme of marriage and partnership, we have what must be a unique privilege to join with two couples in our congregation who celebrate a Golden Wedding anniversary. To Herman and Rachel Neumann and to Gerry and Gladys Rose we wish a hearty *mazal tov* on this wonderful occasion. Fifty years of being together through joys and sorrows, defeats and triumphs, of deepening their love for each other, of companionship and friendship, of raising and nurturing families, is a blessing to be grateful for. We all join them in their thanksgiving: we all have reason to say a sincerely felt *she hekhiyanu*. May they be with us, rejoicing in each other, their families and their friends, for many more years, as an example and a blessing.

And continuing with celebration, at the end of August we join with the Gersher family for their daughter Shayna's Bat Mitsvah. We speak so often of the continuity of Jewish life: this month we shall be living it, with the start of two Jewish marriages, the continuing of that love throughout so many years, and the beginning of a young Jewish life with all its promise and hope. The example of the Roses and the Neumanns is a potent one for Shayna.

And even though we also this month unveil two memorials in the cemetery, it is not in a sense of despair and tragedy. There is always loss when someone we love dies, and there is a time for us to mourn. But there is also a feeling of presence in a different way, and there is then a time to celebrate. And that is what we do when we unveil a memorial in the cemetery: we celebrate life, and we know yet again how blessed we have been in our love, and how eternal that love that binds us together is.

Perhaps that really is the lesson for us, as a community, as we celebrate this August. What we are celebrating is life, hope and love, and the courage to accept that we shall live life, whatever it brings, with joy and celebration, for it is good.

May these summer months before us be a time of renewal and rebirth.

GET MORE OUT OF NORAIM *Vol. 7, No. 1 - Sept/October 1996*

The Holy Days of the New Year and the Day of Atonement are for most Jews the most important part of the Jewish year. This is the time when nearly all Jews, observant and non-observant, try to come to the Synagogue services. While many of the reasons people have for their attendance at this time may be somewhat different from the spiritual imperative that tradition would urge, nevertheless the intuitive feeling that all Jews have of the supreme importance of these days is well founded. They are indeed the *Yemei Noraim*, the Days of Awe.

Ideally, of course, Jews live their lives by the rhythms of Torah. They structure daily life in accordance with Torah and the fulfilment of a mitsvah-centred way of living. In that pattern there are peaks of the spiritual and religious life and the greatest is this time of the *Noraim*. Then the reflection on life that is the mark of the Holy Days arises out of the context of a Torah-focused lifestyle and is a completion of that commitment.

In reality, most of us live our day-to-day lives somewhat short of that ideal. While we are certainly, each in our own way, concerned with our Judaism and its moral and spiritual demands on us, most of us also are caught up in other demands on our energies and concerns. All too often, the Holy Days catch us unawares and to greater or lesser degrees not entirely prepared. But then that is also the reality of life itself: it too often takes us by surprise and doesn't always give us time to prepare.

What can we who are not entirely prepared for the Noraim do to get the most out of this time and give the most to each other as a community?

First, let us be aware of what these Days are about. They form a pattern with a purpose, carefully orchestrated to teach us about life, values and priorities for living, relationship with ourselves and each other, and the nature of life itself. But we do have to listen and be prepared to open ourselves to the message being conveyed and to be honest with ourselves. The Holy Days teach us that there is purpose in our living on this planet. They teach us that we are responsible and the buck stops here, with us. We are responsible for what we do, what we are, for the health of our community, for the well being of each other. And we cannot shrug that off or avoid it in any way. Religion — being Jewish — is for each one of us, and it is very practical, not an escape from the world but an immersion in the world, a world seen differently, in the light of a different dimension of being and possibility.

Second, let us be aware of what is happening in the Services. We cannot seriously expect anything worthwhile to happen if we just come to the Synagogue physically; we have to be present intellectually and emotionally and psychologically as well as physically. It is exceedingly useful, therefore, to have a look at the *mahzor*, the Prayer Book, beforehand. That does not mean a scholarly analysis of a text, but it does mean trying to see what is going to happen and thinking a little about it before it does. In all fairness, we are likely to get more out of the experience if we read some of the program notes before the play starts.

Third, the Noraim are indeed a drama. I chose the word "play" advisedly. But they are a drama in which we all have a part, and not just a spear-carrying part either. The Holy Day services are similar to Greek drama. There are major protagonists, the human represented by the *sheliah tsibbur*, who leads the services, and the divine, Torah, the conscience stimulated in and by the drama. But there is also the Chorus, the community at prayer; and the play cannot develop without that chorus. That is on one level. On another level, of course, the drama is played out within the individual just as much as, and at the same time as, it is being played out on the communal level. There is as much complexity and depth and richness as individuals and communities want, and more, in this multi-dimensional and multidisciplinary process.

Once a year our tradition gives us this time. It is up to us to use it. And, as with everything else, the more seriously we take it and ourselves in relationship to it, the more likely we are to get something from it. In this case, that something may actually transform our whole lives for the better. But that is not a promise, it remains always a possibility and it is for us to make that possibility real. This is the time for reflection, for assessing life and the values that we chose to live by, for accepting personal responsibility for what we choose to do and be and for our community and our society. It is potential renewal and growth. But it is for each one of us, coming together in community, to use that potential and to actualize it.

May these Noraim be realized as a time of renewal, and may they bring for us, for all Israel, and for all humankind, a new year of blessing, peace and growth. Patricia, Jonathan, Danny and I wish for us all a 5757 of health and joy and realization of all our human potential for good.

GOOD REASON TO BE JEWISH *Vol. 7, No. 2 - Nov/Dec 1996*

During the Holy Days I spoke about Jewish continuity. One of the points that I tried to make was that Jews will not remain Jewish unless they want to, unless they find in Judaism some good reason to be Jewish. It is essential that Judaism speak to ordinary Jews in terms of values that will enrich their lives, and teachings that will guide them through their difficulties, and prayers and rituals that make sense and inspire.

If there is any particular lesson that I would want members to carry with them from the Holy Day Services into the new year, it is precisely that. Jews will not want to be Jews and to hand on their identity to their children unless they find meaning and purpose and beauty and truth and guidance and inspiration in Judaism.

Appeals to nostalgia and loyalty to the group, attempts to frighten people with fears of anti-Semitism, Israel, the Holocaust — these will not work in the long run. Nor will threats about out-marriage. Only a positive message that it is good to be Jewish because Judaism offers personal and community enrichment will work.

It is therefore essential for us to work together to that end. We have to try to make a community that will express the highest ideals and values of Judaism, and that will encourage Jews to want to be Jewish, to learn about Judaism and to experiment with living Judaism in their own lives.

We are a remarkably democratic community. There is no attempt by me as Rabbi or the Ritual Committee or the Board or any individual or group within the membership to impose any particular program of being Jewish. Nor should there be. Our essential pluralism of knowledge, observance, belief and commitment is also our strength.

However, we do have to take action to strengthen our Jewish life as a community. The first step is education. Then there is consultation and dialogue. And then there must come a willingness to experiment with ways that we can better express our Jewishness and encourage each other to try to increase our commitment to Jewish living. There must be no coercion. But there must also be no procrastination. Trying things out does not require 100% agreement, merely a broad consensus that the effort is worth making, and that unless we do we shall surely stagnate.

So during this coming year we shall be trying out some experiments intended to enrich and deepen our Jewish commitment so as to find positive reasons to be Jewish and to want to hand on that Jewish identity to our next generation. For if we find in our communal life reasons to be Jews, that will spread to the individual members, and they too will discover positive joy and satisfaction in being Jews. Let this year be one of tolerant experiment to that end. And let there be no personal agenda involved, beyond a willingness to work together in community for the enrichment of us all and the empowerment of Judaism into the future.

DEPTH OF TALENT *Vol. 7, No. 4 - March/April 1997*

Members will have noticed that I have been away from the Synagogue for a while because of illness. I am now recovering quite well, though still in some pain and discomfort and am looking forward to returning from South Africa in much better health and strength.

I am most grateful to so many of our members who rallied round to ensure the continuance of the Services during my absence. I am so impressed by the depth of talent in our community! Perhaps we should sometimes think about that when we bemoan our situation as an isolated Jewish community on the prairies. When need arises, we have many members who can and will respond. A special thanks to Susanne Kaplan and her committee who made the necessary arrangements.

Jewish tradition tries to make connections. There are linkages for all our experiences. So, each of the Festivals speaks to us on different layers: each celebrates the cycle of nature, each also celebrates the historical experience of our people. And each also has then been interpreted as teaching moral and theological principles of Judaism. In addition, the Festivals have been tied into each other by the calendar of the year and by ritual observances that bind them into an overriding pattern.

So, it is with the two Festivals that we celebrate in the spring. Purim and Pesah. Purim marks the end of winter. It enables us to relive history and it speaks to us about the realities of assimilation, out-marriage and persecution. Pesah is the spring Festival of rebirth. It recreates for us the experience of the Exodus from Egypt, and it proclaims the lesson of human freedom.

And the two Festivals are linked by the calendar. They are one month apart. At this time we read special passages from the Torah on four *Shabbatot: Shekalim, Parah, Zakhor* and *Shabbat ha Gadol*, the Great Sabbath. While only two are directly connected with the Festivals, *Zakhor* (Remember) with *Purim*, and *Shabbat ha Gadol* with *Pesah*, all of them form an introduction to and preparation for our observance. We are enjoined in *Shekalim* to take part in maintaining the community; in *Zakhor* we remember Amalek and the hatred we have experienced; in *Parah* we read about the mysterious red heifer and learn about the non-rational dimension of our religious faith; and in *Shabbat ha Gadol* we prepare for *Pesah*.

Judaism weaves disparate experience into a patterned tapestry. It thereby gives us meaning and purpose to our living and radiates a beauty into the ordinary. And that is something that we so desperately need to know and feel.

Patricia, Jonathan, Danny and I would like to wish all the members a happy Purim and a *hag kasher ve sameiah* for Pesah.

REFLECTIONS ON ILLNESS *Vol. 7, No. 5 - May/June 1997*

Dr. Johnston remarked that the prospect of being hanged in a fortnight concentrates the mind wonderfully. A brush with mortality does indeed concentrate the mind: that I can assuredly testify to! It is a time for reassessing values and priorities in life, for considering the deep ultimate questions of life and death, for thinking about religious faith, and about what one has done and still wants to do with life.

Serious illness changes people, often very profoundly, sometimes for the good, and sometimes for the bad. One is forced to consider questions such as: What am I doing with this inestimable blessing of life? Indeed, is there an "I" at all, apart from what I do and the role that I am playing? What is really important to me? And what do I really believe about life and death?

This was not the first cancer scare that I have had. However, it happened to come at a time of great weakness, both psychological and physical, and as a culmination of a truly appalling year of stress and pain. So I had to come to terms with my own spirituality and faith.

When I was lying in bed at night not sleeping, or sitting uncomfortably on my own during the day, I felt very much this need to sort out my relations with faith, with God, with myself, and with the values that I have tried to live by.

In the first place, I have never expected God to do miracles. I am not that arrogant as to expect miracles, not that important as to be worth one. If I were to die, I regretted very much leaving so much undone and saying good-bye to people I love deeply. I did not pray, but I did meditate. In so doing, I came into contact with a deep hidden source of healing and energy. I encountered a presence that was both within me and also at the same time beyond me. I would use the word "God" to name that Presence. It was, and is, a source of warmth and courage, of strength and peace. I do not resonate to mystic experiences, and nor do I believe that this was one; what had happened to me was that illness had stripped away the layers of "busyness," had torn off the masks that we wear, the roles that we play. I was directly encountering God, not as something or someone definable in word, but as a Presence radiating power and serenity. Of course, that Presence is always there, but only times of great stress do we allow the encounter to be a real experience unencumbered by an intellectualizing cloak of words. Prayer was not needed: just a mutuality of Presence. Fear and anxiety remained, of course, because I remained human: but now there was an added dimension — peace. And that peace is deeper because that Presence is more real.

In re-examining values, there is nothing original in the results enforced by illness. We all know perfectly well what are the real values and ultimate priorities in life. But in pain and weakness those ultimate values become more starkly real. The real value in living, what makes life worthwhile, indeed enables us to live at all with any meaning, purpose and dignity, is very simple: Love. Of course we all know this. But there is a difference between intellectually knowing and heart-soul and mind knowing.

Really, nothing that I have done in life is worth anything or will be remembered by anyone. It is what I have *been* in life that counts: someone who has loved and been loved. I have had the wonderful blessing of sharing love with two women: I have had the wonderful blessing of two sons: I have had the wonderful blessing of having loving friendships with men and women and children of all races, creeds and nationalities. In the light of that, what else can matter? Whatever qualities that we have that lead others to care for us and about us we cannot really know. When others refer to our kindness or gentleness or caring, or whatever other qualities of mind, heart or soul that makes them care for us and about us, all that we can do in response is to be grateful that we have been made that way. The fact that they love us and that we are able to respond by loving them, that is ultimately truly breathtaking. And for that love given and received, our thanks are limitless.

It is that love that impels us to try to live well. The moral act is a gesture of love that is a response to being loved. If we were not loved, we could not be moral; if we did not love in return, our acts would be meaningless.

Every moment in life is infinitely precious. We are of necessity greedy. We want time with others, and especially with special others whom we love and are loved by. However long we are granted in life, it is all too short. Death leaves us alone, for when those who are special to us die, part of us dies with them, and when we die part of them dies with us. So it is; and we have to live with that.

A Jew expresses how we live in terms of Torah. We can see Torah in two different ways. Torah can be viewed as revealed legislation: Torah can be viewed as revealed relationship. Buber got it right when he said that we can relate to others in one of two ways: as I-It, or as I-Thou. There are always two partners in any encounter, each an I. And they can refer to the other as either another subject, another I whom they meet as Thou, or as an object, an It. Both have their value. But it is the I-Thou possibility that points us beyond the human and embeds the human Thou into the presence of the divine Thou, and suffuses the relationship with the ultimate empowering love. Then we respond to the other, our partner in encounter, in a being and doing that makes us worthy of the experience of love. And then both of us touch the hem of eternity. Torah is action in loving encounter. It gives us the words, the symbols, the dreams, to articulate the life of passionate loving encounter which is what being a Jew is about.

What I shall be remembered for when I die is not what I did, not the committees that I served on, not the honours that I accumulated, but what I was as a person. It is being a *mensch* that will make me worth remembering. Mourning is the tribute of love to loss. We are frail beings. Our tradition does not require us to try to be a saint, but to accept our frailty, to accept our failures, both the ones that other people know, and the ones that only we know. That knowledge must not paralyse us with guilt. We try to become better; we continually fail. But we personally are not called on to complete the work of healing the world, *tikkun olam*. Neither, though, may we ever stop trying. We cannot prevent others from being hurt, but we can try not to hurt them ourselves. We must never settle for second best, but nor may we become paralysed by our failure ever to achieve the very best. In the last resort, we have to live with ourselves, our own integrity, and with each other and that Presence that I know as God. We have to be a little more relaxed and comfortable with the space and time we happen to be in. Reality imposes constraints, the reality that we make and the reality that others make. Guilt may make us try harder: it may also stop us from trying at all. That is a difficult path to walk.

Being Jewish is to work to heal the wounds of the world. This we do by touching those who are in pain, by hugging those we love; by lighting a small candle in the small corner of the universe where we are, and where we meet and come to know and to love human beings who also know and love us. We accept imperfection because we can learn to place that imperfection in the context of the empowering and loving Presence. We can try, little by little, and without recrimination and guilt, to bring that Presence into the life we live as a blessing for which we shall be remembered with sorrow when we die, but also with gratitude and enduring love. Perhaps if we light a little candle in this small place on earth, we shall be worthy of a small place in eternity.

So, hopefully, I shall continue to live and continue to grow. More I cannot do, or want. In the vast scheme of things that is all, and worrying that I cannot and will not do everything that must be done will not help one iota. So much have I learned from having to confront the ultimate realities of our human frailty and my own fragility in particular. The rest is silence.

RETURN TO HEALTH *Vol. 7, No. 6 - July/August 1997*

There is a lovely traditional custom that after a long journey or on recovery from illness one comes to the Shabbat morning service for an *aliyah* and then recites the *gomel* prayer joining with the community in thanksgiving. It is a custom that we should encourage, for it strengthens the links of caring and concern between members of the community at the same time as it leads the individual to embed a return to life in the experience of the source of life.

I have been delighted to be able to do this on my return to health. In the last *Bulletin* I shared with the members my experience of being ill and its effects on my own spirituality. I should also share my return to health and my feelings of relief and joy and thanksgiving.

I have osteoarthritis in my ankles, especially the right ankle. Compensating for the discomforts that this has brought has resulted in some damage to my hips, but the primary problem is in my ankles. Apparently, the source of the problem is an old sports injury that extends back over 40 years that has become more and more inflamed over the years. However apart from that disability, I am fully returned to health; indeed, I am in very good health now. My recovery has left me feeling renewed, almost reborn. I have a level of energy and zest for life that I have not felt for several years.

Of course, as those who have attended Services know, I prefer to sit as much as possible. Standing for any length of time is uncomfortable. Of course, too, as with all arthritic conditions, even though pain is controlled, there is a slowing down and the disease is tiring. However, I am certainly returned to full capacity in carrying out my duties as Rabbi. There are flare ups of the condition, days when my legs do not function as well as on other days, nevertheless, I am feeling very well.

It is also the case that many members of any community do not know what a Rabbi actually does. There may, therefore, be a temptation to assume that any disability may prevent a Rabbi carrying out the Rabbinic duties at all.

A Rabbi has various functions to carry out in fulfilling the role.

A Rabbi has a "priestly" role, in carrying out the leadership in ritual terms. The Rabbi acts as *sheliah tsibbur*, preaches, reads and teaches Torah, officiates at life-cycle events.

A Rabbi has a "pastoral" role, in advising, counselling, and supporting members in crisis, visiting the sick, comforting the mourners, and sharing occasions of celebration and sadness.

A Rabbi is a scholar, a resource person to the community in Judaism and Jewish traditional insights into the living of life and the values of our heritage.

A Rabbi is a role model for Jewish living for the community. His or her integrity and moral standing must be impeccable.

A Rabbi has an ambassadorial role in representing Judaism and the Jewish community to the general community. A Rabbi teaches not only Jews but must reach out to non-Jews as well. To a large degree, the standing of Jews in the general community depends on the reputation of the Rabbi in that community, if only because the Rabbi is the best known "full-time" Jew in the eyes of that community.

Inevitably, the task is too much for any one human being to carry out, but any serious-minded and committed Rabbi tries to do the best that is humanly possible in his or her situation as an individual human being. Any Rabbi makes mistakes, does some things better than others, and is necessarily flawed. However, the Rabbi also does some things well, derives satisfaction from times when he or she has helped people in need, and tries always to create and maintain links between Jews and the traditional sources of their heritage.

When a Rabbi cannot foresee what demands will be made, he or she cannot plan a week in the ways that other professional people can. The stresses on the Rabbi and Rabbinic family will be enormous.

The telephone, in the office and at home, has to be continuously answered, day or night. The Rabbi has to be on-call 24 hours a day, seven days a week; like a rural physician, he has no locum. The Rabbi has to answer questions from Jews and non-Jews, while retaining unvarying good humour, remembering that even the most "stupid" question is important to the person who asks it. The Rabbi has to welcome visitors to the Synagogue and visit churches and schools. The Rabbi has to visit the sick, at home or in hospital. The Rabbi has to write articles, deliver lectures, produce halakhic responsa, and find some time and energy to read and think and retain a scholarly presence. The Rabbi has to be patient with everyone. The Rabbi has to prepare *Bnei* and *Bnot Mitsvah*, Jews by choice, couples planning weddings. The Rabbi has to sit on committees within the Jewish community and also in the general community. The Rabbi has to officiate at rituals for life-cycle, *beritot milah, pidyone ha ben, shiva* prayers, all Shabbat and Yom Tov services. The Rabbi has to teach, formally and informally, and be available for all social occasions in the community's life. The Rabbi has to be available for counselling when members have needs. Unfortunately in our community, we have large numbers of deaths. Each funeral involves a huge amount of time and energy in planning, being with the family and offering emotional support. This continues through the mourning period. Visiting the sick in hospitals is sometimes easy enough, being with people and families as recovery occurs and involving the pleasure of seeing people return to health. Sometimes, all too often, it is involvement in human pain and fear, being with the dying and comforting those who are waiting for death. That is both the hardest and also the most important thing that a Rabbi does. And any Rabbi is involved in that pain, just as much as in the joy of a wedding or Bar/Bat Mitsvah.

On one level, being a Rabbi is, as the old saying has it, no job for a Jewish boy (or girl). But on the other hand, it is also a wonderful thing to be and to do. It is involvement in Jewish study and scholarship; and it is involvement in the life of individual people, their joys and sorrows, and, occasionally, the immense privilege and satisfaction of helping someone.

On balance, I do not regret the thirty years since my receiving *simihah*. I think that I have done some good in my life, made some contributions as a Rabbi and teacher, carried out my duties as best I could. I have made mistakes enough, but maybe God is more forgiving then we human beings are sometimes inclined to be.

PREPARE FOR THE HOLY DAYS *Vol. 8, No. 1 -Sept/Oct 1997*

Though the Jewish calendar means that this year the *Noraim* are very late and that may be a little disconcerting when we normally associate September with the New Year, we are still preparing to face the preparation for the Holy Day Services even though they do not begin until October this year.

As we return from holidays we prepare physically and psychologically for this period of renewal that marks the month of September. We begin a new year in many different ways; a new school year and a new work year after the lazy days of summer are just two examples. As we prepare in our secular lives, so we begin preparing spiritually for the renewal that comes with the High Holy Days.

Because the actual date of *Rosh ha Shanah* is so late this year, we have extra time for preparation. We can use the whole month of September. There is a temptation to put religion at the bottom of our priorities and to assume that we don't have to bother with these Days of Awe yet: there are other things to do. Yet we should remember that this is not so. Precisely because it is late this year *Rosh ha Shanah* can take us by surprise. And if we come to the services unprepared, we can lose a great deal of the value of the occasion.

How can we prepare for the experience of the Holy Days? I would suggest a 10 stage program of preparation.

1. Think about life and the passages in life, the changes that occur and the way we mark those changes.
2. Think a little about the values that we treasure and that we try to live by and the priorities that we have in our lives.
3. Think about the ideas of renewal and new changes, so that changes don't just happen to us but we make those changes for ourselves. Think, for example, of occasions in the past year when we have perhaps lost touch with reality but have tried to regain control — a serious illness, for instance, or a loss; a death in the family; a relationship that has gone wrong; moving into a new home; losing a job — and how we have coped.
4. Think about the possibility that the Jewish tradition can help to give our lives some direction and purpose.
5. Think about the chances we have missed to do something good. Or the mistakes that we made that we regretted afterwards.
6. Think about what Return can mean. It means saying sorry to others, but also saying sorry to ourselves for not being the best we could be. And then determining to do better, to learn from our mistakes in life.
7. Think about time. If we are to try to change things for the better in our lives and in the way that we live with others, we cannot continue to procrastinate. "If not now, when?" Time slips away so fast.
8. Think about how change happens. Little by little. Over time and not immediately. The important thing is to start. Do we want to change? Are we willing to try? The way to do things is not simple but our tradition gives us guidelines.
9 Think about what we are doing when we come to Services. Are we sitting there for the first time since last year? Are we waiting for some miracle to happen? Are we there because we are there, that's what Jews do? Are we sure that we are going to be bored? Or are we really going to try? Are we really going to start things happening ourselves? There are always choices.
10. Think about what we can do for each other in a community. Can we reach out to each other in our prayers and meditations? Can we stop trying to be one-up on each other, to out-do each other, to gossip about each other? Can we start building each other up rather than tearing each other down? Can we stop criticizing and start celebrating?

We all have to make an effort. But that is, after all, what Judaism is about. It won't happen overnight. But it can happen and will happen if we really try. We all have to try to reach out to each other and work together to make change happen.

Patricia and I wish the members a New Year of fulfilment, blessing and peace.

SHABBAT IN JUDAISM *Vol. 8, No. 2 - November/December 1997*

As the members know, we in this congregation are part of a campaign initiated by the United Synagogue to encourage Conservative Jews throughout North America to introduce the observance of Shabbat into their homes and lives. As a beginning to that campaign in our community, I spoke on *Rosh ha Shanah* about the meaning of Shabbat in Judaism, and I want here to share some of those reflections for those who may not have been able to be in the service on that occasion.

Ahad ha Am, the 20th century Jewish thinker, once remarked: "It is utterly impossible to think of the existence of the Jew without Shabbat. One can say without exaggeration that more than the Jew has kept Shabbat... Shabbat has kept the Jew."

When we observe Shabbat according to the Torah, we are doing two things. We are acknowledging God by resting as God did: and we are acknowledging the unique value of human existence and the right of human beings to rest because we recognize the divine spark within everyone as a result of our own historical experience as a people. We were slaves, objects, who became free, human. Freedom is the birthright of our being human.

The keeping of Shabbat has two aspects. There is a negative: not working. And there is a positive: enjoyment, *oneg Shabbat.* We recreate relationships between families in the community, in prayer and worship, and social interaction in the Synagogue, between human and divine. And for this we need time out of the ordinary world. Positive and negative are interwoven to make Shabbat a foretaste of infinity, a time outside time. Everything is intended to one end: to make us aware of the fact that we human beings have two sides; we are ordinary animals, and yet we are also only little less than divine. We have one foot on earth and the other in eternity.

The eternal yearning within us can illumine the ordinary and earth bound. We can transform the ordinary into the extraordinary. Just once a week on Shabbat we can step out of time and live in the steps of eternity, and then bring something of that eternity, its taste, its flavour, back into the workaday week as we smell the spices of *havdalah at motsaei Shabbat.*

The whole of Jewish tradition is available to us, an incomparably rich resource. We do not need to turn overnight from observing nothing to observing everything. But little by little we can explore Shabbat and find within that tradition the resources that will work for us wherever each one of us is on our own spiritual journey into

Judaism. My suggestions, therefore, are suggestions. I am not attempting to usurp the autonomous conscience of any member, but to offer help and guidance along the way.

For instance, consider this as a possible program to discover and encounter Shabbat.

Let family and friends gather together around the table on Friday evening for a special meal. No appointments scheduled, no TV, no phone. Let the wife and mother light the candles, making the blessing in Hebrew or English. The light of those candles, symbolizing peace and joy and laughter and being together, will frame the whole day. Let the husband and father then make the blessings over bread and wine and the specialness of the day, the ceremony called *Kiddush*, again in Hebrew or English, chanted or said. Then let husband and wife bless each other for the blessing that they are to each other, and together bless the children. A time for personal prayer and meditation is certainly appropriate. The family members can spend time catching up on each other's week and rediscovering each other. Grace following the meal could also be said.

Let families come to the Synagogue services together for prayer and study of Torah and to share with other families in the community in creating circles of love and sharing and caring that transcend aloneness and build community. Being quiet while together, reading and studying, walking, visiting, resting; all of these are forms of *oneg Shabbat*. Maybe too playing games, engaging in hobbies, going on a family picnic: going into the office, housework and unnecessary shopping are not *oneg Shabbat*. And with sunset on Saturday we end the day as we began it, with ritual and drama and poetry, as we make *havdalah*, blessing light, wine and spices and carrying the beauty of Shabbat into the week ahead.

For some Jews the full halakhic definition of Shabbat and how to observe it will be the preferred option. For others this may not be possible or even right in the stage that they are at. Some will experiment with tradition: some will even want to create their own customs. But however individual families choose in their trying to bring Shabbat into their lives, we want to encourage every effort that they sincerely make and help them to do whatever they can to make Shabbat a beautiful and enriching experience that potentially can transform the whole of life for good.

May this New Year be for us all a time of discovering and exploring more of the deep riches of the Jewish tradition, starting with the very core of Jewish identity, the Shabbat that has kept Jews as Jews have kept it.

We have just been celebrating Hanukkah. It is a minor Festival in the Jewish calendar, but it represents a very major theme in Jewish life, a theme that is becoming the focus of Jewish concern: continuity, the continued survival of Judaism. That Jews will survive as human beings there is no real doubt: that Judaism will survive to make Jews uniquely special there is great doubt.

In his recent book *The Vanishing American Jew*, Alan Dershowitz has much to say that is of interest to all Jews. But his essential point may seem a little controversial, itself a sad comment on the health of the Jewish community today.

He says that, given the possible demographic decline in the number of people who want to be counted as Jews, we have to advance strong reasons to convince Jews to commit themselves to the survival of Judaism. And he believes that we can no longer convince Jews to be Jewish for negative reasons, the threat of anti-Semitism in particular. He claims that the level of anti-Semitism is low and declining, despite the perception of many Jews that the opposite is the case, and that in the 21st century we as a community may be confronting for the first time in history the unique challenge of why remain Jews when no one is really stopping us from disappearing into the host society anymore if we should want to.

He is right. There are all sorts of reasons for this assessment, including, paradoxically, the new-found attraction of Jews in the general society as marriage partners. Of course, there always are good reasons for monitoring anti-Semitism carefully, but, regardless of the perception of many Jews, it really is at a low and marginalized level in western society. It is not a factor in the lives of most Jews today in a practical sense.

We therefore have to find some way of presenting Judaism to Jews as an attractive positive option for them, a source of guidance in their spiritual lives and moral decision making. And essentially this means a radical improvement in our educational system, including the Jewish education we present for adults. He does not mean by this that he anticipates a massive rediscovery of Judaism as Synagogue based religion, though he would welcome it. He sees that most Jews will remain secular humanists in the future as they are now. What he wants to see is the presentation to secular Jews of traditional Jewish values derived from the classical sources of Judaism, so that Jews will live at home in both the Jewish and non-Jewish world, deriving from both and giving to both richness and blessing.

He sums it up as wanting to present to Jews now a positive picture of being Jewish, stressing the joy of Judaism rather than the *oy* of Judaism, as he puts it.

It seems to me that Dershowitz is making a correct diagnosis of our situation and prescribing the correct treatment: we must show Jews that being Jewish is a positive experience that can enrich our lives and the lives of others around us. His suggestion that the way forward will begin with a massive investment in education, an encounter with the sources of Judaism as spiritual and moral teaching, is also surely correct. I would add that I think that the way forward cannot be as secular as Dershowitz thinks, but I certainly am happy to work with secular Jews as much as with religious ones.

Perhaps, as we begin 1998 having just celebrated Hanukkah that reminds us of the survival of Judaism as a unique value system, we might renew our determination to survive. Our aim must surely be that every Jew in our world, whether born or converted, should have sufficient Jewish knowledge to be a Jew by choice rather than a Jew by chance.

TALMUD TORAH Vol. 8, No. 4 - March/April 1998

An absolute value of Judaism, a value that lies at the very core of being Jewish, is *Talmud Torah*, study of Torah. For without study there can be no knowledge, and without knowledge there can be no act. As the *Pirke Avot* reminds us so harshly, *Am ha arets lo hasid*, an ignorant person cannot be religious.

Study of Torah is a basic mitzvah of Judaism. Indeed, according to Talmud we should divide the day into three equal parts, one devoted to making a living, one to rest, and the third to study.

Many Jews have fallen out of the habit of study of our sacred texts, the traditional sources of Judaism, and find it difficult, off-putting even, to engage in study of this kind. Though they are often familiar with study in the academic field, they assume that study of Torah involves entirely different skills that they do not have and cannot acquire without investing too much of their limited time and effort.

While it is true enough that study of Torah in depth does demand knowledge of Hebrew and a familiarity with the detailed background of Jewish faith and observance, it is also true that a great deal can be done in English, starting from a minimal base of knowledge, if there is access to a teacher to guide and help.

There are two layers or dimensions of studying a Torah text. There is the analysis of the text from a scholarly perspective, using all the tools of modern academe, so as to understand its meaning and its context in time and place. There is also the existential encounter with the text: it should speak to us in our unique time and place if we open our hearts and souls in an attitude of a willing suspension of disbelief and listen to it.

The two processes should go on simultaneously. The single most important thing is to take the text seriously and read it carefully and then enter into dialogue with it. This is not the same thing as the trap of a fundamentalist literalism.

Beware translation, however, for all translations are, to one degree or another, misleading: and all translations are, without exception, *midrash*. And in "translation" we include the vowelling and punctuation of the Masoretic tradition which is the basis of all printed Hebrew Bibles. The actual text of Torah is the consonants of the Hebrew without the punctuation, and we may vowel and punctuate that text as we wish, within the parameters of Hebrew grammar. It is clear from the use of the Biblical text in Rabbinic literature, that the Rabbis did exactly this, and their reading is often different from that of the Masoretes.

The commentaries, traditional and modern, are an essential part of this process.

But everything must be a tool to understanding Torah for us, now, as conveying to us a deeper understanding of what God requires of us in our daily living. We must listen, question, dialogue, learn and live. For, as the late Rabbi Louis Finkelstein once so memorably put it: "When I pray I talk to God; when I study God talks to me." And a Jew must learn to listen.

SPIRITUALITY *Vol. 8, No. 5- May/June 1998*

One of the buzz words in Jewish life today is "spirituality." It appears to have taken over from "continuity" as word of the month.

Many Jews are puzzled by the word. They do not understand what is meant by it, suspect that it may be somewhat un-Jewish, perhaps even Christian, and see it as a possible threat to community as we know it and to Jewish work for Israel, social justice and inter-group harmony.

First, what is meant by the word "spirituality"?

I would suggest that the definition proposed by the Spiritual Advisory Committee to the Saskatoon District Health Board may be a starting place. (We worked hard enough at it, anyway!)

"Spirituality is the experience of relationship with the empowering source of ultimate value, purpose, and meaning of human life producing healing and hope, and is articulated in diverse beliefs and practices in individuals and communities."

Why has it become a concern of so many nowadays?

Many Jews are looking for meaning and purpose in their lives and a deepening and enrichment of their religious identity. This is not the same as a return to religion in the sense of greater Jewish observance (though it may include that), but a need for a more immediate experience of God. They are finding a secular understanding of Jewishness in modern Jewish life that is lacking for them.

This is not a criticism of those many Jews who see their Jewish identity in terms of cultural and ethnic loyalties, merely a statement that there should be ways of expressing being Jewish that also include the spiritual dimension. Judaism is too broad to be defined in only one way.

Is this a threat in any way to Synagogue life?

Essentially, if Jews see each other as members of a community that is supportive of each person's way of understanding and expressing Jewish identity, however different the choices may be that each of us makes, then it is not a threat. The community should be wide enough in its acceptance of Jews wherever they may be on their Jewish journey, to accommodate Jews who define themselves in cultural and ethnic terms, and Jews who see themselves as being "religious," whether in observance or spiritual life.

Any Synagogue must see itself as community in this sense, if it is to be healthy and if all Jews are to find a comfortable place in it. The narrower our definitions, the more intolerant and exclusive we become. But it would be tragic if we were to go that route.

Some of us are happy defining our Jewishness as a cultural and ethnic identity: some of us thirst for the presence of God. Both aspects are in the Jewish sources and both are valid ways of expressing our Jewishness. A Synagogue must welcome both and support both.

LAST MESSAGE *Vol. 8, No. 6 - July/August 1998*

As this is the last message that I shall write for the Agudas Israel *Bulletin*, I should like to share a few observations for the future.

The Jewish community is under great demographic stress. In general terms, the number of Jews who identify with the organized Jewish community is declining. Various panaceas have come and gone as tactics to reverse the trend of decline: intensified Jewish education, enabling more young Jews to visit Israel, emphasizing anti-Semetic threats. All have failed: the decline continues.

The real lesson is that there can be no instant fix. To rely on a miracle solution is to navigate by a mirage.

When all is said and done, Jewish survival and continuity rests where it always has — in the covenant between the people and God in Torah. Ethnicity, fear of anti-Semitism, remembering the *Shoah*, passionate identification with Israel, trying to resurrect Yiddish: none of these things will work. Only a renewal of Jewish faith and living, the age-old practice of the presence of God, will give Jews a hope of surviving.

The members of this community do not attend Synagogue services. They do not in the main identify themselves as Jews in terms of religious faith and life. And yet this Synagogue is affiliated with the United Synagogue and is officially committed to a traditional form of Jewish religious practice. In all honesty, one has to ask, Why?

Proclaiming oneself to be dedicated to the maintenance of Judaism through the centrality of the Synagogue and loyalty to Conservative Judaism works only if the mass of Synagogue members takes it seriously. They do not. Being a Conservative Jew demands knowledge of the Jewish sources and commitment to traditional observance and life patterns. It will not do to claim to be Conservative as a respectable middle way between Reform and Orthodox and yet do nothing about it.

And do not believe that that situation will somehow change miraculously, that a new Rabbi will fill the Synagogue and inspire commitment to Judaism in its traditionalist, Conservative, form. Things do not depend on the Rabbi but on the ordinary member of the community. If the members will it and come to the Synagogue and organize their personal lives around Conservative Jewish precepts, then Agudas Israel will flourish. If they do not, it will not, cannot.

I have served this congregation for ten years. They have been mixed years, filled with some joy and sense of achievement, but also with some disappointment and a great deal of pain. As a Rabbi, I have failed to share with the members my sense of the beauty and joy of Jewish faith and practice, of the adventure of Jewish learning, of the inspiration of religious faith.

However, with the feeling of disillusion and failure, a feeling that goes deep, there remains a hope and a vision; the same hope and vision that led me to the Rabbinate 31 years ago. The *Shema* and *Tikkun Olam* are the values around which I have structured my life, and I have not been wrong to do so. I was well trained and retain the respect of colleagues, and I know that I am a good Rabbi, despite what you may think. Whatever lies ahead, I still have much to give to the Jewish community, and I hope I have the chance to do so.

I do urge this congregation to examine its attitudes to Judaism carefully. Only if members support the Synagogue because they want to experience Jewish faith and practice can it survive for long. And that will require some changes. If you decide to be real, committed, Conservative Jews, *kol ha kavod*. If that is not really where you want to go, consider the options honestly: your way of being Jewish might be elsewhere.

Rabbi Pavey's contract was not renewed. A search for a new Rabbi began.
Rabbi Pavey returned as our Rabbi in July of 2000.

Throughout history we Jews have been a factious and contentious lot. Our ancestors complained continually about the leadership of Moses in the Torah. Even during the Roman siege of Jerusalem, partisan violence weakened the resistance. *Sinat hinam*, pointless hatred of Jew for Jew has been our besetting sin throughout history.

In many ways, our stubborn refusal to conform, our continuing willingness to question, has been one of our great gifts to humankind: it has made us the eternal dissenter, and without it we and Judaism would have stagnated.

But in times of emergency and crisis there has to be a limit to this fissiparous tendency. Dissent can become a self-indulgence that we cannot afford.

We are in such a situation of crisis in our community. The continued healthy survival of our community is threatened: there is an increase in *sinat hinam*. The injunction of *al tifrosh min ba tsibbur*, don't withdraw from the community, now becomes the prime imperative. The personal agenda of members of the community, however strongly held, must give way to that. We must work together to ensure the continuance of Jews and Judaism in Saskatoon for the future. We must restate the real moral and spiritual values of Jewish tradition. All political games must be subordinate to that.

I therefore want to make it clear where I stand.

First, I support the leadership of the Congregation, and commend those who are working to maintain the range of services to satisfy the Jewish needs of the members. Second, as a Rabbi, it is my moral duty to do whatever I can to help at this time. I am personally committed to a liberal perspective on Judaism. But the Congregation is affiliated to the Conservative Movement, and I respect that democratic choice and am able to work within those parameters. A Rabbi should be a person of intellectual scholarship and moral integrity, a leader and teacher, not a dictator. This is what a Rabbi should offer to the community.

There are areas of Congregation life that I can contribute to as a Rabbi, and I must do so. I think of study courses, life-cycle ceremonies, campus chaplaincy, representation of the Jewish community in the general community, help with Shabbat and Festival Services, conversions, as examples.

You and I, as members of this Synagogue, need each other. You need to be able to guarantee Rabbinic support and expertise so as to maintain the full range of services offered by a Synagogue. I need a viable community of Jews with whom to pray and study. Our partnership is mutually beneficial. At the present, I would envisage such a partnership on a limited time frame designed to help the community to help itself by helping to train a cadre of "para-Rabbis." But I could never refuse to help fellow Jews whenever specific Rabbinic expertise is needed, without time limit, and within the constraints of my own health.

All of us as human beings have to learn to let go the negative baggage of the past and look to building for the future. All of us make mistakes as we go through life. There are times when we must learn to work together in partnership for the greater good of the community. This is such a time.

THE RABBI AS A RESOURCE Vol. 11, No. 3 - Jan/Feb 2001

As the members will see elsewhere in the President's message, the Board of Trustees and I have formalized the relationship between Congregation Agudas Israel and myself to spell out the areas in which I can help the Synagogue during this difficult time.

It is essential that the Congregation have access to a Rabbi for several reasons. A Rabbi is a fundamental resource for the community to give advice on halakhic matters and to ensure that lifetime observances are available, such as *beritot milah*, baby blessings and namings, *bnie/bnot mitsvah*, weddings and funerals. In addition, a Rabbi provides programs of adult education, and can be involved in Shabbat services as *baal koreh* and in giving *divre Torah* and the occasional sermon. The Jewish community must also be represented in the general community, especially in multi-faith activities and chaplaincy on campus. And the members must be able to turn to a trained professional for counselling and advice.

But there are more than just practical matters involved. Regardless of the things that a Rabbi does, it is just as important what the Rabbi symbolizes for the community. A Rabbi can be and should be the core of the community. Having a Rabbi gives the community a sense of continuity and survival, a resource that members can turn to when needed. No Rabbi will ever refuse to help a fellow Jew when called on.

My view of the role of the Rabbi is precisely that: to be the Jewish resource to the community in every way. The relationship between Rabbi and community is built on trust, the feeling that both can rely on the other, because they are both committed to the survival of Judaism. There are needs that tie them together, personal needs, the need to get things done and to ensure that the Synagogue goes on, and the need to ensure the survival of Judaism in Saskatoon. There is a need to let go the traumas of the past year and to heal.

I hope that we can work together to that end. Now is the time to look to the future. The community has been in a state of shock for some months, and that is understandable. But it cannot continue in that way. We must plan together for the future and make our Synagogue into a vibrant centre of Judaism. Our services and our educational programs have continued, and we all owe a deep debt to those who have helped in so many ways to maintain those services and programs. Now is the time to expand and deepen our efforts. Our concerns must be the health of the Jewish community of Saskatoon, and to ensure that every Jew in Saskatoon can look to the Synagogue to satisfy their Jewish needs and make their own contribution to Judaism. We must strive to be inclusive and to welcome everyone who wants to be part of the community. My task as a Rabbi who is a resource for that community must be to initiate, help and support, and be available to all members at all times.

Let us go forward in partnership and trust.

BEACON OF JEWISH VALUES *Vol. 11, No. 4 - March/April 2001*

The core of any Synagogue is and must be three things: as the *Pirke Avot* says, *Torah, Avodah* and *Gemilut Hasadim*: worship, study and the living of Jewish moral values. Everything else is a means to that end.

Therefore the health of the Synagogue can be judged by the quality of its programming to those ends. That must be the criterion by which we can judge. Are our Services fostering Jewish spirituality and bringing Shabbat and Festivals alive, giving us the foundation of prayer so that we live everyday life in the presence of God? Does our study, both for the young and for the old, open up for us a genuine dialogue with the classical sources of Judaism, so that our minds are enriched with the knowledge of how to live well? And as a result do we reach out to the world in a spirit of *tikkun*, dedicated to creating love and justice in our community and among all humankind?

There is a time for each of us to engage in an honest and deep appraisal of where we stand in life and where we want to go so that we do not waste the infinite wondrous gift of that life. This is the Holy Days each year, a time of ending and beginning anew. For the community as a whole there is such a time, too. We cannot just drift: we must engage in a moral and spiritual audit of what we are, what we should be and where we are going. And when we do so, we apply those three criteria, for they are the focus of Jewish life, for each of us and for our Synagogue community.

I would suggest to our members that we should begin to let go the traumas of the past and begin the healing process. Essential to this is for us all to look at the long term health of the Synagogue. To ask the simple questions that I posed above, and to struggle to find the right answers.

Can we make our Services better and involve more of the members? Can we open up the Services to the talents, needs, questions, of all the members? Can we use them better to pray, to study, so that we fill our lives with meaning and purpose and beauty and hope and courage? Can we attract those who feel that they are not knowledgeable enough to come to services and feel frightened or embarrassed because they don't know Hebrew or lack Synagogue skills?

Can we make our educational programs better and make Jewish learning a joyous voyage of discovery for all? Are there talents that we have not yet tapped? Can we overcome the sense of fear that afflicts those who, for whatever reason, feel disenfranchised and unwelcome because they do not know enough even to start, or feel discouraged because learning seems so difficult, Judaism so immense to grapple with?

Can we make our Synagogue a beacon of Jewish moral values in action, leading and encouraging members to experiment with bringing Judaism into their lives, and representing Judaism to the non-Jewish community? Can we be involved — as Jews not just as individuals — in the needs of our society around us, with its enormous problems of racism, poverty, homelessness, violence, and marginalization of minorities of all kinds?

In short, is it now time for the community to come together in a Congregational *Kallah* to draw up a "mission statement" for our Synagogue? We can discuss together in friendship and share in love our vision for what Synagogue is for and how best to get there. What is our Synagogue? Why do we want it? What services does it and should it provide? How can we have the best possible worship services and education programs? And how can the Synagogue become a light of Jewish moral and spiritual values for ourselves and for the community we live in.?

I believe that the time is ripe to do this. The reason is given us by the Psalmist: *Hineh ma tov umah na'im shevet akhim gam yahad*, See, how good, how wonderful it is, when siblings come together united!

PESAH AND SHAVUOT *Vol. 11, No. 5 - May/June 2001*

With Pesah we begin the journey to *Shavuot*. At Pesah we become a free people. We are free from slavery, but as yet we do not know what that freedom is for. When we come to Sinai seven weeks later we receive Torah and we enter the covenant with God that makes us a specific people, an *am kadosh*. At Shavuot we receive Torah, we say again each year as our forebears said "*Naaseh ve nishma*, We will obey and we will listen." *Zeman herutenu*, the season of our freedom, becomes *Seman mattan Toratenu*, the season of the giving of our Torah. And freedom from is transformed into freedom for.

There is no complete freedom. That way is anarchy and chaos. There is only the freedom to be and to do in service to others. Our freedom at Pesah is the freedom that all human beings will have in the Messianic time. But that freedom will only be worth having when it is transformed by Torah, the freedom to be special, to be fully human.

Our calendar confirms this for us. From the second day of Pesah on we count the days, and as we count days as beginning in the evening as in the story of creation ("it was evening and it was morning") we count as part of the *Arvit* service in the evening. The act of counting the *Omer* builds into our liturgical practice the unimpugnable linkage of Pesah with Shavuot. We cannot avoid the working out of our freedom in Torah.

And the counting is not just of numbers, it is of the *Omer*, a bundle of grain brought to the Temple in Jerusalem each day. For Pesah and Shavuot are also Festivals that link us with nature and its fertility through the harvest. And nature is embedded in history, in the Exodus from Mitsrayim, the narrow place of hardship, and in the receiving of Torah at Sinai in the desert.

For the Jewish Festivals are our calendar, the fundamental textbook of Judaism. For Judaism is the sacralization of time. In many Jewish traditions the Pesah music is used throughout the Omer and for Shavuot to remind Synagogue goers that they are really one.

A KALLAH FOR THE FUTURE *Vol. 11, No. 6 - July/August 2001*

I mentioned in the last *Bulletin* that I feel that the time is now right for the Synagogue members to come together in a *Kallah* to start building for the future. Regardless of how immediate events will play out, we have to lay the foundations for the survival of the Synagogue as a viable centre of Judaism in our community and now is the time. I want to say a little more about the idea.

Such a *Kallah* will have several purposes. It will enable the members to come together to brainstorm, to assess the Synagogue programs, to look at the Synagogue's resources, and to make plans. Especially, it will enable the Synagogue to draw up a mission statement, so that it can serve the needs of all Jews in Saskatoon and bring Judaism into their lives.

One of the essential things to do is to consider the priorities of our Synagogue life. Inevitably, Agudas Israel will have fewer resources to call on — the demography of Jews in Saskatoon cannot but be one of decline. At the same time, the Synagogue has resources of personnel and talent that we must assess and then use effectively.

It seems to me that the essential priorities of any Synagogue must be the following, and I place them in strict order.

1. To maintain regular religious services for all *Shabbatot. Yamin Tovim*, special occasions and life-cycle events of members.
2. To maintain a full program of religious education for both children and adults.
3. To represent the highest values of Judaism to Jews and non-Jews in Saskatoon.
4. To be involved in programs of social justice.

5. To provide social programs to enrich the Jewish life of members of the community.

In these fields we cannot compromise if we are to remain a Synagogue at all. Anything more is a bonus. In relation to these needs we have to look to the members and their talents and abilities and willingness to offer them to the community and to work with each other in the cause of the maintenance of Jewish presence in Saskatoon. We need to know what all our members could offer the Synagogue. It is unlikely that Saskatoon is going to be able to look to the outside Jewish world for help. At the same time, we must beware of the dangers of "doing our own thing" without reference to the outside Jewish world. There is a difficult balance to be aimed at.

There is a further point that I believe must be accepted by all if there is to be a future at all. That is the necessity of compromise. No member may impose his or her view on what is Judaism on any other. While the Synagogue will remain a member of the United Synagogue of Conservative Judaism and will be guided by its norms and practices, we must remember that the tent of Conservative Judaism is a broad and tolerant one and there is always place for scholarly discussion of *halakhah*. All Jews must be able to find a home in the Synagogue. Our intention is to enrich the Jewish experience for our members, within the broad parameters of Conservative Judaism but without excluding any Jew, or insisting that everyone conform in every detail. That is the way that we have functioned in the past and it should continue to be our way.

I look forward to the coming together of all members of the Synagogue in a *Kallah* to discuss building for the future of our community in the spirit of tolerance and *ahavat Yisrael*. And the first task is to draw up a mission statement that will describe us, what we are and what we want to be, as a Synagogue, and how we are to serve the needs of all Jews in Saskatoon.

ANOTHER NEW YEAR *Vol. 12, No. 1 - September/October 2001*

As we begin preparing for the Holy Days, there are several aspects of the Festivals that we need to recognize. First, we are starting a New Year. We have to assess our lives and the values that we want to base them on. Judaism is not just a list of ritual dos and don'ts, it is a way of orienting oneself to life and ways of moving from what is to what ought to be. We are given time at New Year to think carefully about what we do and what we are, in relation to what we should be and what we ought to do.

Second, we are engaging in a moral and spiritual audit of our lives, with special reference to our relationships; with ourselves, with our families, with our friends and with our community, all from within the perspective of the moral and spiritual teachings of our Jewish tradition.

Third, we must be aware that this process that we begin on *Rosh ha Shanah* and come fully to terms with on Yom Kippur is both difficult and perhaps painful for us. It takes preparation and involves hard work. It is difficult because it demands *kavvanah*, the willingness to work at the task: and it can be painful because it brings us face to face with things that we may prefer not to recognize — our own inadequacies and the fact that we have made mistakes, many of which have hurt ourselves and those we love. Wittingly, or all too often, unwittingly, we have done things we should not have done or not done things that we should have done.

And fourth, we have to realize there is a difference between what is, what it means just to drift through life taking one day at a time, and what ought to be. Living day to day causes us to forget we need a broader vision for life and not just to react to the passing events. Indeed, we need to recognize that there is such a thing as "ought," an absolute moral demand on us. Judgement is not just a word: it can and should be a reality.

The month of *Elul* that precedes *Tishri* and the *Noraim* is traditionally such a time for preparing for *teshuvah*, returning to the core of Jewish identity which is Torah. At this time especially, however ideal it is at all other times, it is crucial to turn our lives to prayer and study. To come to the Services for the Holy Days totally unprepared is to guarantee failure. Beginning now, it is essential to put aside some time every day for being alone in prayer and meditation. It is good to read through the *mahzor* for the *Noraim* and think seriously about the meaning of the words that we are going to say as a community before God. The impact of the Holy Days Services on the quality of the life of our community and all its members rests on the sincere willingness of everyone who comes to pray to help everyone else. We are fortunate that Nattan and David Green will be leading us in our worship during this special time. With the support of all members our services can be truly transformative in our lives.

Patricia and I wish every member of Agudas Israel a New Year of health and happiness and fulfilment. May 5762 be a good and sweet year for all Israel and all humankind.

SEPTEMBER II, 2001 *Vol. 12, No. 2 - November/December 2001*

As I write, the world is again at war. US and British forces are bombing Afghanistan in the beginning of a campaign to root out terrorists and terrorism. For the moment at least, a large majority of world opinion supports this action, seeing no alternative adequate response to the events of September 11, in the United States.

Our hopes are that the campaign will be successful in achieving the purpose. And our prayers are that events will not get out of hand. We are aware from historical experience that any and every act will have unforeseen consequences, and in our volatile world actions may well not be what we anticipated or intended. Many of the potential consequences of what is now happening could be horrendous, and as people of faith we should pray that this will not be so. We should also pray that while the guilty may have to be punished, the innocent should not suffer. We particularly think of the ordinary Afghan people who have suffered so much and our duty to help them to rebuild their lives when peace returns.

There are several things that we should keep firmly in the forefront of our thoughts and prayers at this time. Every effort must be made to root out terrorists and those who live by indiscriminate acts of violence and murder. Equally, every effort has to be made to preserve our human rights and not allow terrorists to push us into hysterical and ill-thought-out responses. We must further protect the innocent. We must look beyond a simplistic military solution. And, most of all, we must look hard into our own hearts and consciences and determine to tackle the problems of poverty, disease, injustice, frustration and despair that are the feeding grounds of terror. None of us are entirely innocent: all nations in history have committed acts of terror on others. History is a long tale of human savagery, racism and violence. Now, perhaps, is an opportunity for us to heal wounds of humanity as we deal with the latest barbarians in our midst.

The prospects are not entirely optimistic. War has a tendency not to be surgical and confined. It spreads. It is destabilizing politically, socially and psychologically. Once unleashed, no one can know where it will go. The Muslim world is filled with injustice, dominated by corrupt regimes. The whole situation can collapse like a house of cards. And none of us should welcome the resultant chaos.

On the other hand, the collapse of the present regimes in the Muslim world would ideally be a good thing. The arrival of true democracy and social justice in *dar al Islam* is a consummation devoutly to be wished. It would, among other things, be the ultimate guarantee of peace and well being for Israel. And that perhaps should be also in our prayers.

May God protect the innocent and bring the guilty to justice. Out of the evil of war may there come the blessing of genuine peace, a peace that will transform our world into a place of justice and security, where all may dwell beneath their fig tree and their vine and none shall make them afraid. May the God who dwells among us cause to dwell among us, all humankind, love and fellowship, peace and friendship. May that be God's will. Amen.

WORK FOR RECONCILIATION *Vol. 12, No. 3 - Jan/Feb 2002*

Our world is a hugely depressing place. On the broader sense, we have watched events in Afghanistan. None of us will mourn the end of the Taliban regime, the most evil and repressive government that existed in our world. But the events of war, however justified, should cause us to mourn the inevitable loss of life, the inevitable human suffering. Perhaps we had no choice, but we still are aware of the human cost of our actions. And of course, we cannot know the future and most have some foreboding, given the facts of Afghan history. Civil war, revenge and reprisal, tribal violence — all remain real possibilities. And liberal democracy, western style, is a frail plant in Afghanistan.

Nearer to home, we are seeing a rapid deterioration of the situation in Israel. It is clearer and clearer that our human desire for peace is doomed to be frustrated by the intransigence of political and religious commitments. Not all people actually do want peace, and we live in a world where moral evil exists and all too often flourishes. Our hearts are bound up with our fellow Jews in the Land of Israel: we share their hopes, their fears, their pain. We still pray for peace and justice and mutual acceptance of Israelis and Palestinians, but we know that our prayer is not enough.

The whole world is entering economic recession. For many of the more marginal in our own society the future is increasingly bleak as a consequence.

And we must face the real possibility of a kulturkampf, a conflict of civilizations and religion-based cultures, specifically our western liberal democracies versus the Islamic world. We must continue to work for reconciliation and mutual understanding, for we are all human; but we are acutely conscious of the barriers to understanding, the difficulties of dialogue, in a situation where the language we use is not understood in the same way by the partners in that dialogue process. Where one side really does believe that it and only it has absolute truth, and all others by definition are wrong, it is increasingly hard to see how any conversation at all is possible. We should remember the words attributed to the early Islamic conqueror of Alexandria in Egypt when the famous library there was burned: if those books agree with the Quran they are unnecessary: if they do not, they are blasphemous. Either way, they should be burned.

But it is forbidden for a Jew to despair, however rational despair might seem to be. We must retain our hopes and nourish our dreams, for there will come a time of peace and justice between human beings. That is the faith of Jews throughout history. It must remain ours too.

REBIRTH OF LIGHT *Vol. 12, No. 4 - March/April 2002*

This is an exciting time of the year for us as Jews. We celebrate Purim and we look forward a month later to Pesah. And both are important to us.

Purim expresses a profoundly human emotion: we turn away from the winter darkness, a gloom both physical and emotional, and we look forward in renewed hope to the rebirth of light and life in the spring. As Jews we direct this through the story of Esther and Mordechai and the saving of the Jewish people from planned genocide. Purim is the Festival of our year that is totally unambiguous: it is unalloyed celebration and joy. It is the only Festival that will continue into the *Olam ha Ba*, the world to come.

A month later, we celebrate again at Pesah.

The historicity of the events recorded in the Book of Exodus, the ten plagues and the escape of the slaves under Moses from Egypt, may be challenged. But that doesn't matter. Things happen on many different layers of human experience. What people "know" happened is much more important than what actually happened. And history is not, as the German von Ranke thought, what really happened (which we cannot ever really know), so much as what existentially happened. The Exodus from Egypt, *yetsiat mitzrayim*, is at the very heart of our Jewishness, because it brings us into direct encounter with our identity as a free people in covenant with God, the God who acts in human history because God cares and is involved with us and our sufferings and triumphs. God will not let evil win, and because we have known that fact in our history, we are called to be God's agent in healing all of history for all people.

Pesah has three dimensions: it is the spring harvest when we rejoice in the wondrous rebirth of nature; it is the historical event of transformation from slave to free, a process completed seven weeks later at Sinai when we accept the covenant of Torah; and it is the lesson of freedom and what it means, and therefore what it means to be human, that we Jews proclaim to the world, reluctant though so many are to accept it.

Pesah is the time when a people is transformed from slave to free, and Pesah is the time when people find their purpose: to be Jews. The birthday of all people becomes the birthday of Judaism.

Patricia and I wish all the members a *hag kasher ve sameah*.

ISRAEL WILL SURVIVE *Vol. 12, No. 5 - May/June 2002*

The situation in Israel deteriorates daily. The murder of innocent civilians continues, and now Israeli soldiers are being killed as well. In effect, the Palestinian Authority has ceased to exist, and the social and economic impact on the Palestinian people has been enormous. Even the Israeli economic and social fabric has been put under intense strain. There is always the possibility of the spreading of violence into a general war and resultant chaos.

There is no question that Israel will survive. The military and political strength of Israel far exceeds that of any Arab state or any combination of Arab states. But the damage could well be immense, the loss of life intolerable. And following the events of September 11th and the Coalition war on terrorism, we cannot foresee the possible fall-out from other theatres of war nor can we be optimistic that terrorism can ever be defeated finally. As long as there are grievances, whether justified or not, it will always be possible that people will turn to violence against the innocent to vent their frustration and to advance their cause. We have to be ever vigilant to protect ourselves. And it remains always the first duty of any government to defend its citizens against such threats.

But in the long term we have to search for answers to the underlying issues that are the breeding grounds of violence and terrorism. Not all grievances are justified; but some are and must be addressed if we are ever to live in peace. Many terrorists are so bigoted, irrational and even insane or evil that no solution will stop them, and they have to be suppressed. Even so, we have to beware lest they force us to become as evil as they are, as addicted to violence. We can only try not to make things worse by our own words or acts, and to continue to pray for and to work for real peace and justice as best we can and in our own little way.

Similarly, in our own community, we have met something of this meaningless violence and hatred, with the bombing of our Synagogue building and the destruction of much of our library. We have been comforted by the massive outpouring of loving support from so many in our community. It has been incredibly heartening. And it has restored some of our faith in the essential goodness of most people. Perhaps we can build on this solidarity and determination not to allow the twisted agenda of hateful and hate-filled folk to determine our lives, to create an ongoing coalition with all people of good will to resist violence. We must renew our commitment to the democratic solving of problems through peaceful argument that respects all parties, and the Biblical tradition on which that democratic commitment is based that we are all created in the image of God.

We are truly grateful to all who have contacted us with messages of support. And we are determined as a community that we shall go on *me hayil le hayil*, from strength to strength.

PREPARE FOR THE HOLY DAYS   *Vol. 13, No. 1 - Sept/Oct 2002*

As we reluctantly turn away from the delights of summer and the many forms of rest and enjoyment that flow from those long and lazy days, we confront the New Year. It always takes us by surprise: this year more so because it falls so early in September. Suddenly we realise that the time is on us to return to the Synagogue and to profound examination of our lives.

Now is the time to prepare for the Holy Days. Now is the time to begin to think about our lives, what has happened to us since the last time we stood in the Synagogue to hear the call of the *Shofar*, what we have done, and the values of which we have tried to live.

Each of us looks back on the past year with some sense of disappointment at failures and setback, sadness for illness, pain and loss, but also remembering some occasions of joy and celebration. And that applies, too, to our community. We have mourned death. We have rejoiced with Bnei and Bnot Mitsvah. We have celebrated with bride and groom. In short, we have lived life in all its bitter/sweet variety, with tears and laughter co-mingled and inextricable, our community, and each of us as individuals. And now is the time for turning, for returning, to the Synagogue, to prayer, to study and meditation.

We congratulate once again, the *Bnei* and *Bnot Mitsvah* this past year, all of them so accomplished, each in their own way. We lift our glasses once again to brides and grooms. In the silence of our hearts we remember again loved ones who have gone on into eternity. And we turn to the Holy Days, determined to examine our lives, as individuals and as community, so that we may return to Judaism and Torah. Some in our community have gained honours this past year, especially for *Gabbai*, Dr. David Kaplan, newly inducted into the Order of Canada, and the chair of our Ritual Committee, Dr. Cindy Hannah, freshly minted Ph.D. Most have gone through the year only honoured in private by their families and friends. Many of our members have served our community unceasingly and wholeheartedly, their work seen in the quality of the Synagogue and our community life. All too many have known pain and illness. Now is the time for all of us to turn back to discover again the Presence that underpins and supports life itself.

Elsewhere in *The Bulletin* you will find details of our services this year for *Rosh Ha Shanah, Yom Kippur* and *Sukkot*. We shall be welcoming back to our community Noa and Natan Recht: *berukhim ha baim*, welcome! Natan will be acting as our *Sheliah Tsibbur*, together with Dr. David Green.

Patricia and I would like to wish everyone a 5763 filled with blessing and health and above all peace, a *Shanah tovah umetukah*, a good and sweet year.

A NEW BEGINNING IN LIFE *Vol. 13, No. 2 - Nov/Dec 2002*

There is often some sense of anticlimax after the Holy Days. While the month of *Tishre* is filled with Festivals, one after another, so that many Jews begin to feel "shuled out", the month that follows, *Heshvan*, has no celebration at all.

But surely this is psychologically and spiritually right. *Rosh Ha Shanah, Yom Kippur, Sukkot* and *Simhat Torah* have filled our hearts and minds with so much that we need a month to digest our experiences and learning. We have to integrate into our lives the reality of a new beginning in life and the values by which we shall live for the future; the serious moral responsibility that is the fundamental lesson of the *Noraim*; the sense of gratitude for the relationship with each other and with nature that is the lesson of *Sukkot*; the joy in Torah and the community that we learn from *Simhat Torah*; these are things that need sober reflection.

And even so, *Heshvan* is not entirely a festival blank. Each week there is Shabbat, the very core of our identity as Jews. The effort that all made to be in the Synagogue for the Holy Days is often enough not continued into attendance at the Shabbat services. That is a pity! There are many reasons to come to services weekly on Shabbat. We want to maintain the community, we want to ensure a *minyan* so that fellow Jews who need to say *Kaddish* can. We want to keep up the numbers so that when we welcome visiting groups, Jewish hosts are not outnumbered by non-Jewish guests. But, far more important, regular Shabbat service attendance is our weekly recharging of batteries. It is our chance to reopen contact with Jewish ideas and values, to explore our own spirituality in supportive community, and to rediscover our relations with fellow Jews.

Our guest Cantor, at the beginning of October reminded us of the importance of Shabbat worship by his teaching and through his leading of musical setting of services. Jewish music is so rich that it enables us to transcend our mundane concerns and leads us into a journey of Jewish historical faith. Cantor Shalowitz showed us how precious that journey is and how beautiful and spiritually moving it can be.

Perhaps the major New Year resolution that we could make, and the one that we are most likely to keep, is to come to Shabbat services once a month regularly and discover for ourselves what a blessing that can be. Of course, we must always remember that, as with all human experience, we shall get out only what we are willing to put in. If someone comes to a religious service in a critical mood, resentful, with no intention to make an effort to contribute to the communal pool of prayer, then that person will find the experience boring and useless. But if someone comes intending to explore and discover, open to the surprise of discovery, eager to be a real part of the community at prayer, then wonderful things can happen, for that person and for us all.

So, in this seemingly empty time after the Holy Days, we might all try to do just that.

MEMBERS HONOURED *Vol. 13, No. 3 - Jan/Feb 2003*

It is a quite astonishing fact that our small congregation includes a number of people who have been honoured by the general community for their contributions to Saskatchewan and Canada that is totally out of proportion to our numbers in the population as a whole. We have four members of the Order of Canada and two recipients of the Queen's Jubilee Medal. And that of course does not include the large numbers of our members who have made enormous contributions to the welfare of the general community but who have not as yet been recognized for those contributions.

This is a source of pride for us as a Jewish community. First, because of the personal achievements that have been honoured. And second, because of the honour that our achievements bring to the Jewish community and to Jews and Judaism. This quite-tiny Jewish community has born witness to Judaism and to Jewish values in the non-Jewish community.

One of my favourite *Midrashim* is of the Sage who bought a donkey from a non-Jew who agreed to sell not only the donkey but to include everything attached to it. On getting home, the Sage removed the donkey's saddle and discovered a precious gem. The Sage's students argued that, as the donkey had been bought and sold in good faith "as is," it was perfectly in order for the Teacher to keep the jewel. The Sage demurred and insisted on returning the jewel to the non-Jewish seller, who obviously had not known about it and clearly had not intended to include it in the sale. To take advantage of the man's ignorance would clearly break the Commandment not to steal. And, even more important, the Sage's act of honesty would bring credit in the eyes of the non-Jew for Judaism and the God of Israel.

Each one of us is responsible in the moral way in which we live for the standing of Judaism and the Jewish people in the eyes of the non-Jewish world. And I quoted the *Midrash* to show that this is not a new idea. Nor is it a fear of the non-Jewish world and the possibility of anti-Semitism, the "what will they think?" syndrome, as some Zionist thinkers have claimed. Rather, it is legitimate concern for the reputation of the God of Israel. By bringing credit in non-Jewish eyes for Judaism, we fulfill the *mitzvah* of *keruv*, of bringing non-Jews to the Torah, whether directly, or indirectly, by strengthening the moral code that, derived from Israel, applies to all humankind.

So our good wishes and congratulations to the recipients of awards, and our gratitude to all our members who make such wonderful contributions to the quality of life in Saskatoon, Saskatchewan and Canada, and thereby radiate the values of Jewish tradition into the non-Jewish world. Truly are we called to be a blessing to all the families of the earth.

PREPARE FOR PESAH *Vol. 13, No. 4 - Mar/Apr 2003*

Now is the time to prepare for Pesah. There are two aspects of our preparation. First, we look to the practicalities of observance. Judaism teaches through the act, not the thought. The cleaning of the home and the laying in of *kasher le Pesah* supplies cannot be avoided, and other traditional observances, such as selling of leaven, *mekhirat hamets*, should be seriously considered as part of our Jewish life. Second, we meditate about what lies behind the act. Thought without action is futile, but action without thought is stupid.

So it is in order to reread the *Haggadah*, and re-familiarize ourselves with what we are going to experience at the *Seder*, so that it becomes for us not a boring recital of the past but a reliving of leaving behind slavery and becoming free. Every year is the first time. And for this we need to have a good edition of the *Haggadah*.

Of the making of *Haggadot* there is no end. What we should be looking for is an edition that is beautiful to look at, well illustrated, well annotated, with new readings, and guidelines about what to do and when and why; in short, user friendly. The non-Orthodox groups have all issued remarkably good Haggadot that are both religiously inspiring and wonderful teaching tools. The Conservative Haggadah guides the user through the Seder service and has sensitive notes and new readings; the Reform Haggadah is well illustrated and includes music; the Reconstructionist Haggadah weaves tradition into contemporary themes and readings seamlessly. All can be recommended, and there is no reason why we cannot use them all to involve everyone present in the Seder, regardless of knowledge or commitment.

The lesson of freedom itself has two parts: there is freedom from, and there is freedom for, and the one is incomplete without the other. We did not leave Egyptian slavery just to become free to do our own thing; we became free to enter into the covenant of Torah and to share purposeful freedom with everyone.

A final note: if we believe in the Exodus as literal history, we have reason to rejoice at the Seder; but if we do not believe that it actually happened, we still have good reason to rejoice. For Pesah is part of being Jewish. Even if it didn't happen as the Torah says, it still happened in the heart and soul of the Jewish people, and it still happens magically every year as we relive the experience.

Patricia and I would like to wish all our members, and the whole Jewish community, a *hag kasher ve sameah*, a *Pesah* filled with joy, peace and renewed hope.

COUNTING THE OMER *Vol. 13, No. 5 - May/June 2003*

We are now counting the *Omer*. Each day between *Pesah* and *Shavuot* in the evening service we count down the days from 1 to 50. This is a very practical link that we make between the two *hagim*. The obvious question is: Why do we do this, and particularly why seemingly so mechanically (this is day one, two etc.)?

We count because in ancient times our ancestors brought each day an *omer* (about a litre) of barley to the Temple in Jerusalem in thanksgiving for the harvest. But there is more to it than that, and we are not merely remembering ancient history. We are actually linking the two Festivals. *Pesah* and *Shavuot* are not really separated; they are the beginning and fulfilment of a process. We are celebrating freedom. At *Pesah* we remember and actually relive the experience of standing once more at Sinai and receiving Torah and so entering into a covenant with God. And the connecting link is freedom.

At *Pesah* we become free from, and at *Shavuot* we become free for. We become free from slavery to others; and at Shavuot we become free to serve others.

Freedom is not license. Freedom is not the chaotic ability and right to do whatever we want (even provided that we do not impinge on the freedom of others to do likewise). Freedom is not libertarianism. Freedom is, first, the ability to make our own decisions and choices. But it is second, the ability and right to make those choices and decisions in a larger context than our own personal will. It is the right freely to choose to exercise freedom within the parameters of the moral universe that includes others in relationship, this society. The parameters that guide and structure our choices and decisions are laid down by Torah and the responsibility of covenant. And freedom from must become freedom for: Pesah is not fulfilled until Shavuot. Our path is from Mitsrayim, the place where we are constrained by human agency, to Sinai, the place where we are constrained by nothing more than our free choice to enter into covenant with God. And this understanding of freedom is uniquely Jewish.

Most Jews observe Pesah, primarily because the seder is the occasion par excellence of family togetherness. Not so many Jews observe Shavuot, primarily because it is not marked by families coming together to eat, celebrate and share love and joy. Yet the one is not complete without the other. Shavuot, often falling as it does on a weekday, is often lost; it becomes a sort of orphan festival. And that is a tragedy. Because it is actually a major Festival of our year. This year, why not try it? Why not come to the Synagogue and forge another link in the chain of tradition as we stand again at Sinai with all Jews who ever were or ever will be? That is what our freedom, so hard won at Pesah, is really all about.

READING AND VISITING *Vol. 13, No. 6 - July/August 2003*

During summer our thoughts turn to holidays and recreation. We anticipate days of glorious weather when we can forget everyday concerns about the office, appointments, committees and the general business of making a living: days at the lake, on the beach, travelling to exotic places, enjoying family and friends.

But we do not give up being Jews during the summer months. Even on holiday we are influenced by our Judaism. Indeed, we have more time to think about it, leisure to experiment with bringing it into our lives. Consider just two things, for example.

We have the opportunity when on holiday to read. Maybe we don't want to read "heavy" scholarly tomes, but there are many Jewish books that are appropriate reading for leisure time. There is fiction with a Jewish theme, there is easy history, thought-provoking books that raise issues from a Jewish perspective, books about Israel. And we have our Synagogue library as a rich resource available to all members. Why not think about coming into the Centre and picking out a few books to take with you on holiday? After all, unfortunately, not all the summer will be perfect weather, and there will be rainy days when reading a good book will be welcome: why not a Jewish book?

And second, wherever you may go on holiday this summer it is highly likely that you will find fellow Jews, even a Synagogue. Why not visit the Synagogue and make contact? It may be that the local community is small like ours and needs you to help to make up a *minyan*. Why not help fellow Jews to say *Kaddish* by joining them when they need you? The world is filled with Jewish communities scattered throughout all countries, sometimes in places where you would least expect it. To make contact during one's travels is to fulfill a *mitsvah* by creating links between Jews all over the world. If you would like to have information about local communities where you are going to be during the summer, contact me and I will let you have some information.

There are so many other ways to keep in touch with our Jewishness while away from home during the holiday period: take candles for lighting on Friday evening; take a *siddur* and say some prayers while freed from day-to-day pressures; look for sources of kosher food. But reading Jewish books and making contact with local communities are things that will give pleasure and take little effort other than looking up an address, but will give lasting satisfaction.

Patricia and I wish all our members happy holidays, and a summer filled with perfect weather. Good reading and may you make new friends in fa-flung communities!

Ready for the New Year *Vol. 14, No. 1 - Sept/Oct 2003*

We are now beginning to realise that we shall soon have to turn back from the summer holidays to the business of what for many is a New Year. Plans for a new term are under way; businesses begin a new year. It is time to get back to day-to-day living focused on the harsh realities of making a living, getting children back in school, planning another year of hectic activities.

And that applies to the community as well. It is a New Year for us Jews that is coming up soon. And that too forces us to make plans. For *Rosh ha Shanah* begins the Days of Awe, the Ten Days of Return that culminate in Yom Kipper. Actually, the process begins even earlier with *Rosh Hodesh Ellul*, when, traditionally, we blow the *shofar* in each weekly service. Time suddenly seems to accelerate, and the New Year overtakes us before we even notice. No Rabbi I know, and certainly not this one, ever gets sermons written in time for services prepared properly, before Rosh ha Shanah is tomorrow already.

Perhaps this year, as *Rosh ha Shanah* is late, we might take control of the mad passage of time and actually be ready.

We all need to get ready for the New Year, not just Rabbis and Cantors. If we do not prepare ourselves, practically, emotionally and psychologically, we shall find that we do not get as much spiritually out of the experience as we ought to, or help our community to give to its members what it should.

What, for example, do we need to do to prepare?

We need to make practical preparation in terms of house cleaning and preparation of traditional foods that give this time its special *taam*, flavour. We need to make spiritual preparations in terms of familiarizing ourselves with the format of the services that are unique in our tradition. We need to meditate on the spiritual themes of this time, *teshuvah*, "return of God"; responsibility for moral choices and ethical living; letting go of the past, yet also integrating our lives with the lessons we have hopefully learned over this past year; rebuilding relations between us and family, friends and community that have been frayed over this year; rediscovering the moral and spiritual values of our Judaism. Putting aside 15 minutes a day in such preparation will produce inestimable results. Prayer, study and meditation is an investment that pays better dividends than the stock exchange has for many months.

There is much more that we can do to make ready for the New Year, but this is a useful start we could make.

Patricia and I would like to wish all our community a New Year of renewed hope and courage and reborn vision, a New Year of peace and love and justice, for us and all humankind.

RELIGIOUS SATURATION? *Vol. 14, No. 2 - Nov/Dec 2003*

As we look back on the three weeks of *Tishri*, many of us will confess to a feeling of religious satiation. *Rosh ha Shanah, Yom Kippur, Sukkot, Simhat Torah*, one after the other, and all requiring from us attendance in the Synagogue and intense concentration on worship, study and a spiritual agenda: enough already!

At no other time do we appreciate the jarring disjunction between our calendar and the secular calendar. At no other time do we know so acutely the feeling of being out of step with the majority. Together with everyone else, we go back to work and school after the summer holidays, only almost immediately, unlike our colleagues and friends, we have to take time off again. This is the time when a Jew understands just how different he or she is from all others.

And that is precisely the point. Like *Shabbat*, these three weeks in *Tishri* are telling us very clearly that we are different. We are different because we are Jews and our tradition demands of us sacrifice. As close as we are to the rest of the world, we still have to acknowledge that we have a special role to play in our world, to be a prophetic people dedicated to *tikkun olam*, healing the world.

And, also like *Shabbat*, these Festivals say bluntly to us that we are not the roles that we play in ordinary life — client, customer, professional person — we are human beings, called to recognize our humanity as a clear link with our divinity. We wear many masks in our day-to-day lives, but we are not those masks; we are to be defined as a people in covenant, a *kehilah kedoshah*, a holy community.

This is the lesson that we can take with us as we move into these days of deepening gloom and winter. We sanctify time, we fill the passing moment with meaning and joy, we are not bound to the unending wheel of work, the illusory hope of becoming: we have arrived, we are. We and our families are holy agents of healing and holiness if we want it.

SEVERAL NEW YEARS *Vol. 14, No. 3 - Jan/Feb 2004*

We begin a secular new year. It may seem that this has little to do with us Jews, at least religiously. This is not entirely so.

The Jewish calendar has several new years: the one we know best, *Rosh ha Shanah* (which oddly comes in the 7th not the 1st month of our calendrical year), *Tu biShvat*, the new year for trees, and *Rosh Hodesh Nisan*, being the main examples. So does the secular year: January 1st, the tax new year in April, the academic new year in September, to name but three. We should remember, too, that the secular new year has not always been in January: in the Protestant parts of Europe until the middle of the 18th century the new year began in March.

There are links between the Jewish and the secular calendar.

Every human tradition has marked the passage of time and celebrated moments of transition. We have divided up time — into the obvious days added together to give us weeks, and most obviously into months that correspond to the phases of the moon. Most peoples created a lunar calendar because it was so easy to see those phases, and they corresponded with human biological phases, such as the menstrual cycle. Later, the connection was made with the cycle of the sun, and, for Jews at least, the lunar and solar years were synchronized by intercalating a month seven times in a 19-year cycle.

But every calendar is still marking significant times of transition in human experience. Especially is this so with a new year. *Rosh ha Shanah* is the time when Jews mark the most significant transition, look back on the year past and forward to the year now beginning, and associate the period with change in human behaviour, from doing what is wrong to—hopefully—doing what is right. January 1st for many of our friends is much the same. It, too, is a time for looking back and assessing life, and then looking forward into the unknown about to be born in an attitude of hope and determination to do better: it is a time for celebration and for wishing for ourselves and others good for the year to come.

In that spirit, let us wish ourselves and others a good New Year, 2004. Whatever it may bring to our world we do not know, but we can pray for peace, health and happiness, and we can determine to play our part that it may be so. Patricia and I wish everyone a good 2004. If the beginning of 5764 seems already a little remote, perhaps this is an appropriate time to renew the hopes and prayers of *Rosh ha Shanah*.

SPRING APPROACHES *Vol. 14, No. 4 - March/April 2004*

At last we are nearing spring. We know it because we are celebrating *Purim*, and between *Purim* and *Pesah* there is only a month. And with *Pesah* we really are rejoicing that winter is over and gone and the voice of the turtledove is heard in the land. So, though there may yet be weather surprises in store (this is Saskatchewan after all), the end of the harsh winter is now in sight.

Purim is an odd Festival. It really has very little to do with religion. I know that it has been seen as a paradigm of Jewish life in Diaspora and the continuing threat of anti-Semitism. Esther has been seen as a Jewish girl who was highly assimilated and who awakes in the emergency to her Jewish identity. This may be true. But *Purim* remains an odd Festival. It is, after all, a sort of Mardi Gras, a carnival marking the imminent end of winter and the rebirth of spring. And I have a feeling that we are fully aware of the sorrows of Jewish history already — how could we not be? — and we need to rediscover some of the triumphs of that history. As Alan Dershowitz has reminded us, we need to be more conscious of the joy of Judaism instead of the '*oy*' of Judaism.

And Purim does that for us. It is a time for letting our hair down (for those of us who still have hair!), and just being happy. It is good to be Jewish, it is good to be alive: we have survived winter darkness to enter the light and warmth of spring. So let us rejoice at Purim and not bother too much to find deep meaning and the lessons of anti-Semitism in our history. Enough already! What is wrong with having fun?

And in only a month's time we shall celebrate the Festival of Freedom: Pesah. We shall remember our history, we shall rejoice in our freedom from slavery and we shall look forward to the working out of that freedom in the future. Our families will come together, and all the prayers and symbols of our celebration will be filled with memory and hope. We will talk and pray and sing together; we will remember good and bad, and we will renew the fundamental hope and courage that makes us Jews.

So, a happy *Purim* to all. And a *Pesah* that will truly be a *hag sameah ve kasher*, for us all.

In our liturgical year we now reach *Shavuot,* the fulfilment and completion of what began at *Pesah.* We have counted each day from *Pesah* during the *Omer* period to remind ourselves that the two *Hagim* are linked together. At *Pesah* we became free, but we remained an *erev rav,* a rabble of former slaves: seven weeks later we came to Sinai and we became a people with a purpose, an *am kadosh.* We entered the covenant with God, symbolized by Torah.

But, as with all our Festivals, there are two aspects of Shavuot. Pesah was the time of freedom, *zman herutenu.* But it was also the time of spring and the renewal of life after winter. Both aspects are of the *seder* table before us in the symbol, for example of the *zeroa,* the lamb bone. This is a reminder of both the Temple and the history of the Jewish people entering freedom; and also a reminder of the new born lambs of the flock in the spring. So, too, is it with *Shavuot.* This is the time of the revelation of God to Israel at Sinai, *zman Toratenu*; it is also the summer harvest. So we read two parts of the *Tnakh*: we read the Ten Commandments, the *aseret ha dibrot,* reminding us of the covenant between Israel and God; and we read the book of Ruth, *megilat Rut,* a book that breathes the atmosphere of summer and harvest. Brilliantly, Ruth conveys indeed both messages about Shavuot, for it is also the story of a young woman who becomes a Jew by choice, who loves Torah because she loves Jews.

Shavuot is a very important Festival in our calendar. It teaches us two very profound truths. It teaches us that we are bound up with nature and the cycle of the seasons and the fertility of the earth. And it teaches us that we are a people created by covenant. Our identity is as a community bound to God by Torah. Both are the same lesson. Without Jews there is no Judaism; but equally, without Judaism there are no Jews.

Summer – Return Refreshed Vol. 14, No. 6 - July/Aug 2004

These summer months are a time for holiday. It is a time for refreshment of body, mind and spirit, so that we can return to normality in the autumn renewed, with new ideas, new energy, reinvigorated body.

We need such a time of being away from the normal, a time when we are not dominated by the demands and pressures of the everyday. We are not machines that can be run without a break: we become very easily and quickly burned out. So let us all enjoy time to be away, away from phones and faxes and e-mails, away from having to work eight hours every day, away from deadlines and responsibilities.

Yet, while we are away, let us not entirely vegetate. Our minds and spirits, like our bodies, need exercise to stay healthy. We are not built to endlessly lie on a beach, to do nothing at all. Summer is a time to catch up with other things in our lives that we tend to lose sight of in our workday lives. By all means, catch up with tennis and golf, walking, lazing, soaking up sun. But humankind cannot live by golf alone!

These summer months are a time for us to read and meditate, to enjoy the world around us and think of our relations with nature, to walk around museums and art galleries and re-establish our links with history and art and human creativity, to be with family and friends without pressure and hurry and rediscover the links of love that are so easily frayed in making a living. And they are a time, too, to think about our Jewishness, to read Jewish books, to visit other Jews as we travel to other parts of the world. We all welcome and value the chance to meet fellow Jews from other countries. So, if you are travelling, don't forget to call in to a local Synagogue and make up a minyan.

Patricia and I wish all our members a restful and enjoyable summer. If anyone would like details of a Jewish book they may like to take with them, or the address of a local Jewish community where they may be staying so that they can call in, get in touch and I would be pleased to give the information. Let us all have a profitable holiday period and return refreshed to a new and busy year in our community.

A Time for Spiritual Audit *Vol. 15, No. 1 - Sept/Oct 2004*

Elsewhere you will find the dates and times for the High Holy Day Services. Here there are just a few explanatory notes to ensure that you, the members, have as much information as possible.

The evening Services will be less than an hour in length, except for *Kol Nidre* which will be about one and a half hours. There will be sermons on *Rosh ha Shanah*, both days, and on *Yom Kippur* evening, morning and *Neilah*. The sermon on the second morning of *Rosh ha Shanah* will be, as is our custom, by our President, Susanne Kaplan: the others by me.

Please try to be on time so as to preserve the special atmosphere of these Days of Awe. If you are late, please do not enter the Sanctuary while the Ark is open or during a sermon. In addition, please plan to remain throughout the Service.

You will note that we do not intend to put out seating for more than 150 (we can always expand the space if we have a massive influx), so people will have to fill the seating available and not disappear to the back.

Services always give to worshippers in proportion to their input. Participation in singing and reading by all members works together with the efforts of those leading the Service to create an experience worthy of the occasion.

It is also useful in getting the most out of these Days to come to Services with some preparation. This means having a look at the Services themselves and the themes of these Days, and also thinking a little about what we are actually trying to do. This special time of the year is a sort of spiritual and moral audit that we are carrying out for ourselves and for our community. It is a chance to come to terms with our lives, *Liten din ve heshbon lifne khise khododekha*, to give an account of ourselves and our deeds before the Divine throne, as the Sefardi liturgy puts it. It would be profoundly missing the point if we didn't use it.

Note, too, that we go immediately from *Yom Kippur* to *Sukkot*, from solemn meditation on life and our values to joyous celebration of the harvest and beauty and bounty of nature. So plan to be with us for Sukkot and join us in the *sukkah* as well as for the Days of Awe. Joy is as acceptable to God as our repentance. It may even be a sign that *teshuvah* is really sincere!

Patricia and I wish everyone a joyous New Year. May we all be inscribed and sealed for life, health and peace in 5765.

ASSIMILATE THE LESSONS *Vol. 15, No. 2 - Nov/Dec 2004*

After the run of Festivals in Tishri, we enter a long period without Festivals. For many of us, especially those involved with the services for these Festivals, this is a welcome break. However, we should see this period as something more than just a breather after the *Noraim* and *Sukkot/Simhat Torah*. It is rather a fallow time when we can assimilate the lessons of what we have just lived through. We can integrate the religious and ethical themes of the Festivals more and more into our lives. So we need time to think about our experiences during this special time of our year, and see how we can apply what we have learned to our world.

This is obvious enough with the lessons of *Sukkot*. We experience our frailty as we stand in the *sukkah*; we remember loved ones with whom we have shared the celebration of the harvest and who are now dead; we see in our lives the cycle of the seasons, the cycle of nature and life itself. We know that our emotions of joy embedded in sadness will be with us as we go on into and through the winter. Nature will be reborn, and so will life even at the darkest moments.

And the lessons of *Rosh ha Shanah* and *Yom Kippur* also stay with us and mould the way we will live on. We know that we fall short of what we should be and could be, and yet, even then, there is always hope renewed, for we can always become different if we want to, always react more imaginatively and more intelligently to life if we want to. We will respect our fellow creatures more because of what we have learned. Maybe we will love more, give more, be more open to the mystery of divinity.

These winter months are therefore a time for us to reflect and to try to change in the light of what we have learned.

After all, why when we end *Sukkot* do we straightaway add *Simhat Torah*?

Because when we rejoice in the beauty and bounty of nature, we immediately link that to Torah which is the anchor of our lives. We have not only life itself, but we also are given instruction on how to live that life at its richest. As we are blessed by life, so should we be a blessing to life.

TIME OF BEGINNINGS *Vol. 15, No. 3 - Jan/Feb 2005*

We cannot complain of not having enough chances to make new year resolutions. Quite apart from our own *Rosh ha Shanah* and the various New Years in the Jewish calendar, we also have a secular new year, indeed several of those, too. But specifically I refer to January 1st, the beginning of the secular year 2005.

Although this date has no resonance in Judaism, it is still a time of beginnings. We live in two worlds, our own Jewish year, based on the lunar calendar; and the secular year, based on the solar calendar. January 1st is a time when we can link these two aspects of our identity. We can celebrate with our neighbours of all religions the start of a new year when we can look back on what was and what it meant to us, and look forward to the unknown, with hope for peace and happiness for our world and all its people.

It is a time when people come together to share their thoughts and hopes in fellowship. There are times when we can forget our differences and look at life as something that we all share, and this is the major time for coming together. It doesn't have to be an occasion for drunkenness—as all too often it is, but coming together socially in family and friendship groups is to be encouraged.

New Years are often times for making resolutions to improve the way we live. Unfortunately, resolutions rarely survive far into the New Year, perhaps because we tend to be somewhat unrealistic in our intentions to improve our lives, heartfelt though those intentions are at the time. Even so, some more realistic resolutions are worth making.

We can, for example, determine to be more tolerant and less judgemental, both of others and ourselves. And perhaps this is the resolution that is hardest to keep, yet also the most important for us to try to keep. Just imagine what a better world it would be, for us and for the world around us, if we could be a little more tolerant, and a little less quick to judge!

It would also ease our own burden of frustration, stress and high blood pressure. It might, therefore, be highly worthwhile to make that particular resolution, enter it into our diaries on each page, and continually remind ourselves of it through the year to come. So, let us resolve to lighten up, be more gentle with ourselves and those we live with, accept the range of human difference as a delightful mystery rather than a challenge, and refuse to judge others too quickly. And remember, too, that this is a good Jewish attribute to strive for. As Shammai, of all people, says, "Receive all people with a cheerful face."

Patricia and I wish all our fellow members of Agudas Israel a peaceful, healthy and happy New Year. May 2005 see the fulfillment of all our intentions and desires for good.

PESAH – A FAMILY TIME *Vol. 15, No. 4 - Mar/April 2005*

We are approaching the coming of spring, hard as it may be to visualise as I write this at the end of January. And with spring comes Pesah, when we celebrate the birth of the Jewish people and the freedom hard won in the Exodus. And with Pesah we begin to count the *Omer* toward our symbolic arrival at Sinai and our entering into covenant with God that we celebrate at Shavuot.

This is a marvellous time for us. We have survived yet another winter. And we begin again to relive the historical experiences that make us a special people and that declare the purpose of that specialness: to be a people of God living Torah and struggling continually for *tikkun olam*, the healing and making whole of our world.

Pesah is also the time for being with family and friends at the *seder*. It is also the time when we drive ourselves mad worrying about spring cleaning (physical and spiritual), and food. The whole of *kashrut* moves into a higher gear. We become concerned with whether or not leaven is present in what we eat. This is not to be a neurotic ritual (and it can be obsessive if you let it), but a search for a higher dimension of holiness. For the week of *Pesah* we are trying to live on another level of holiness. Why? Because we are especially conscious of who we are and what we are. Leaven is a symbol of everything that restrains us from being true to our Jewish identity. By removing it from our diet and our homes even if only for a week, we are teaching ourselves that we have a higher purpose in our lives as Jews.

Just consider the beauty of our calendar. After the quiet of winter, a time of mere survival, we suddenly burst into the light of spring, with the simple human joy of survival proclaimed and celebrated at *Purim* and then, a month later confirmed by the becoming free at *Pesah*, that freedom confirmed in the covenant of Sinai that we remake every year as we link the generations of Jews together, at *Shavuot*.

If you would like to sell your *hamets* for *Pesah*, please contact me to do so. And if you need advice about Pesah foods — what is and what is not *kasher le Pesah* — please contact me and I will help. Remember, it isn't as complicated as some like to make it, and the effort is well worth while.

Patricia and I wish all our members a *hag kasher ve sameah*.

What Unites All Jews? Vol. 15, No. 5 - May/June 2005

Over the past few months we have been looking at the choices that Jews make in terms of Synagogue membership and "denominational" affiliation. We have seen a wide range of differing interpretations of Jewish faith and practice. And a question arises out of this: Is there a common core of belief and practice that unites all Jews, regardless of the style of Synagogue they choose to belong to?

I think that we can discern some such core if we look carefully.

All Jews would agree on the centrality to their Jewish experience of the Shma. The statement of the unity of the Divine Principle in the universe is a given for all Jews. From that principle flows both the basic attitude that has produced modern science in its search for the unifying factor of the four forces in the universe; and also the moral statement of the unity of all humankind.

All Jews would agree on the Jewish calendar and the Festivals that mark life during the year. Shabbat is one of the greatest Jewish gifts to the world; and the other Festivals have been important to the forming of the Christian year as well as ours. The celebration of the three harvest Festivals, and the marking of the New Year and Yom Kippur, are essential to human understanding of the passage of time.

All Jews would agree on the marking of the life cycle, from birth to death. The idea of the covenant that underlies circumcision and marriage, the celebration of life at the time of death, and the customs of mourning that lead to healing after death, all are part of a united people and faith.

All Jews would agree on the importance of prayer and the basic way in which Jews have prayed. Prayer Books have differed in detail, some use more English than others, but the basic format remains accepted by all.

All Jews accept the importance of *kashrut*, even when they differ in detail. All Jews accept the overriding importance of study of the traditional texts, even if they do not find themselves able to engage in study: it should still be done.

And there are values that all Jews share. Few would deny the supreme importance of *tsedakah*, justice in human relations; or *tikkun olam*, the striving for social justice, harmony and healing. All would agree that Jews are called to be compassionate as God is seen to be compassionate.

And above all, all Jews would accept that we, the Jewish people, are a special people, in covenant (*brit*) with God, and called to the task of proclaiming that God to the whole world, by witnessing through our continued existence to God's demand that we shall be *kadosh*, special. That covenant is detailed in Torah, both the written text of the Hebrew Bible and also the oral text of the Rabbinic tradition in *Talmud, Midrash, Halakhah and Haggadah*.

Despite all our differences in the detail of how we express our Jewish identity in faith and practice, what we still have in common far transcends those differences. We have to keep open the dialogue with each other, stressing our commonalities, while also accommodating our principled differences in a spirit of integrity and *ahavat Yisrael*, love and respect for each other as Jews.

RECHARGING ENERGIES *Vol. 15, No. 6 - July/Aug 2005*

The summer months are a time for rest and reflection, a time for recharging energies. All of us need this time away from daily pressures to regain a healthy perspective on life. So, however you will be spending this time, on holiday, away from home, with friends and family, Patricia and I wish you health and rest.

However, rest does not necessarily mean just lazing on a beach doing nothing: that is important: as the Italians so correctly put it "dolce far niente," it is good to do nothing: but there are other important aspects of resting. As the English proverb says, "A change is as good as a rest." These holiday months of summer are also a chance to catch up with things that we have lost sight of during the hectic times. There are books that we always intended to read, music that we always intended to listen to, places we always wanted to visit. This is our chance.

And as we try to fit these things into our schedule, we should not forget Jewish things. Being Jewish is not just for the rest of the year: it includes the summer holiday period as well. There are Jewish books to read, Jewish music to listen to, Jewish places to visit, and fellow Jews all over the world to meet. So, when you go on holiday, consider taking a Jewish book with you, especially one you always wanted to read but never got round to. And if you travel to far off places, put aside a little of your time to make contact with Jews and Jewish sites wherever you may be. Jews are a world-wide family, always pleased to meet other Jews from different places. You will always be welcome if you call in at the Synagogue, perhaps help to make up a minyan, have a meal in the local kosher restaurant. Introduce yourself and bring greetings from snowy Saskatoon. You will be appreciated. If you need help with addresses for communities where you are intending to be, please contact me at the Synagogue and I can probably help.

Wherever you go and whatever you do in these summer months, come back refreshed and reinvigorated and inspired to play an active role in your own community here in Saskatoon in the new year.

We are now preparing ourselves for the Holy Days. I sometimes think that we as modern people are a bit overwhelmed by the ideas that underlie this time of the year: sin, atonement, prayer. The concept of prayer is one that we find especially hard to make sense of. It seems perhaps a little old fashioned, redolent of magic.

Most of us think of prayer as petition, asking for things, particularly things that are outside our ability to do for ourselves. It is true enough that petition is a part of the pattern of prayer in tradition. In a world where so much seemed beyond human control and arbitrary, even chaotic, this is not altogether surprising. But not everything in the traditional prayer book is petition, in effect asking for God to do miracles: far from it. There are many other aspects of prayer.

The Hebrew word for prayer, *tefillah*, connects to the grammatical root PLL, which means "struggle, wrestle." An insightful translation of *tefillah*, therefore, is Judith Plaskow's term "God wrestling." That is exactly what prayer is — struggling, wrestling, with God. Or maybe wrestling with oneself, trying to discover meaning and purpose in our human experience. We try to relate our experience to past human experience, and particularly the experience of the Jewish people, and so find some lesson that will give us courage, hope and inspiration to live better. Life, after all, is not just to be passively experienced, it is to be learned from and given a moral anchor.

If we apply this insight to what we are engaged in over the Holy Days, perhaps it will make some more sense of what is going on. We shall be coming together to do many things. We shall be restating our Jewish identity and trying to find some meaning in being Jewish for our modern living. We shall be trying to come to terms with what we have done and what has happened to us in the past year. We shall be trying to learn from our experience so that we shall be, hopefully, better and more sensitive human beings in the year that is beginning. And we shall be investigating important ideas handed down to us from our tradition. And perhaps the most important single one of these is the significance and meaning of prayer.

Why is this last so important? Because, in the last resort life has to be founded on prayer in order to be lived most fully and richly. Not prayer in the sense of manipulating a higher power to do miracles for us: that isn't important, because not one of us is important enough for the universe to be disrupted for us — how self-centred that idea is! But prayer in the sense that I have suggested — wrestling with experience to find meaning. Unless we have meaning and purpose in our lives, we are merely flotsam, cast hither and thither by events. With that meaning, we live with purpose, and most important, we have the courage and hope to live well.

It is therefore worthwhile to spend some time thinking about prayer as we prepare for *Rosh ha Shanah* and *Yom Kippur*. Perhaps this year our experience may make sense and not just be an exercise in nostalgia, tribal identity or, *has ve shalom*, mere boredom. A prayer-based life, the search for purpose and meaning, is what calls us to be truly human.

May we all be blessed with a New Year of blessing and *shalom*.

A BUSY COMMUNITY *Vol. 16, No. 2 - November/December 2005*

We have been very busy during this period, with the Holy Days immediately followed by Sukkot. We have also said a special farewell to a special person with the dinner in honour of Gladys Rose: we hope that her life-long commitment to the community in Saskatoon will continue, and that the farewell will be more *lehitraot*, until we see her again, which God willing, will be often. Our congregational cup is overflowing: we have celebrated the Bar Mitsvah of Noah Fenyes, well done and deserving our hearty "*mazal tov*" to him and to his family and friends.

Our busy time is not done. On November 26 our Shabbat morning Service will be very special. To mark the Centennial of the Province of Saskatchewan and the next year's Centennial of the City of Saskatoon, we are celebrating the contribution that our Jewish community has made to the broader community over the last century, and also looking forward to our own renewal over the next hundred years. We shall be rededicating our Synagogue for the new century. Our service will be marked by the presence of the Lt. Governor of Saskatchewan, Her Honour Dr. Lynda Haverstock, and will involve a large number of our members. It will be followed by a *Kiddush* lunch. The celebratory weekend will continue on the Sunday with a special Concert. And during the week there will be a reprise of the well-known operetta "Love and Latkes." Our celebration of our Province, our City and our Community will be a heartfelt one.

Our members are invited to join us and our many guests for all these events.

We are a small community. Jews never constituted even 0.5% of the population of Saskatchewan, or of Saskatoon. Yet our contribution to both the Province and City has been enormously disproportionate to those numbers in all fields — the arts, business, the University, voluntary work, medicine, and many others. For the next year's centennial of the City we shall be putting on an exhibition of 100 Jews who have made a difference to the quality of life in Saskatoon over the last 100 years, and we hope that many — Jews and non-Jews — will come to see this source of pride to our Jewish community. We pray that the next century will be just as rich and productive. Truly does the Torah promise us that, "In you shall all the families of the earth find a blessing."

At the end of November we celebrated the centennial of the Province of Saskatchewan and also rededicated our Synagogue for the next century. We were privileged to have the Lt. Governor, Dr. Lynda Haverstock, with us for the occasion.

The Service was most successful, and I should like to thank everyone who took part in the Service for their contribution on that Shabbat morning. Dr. Haverstock spoke eloquently and movingly about the Jewish contribution to Saskatchewan and her words were most welcome. This was part of our community celebration of the centennial which also featured the remarkable musical and theatrical talent of our community. Small as we may be, we have so much still to give, and this was made obvious in these special events.

What, members may ask, was the purpose of all this? Why did we ask so many to put themselves out and work so hard, and invite the general public to share with us?

The answer is simple. We are so aware that our numbers are declining, and that our volunteers are becoming fewer and have less energy, and that we are stretched thinner and thinner, that we sometimes feel that we have no future in the long term, and are doomed to extinction. It is important, therefore, to take the time and make the effort to show ourselves that we are seen by the outside world as an important part of our City and Province, that we have made an immense contribution to the well being of our neighbours, and still have so much to give to our community that we live in. It is important for our members to hear the Lt. Governor of Saskatchewan telling us that Jews are essential to the fabric of our Province. Somehow, we Jews don't believe it when we say it: somehow we Jews are so good with bad news!

This was a time for us to show ourselves at our best to the outside world. It was a time for us to be proud of ourselves and of our Jewish community. It was a time for us to realize that we are not dead yet. And I think we did this, and more. Once again, thank you to all our members who took part, and all our members who attended.

Next year, we shall celebrate the centenary of our City with an exhibition of the 100 Jews who have made a real contribution to Saskatoon over the century. A sincere thank you in advance — to those 100 members and former members of our community, and to those who will carry on their work!

OUR PAST AND FUTURE *Vol. 16, No. 4 - March/April 2006*

The Jewish years seems a little unbalanced. There are two periods of busyness interspersed with months that are fairly quiet. In the autumn we have *Rosh ha Shanah*, *Yom Kippur* and *Sukkot* that follow each other seamlessly, so that by *Simhat Torah* we are breathless and davened out. And now in the spring we have *Purim* and *Pesah* leading into *Shavuot*. The spring busyness is over a longer period and perhaps therefore less breathless, but the Festivals still come one after the other. And in between there are quiet months marked only by the inexorable regularity of *Shabbat*.

There are lessons here. We need quiet down times: we cannot live in perpetual excitement. The comfort and serenity of *Shabbat* punctuates the passing time, but in essence, our religious life is like life itself, a time of preparation and waiting. We need the passion of the spring and autumn times of doing. Our religious life, like life itself, also includes a time when preparation is discharged as the time we have waited for finally comes.

With spring we reawaken from the little death of winter. We give thanks for survival in the passionate celebration of Purim. It isn't really religious so much as an existential rejoicing in life itself: so we dress up, we have fun, we celebrate unrestrainedly. That is it: it isn't really a serious meditation on anti-Semitism, just an explosion of fun and laughter.

And then we turn to more serious things. We relive another rebirth experience. We become a people again, free, rooted in a historical identity and destiny. We clear our homes of *hamets*, everything that corrupts the primeval integrity of our being. We prepare for the *seder* when we re-enact what it is to be a slave who suddenly becomes free. There is still laughter, but we now know that there is a more serious side to celebration; sometimes people have to die to earn the right to laugh.

And then, counting down the passing days, we arrive at *Shavuot* and realize the meaning of our identity and freedom: we stand at Sinai, accept Torah and become a very special people. Many peoples have found freedom: not many have discovered what freedom is for, to be a God-intoxicated people, as Spinoza called us Jews.

If you need advice on *Pesah*, the complexity of the special dietary laws, how to arrange the seder, how to sell your hamets, what to look for in a *haggadah*, please contact me. In the meantime, from Patricia and myself, *hag sameah*, may you have a spring celebration time of joy and peace.

PASSOVER TIME AGAIN *Vol. 16, No. 5 - May/June 2006*

Pesah is a Festival that is very popular with Jews. It is a time when families come together for the seder; it lasts for a week; it is marked by a multitude of symbols; we eat matsah and avoid eating all forms of hamets for the whole period.

It is easy to take *Pesah* out of context, and to see it as isolated. But it is linked to the next Festival of *Shavuot*, both by ritual observance and by meaning. On the second night of Pesah we start to count the *Omer* and we count until we reach *Shavuot*, because *Shavuot* is the completion of *Pesah*; the two have to be taken as a unit and they are meaningless without each other. *Pesah* is the *zeman herutenu*, the time of our freedom from slavery; Shavuot is the *zeman nattan Torah*, the time of the giving of Torah, the time when freedom from is transformed into freedom for, freedom from slavery into freedom for Torah. It is not being free that defines a Jew, it is being free to enter the covenant with God that is Torah that defines a Jew.

I hope, therefore, that this year everyone will make a special effort to celebrate *Shavuot*. It is an old custom to come together on the eve of the Festival in study and preparation for receiving Torah in the morning, the *leyl shel Shavuot*. It is also a *milkhig* Festival, a time for eating milk products, for the laws of *kashrut* have not yet been given, so eating meat is inappropriate.

So let us come together as a community on Thursday, June 1, the eve of *Shavuot*, for a potluck dinner (dairy) and a period of study; and then on the morning of the second at the Service we shall stand as we read the Ten Commandments, *Aseret ha Dibrot*, and symbolically receive the Torah at Sinai once again, as the generations of Jews have done throughout history.

A FULL-TIME COMMITMENT *Vol. 16, No. 6 - July/August 2006*

So we are now heading into what we all hope will be a brilliant and restful summer. This is a time for relaxing, a time for holidays, and also a time for catching up with our Jewish reading. Judaism is a full-time commitment. Wherever we travel on vacation, there are Jewish communities to make contact with, Jewish books to read. Even on holiday, we can always fulfill the wonderful *mitzvah* of helping to make up a *minyan* so that a fellow Jew can say *Kaddish*.

Many of us are, I am sure, disappointed that the Ahenekew appeal was granted, and that we shall therefore possibly have to go through the whole trial process again. Non-lawyers may be puzzled as to why. After all, no one denies that the remarks were made, made in public, and were not only offensive but a clear incitement to hatred and violence. But lawyers have more subtle minds than the rest of us. We now know that the Province has challenged the appeal and it will be determined whether or not the original judgement will be upheld. In the meantime, let us console ourselves with the thought that Mr. Ahenekew's career is over, he will always be seen as a bullying anti-Semite, and most people will remember only the initial guilty verdict, regardless of appeals. We should remain satisfied that the Province acted and acted correctly.

Now, though, is the time for us all to relax and enjoy the summer.

Patricia and I wish all our members happy holidays. Let us return refreshed and ready for the New Year.

SUMMER DOMINATED BY WAR Vol. 17, No. 1 - Sept/Oct 2006

Time seems to pass so quickly. Another year has gone by. We are confronting a new *Rosh ha Shanah*, a new *Yom ha Kippurim*. The Days of Awe are upon us again.

It is difficult psychologically to turn from days of summer and relaxation on holiday to confront these days that thrust on us considerations of moral and spiritual challenges. At any time and in any year it is hard. But this year has been different from other years. Our summer has been dominated by war. All of us have been devastated by the harsh realities of what war does to everybody. Death and destruction and the unknown implications of war once unleashed have led us into a dark world dominated by fear and foreboding. We cannot know what will come out of war. Every one of us is troubled and moved to the depths.

But we still must face the challenge of these Days of Awe. We must look at our lives, what we have done, what we are, how we stand in the moral balance weighed against what we should have done, what we should have been. If we are to remain Jews we cannot avoid it. In the passions of war many things are done and said, many positions taken, that should make us uncomfortable in that balance. We are always in danger of losing sight of humanness, our own and other's; even more so in war when reason is lost in emotion.

May we and all our fellow creatures pause these days to draw spiritual breath. May we recount our faults honestly, feel our pain and the pain of all human beings sincerely, and experience genuine repentance. May we feel compassion for everyone who suffers, including ourselves, and find real peace in our hearts and in our minds.

Shanah tovah u metukah, a new year of good and sweetness for us all. A new year of peace.

NEED MEMBER INVOLVEMENT Vol. 17, No. 2 - Nov/Dec 2006

First and foremost, I would like to thank everyone who took part in our Services over the High Holy Days and whose participation was essential in making our Services so moving and inspiring. Especially, of course, our thanks as a community and my own thanks specifically to Irwin Huberman whose chanting added so much to our *kavvanah* and *devekut*. It was a pleasure to work together for the Congregation.

Of course, things do not stop after the spiritual intensity of *Tishri*. There are still Jewish books to be read, Jewish sources to study, Services to come to. The attendance at our Services for the Holy Days this year was dramatically up on last year. It would be wonderful if the spirit of these days were to continue; if everyone who came were to come back for an ordinary *Shabbat* Service, say once a month; if new people were to come to our Lunch and Learn sessions on Mondays; if every member were to study a Jewish text, read a Jewish book; if everyone would determine to learn more Hebrew; if..... The *hesbon ha nefesh*, the spiritual and moral audit of the Holy Days, is not just for *Rosh ha Shanah* and *Yom Kippur*!

Seriously, the need for all our members to involve themselves in the Synagogue is even more important now than it usually is. 2007 will be a difficult year for the community, if only because I am of necessity curtailing much of what I can do. While I hope to be still active in some aspects of our communal life, there is much that I am having to give up at the end of the year. We all get older, and as we get older there is a certain degree of infirmity: what we used to do so easily now gets harder, as the joints get creakier and the eyes dimmer and the memory less reliable. I wish the community well and hope that they will find another Rabbi to fill the gap. But, whatever happens, more and more will have to be undertaken by members who are willing and able to accept responsibility for the Services. I am remaining in Saskatoon, and will give as much help and advice as I am able to. But, as the English saying is: the Lord helps those who help themselves. I am completely selfish here: I want and need a viable Synagogue where I can come and *daven*. I need you to ensure that I can do just that.

Finally, I want to add a few words to what our President said on Rosh HaSanah about our Schlichim. Yael and Yishai are a wonderful partnership. Individually, they are charming, energetic and deeply sincere in their devotion to Judaism and the Jewish people. Together, they are breath-taking in their willingness to teach and learn, and are a partnership that we are blessed to have with us. But they, too, need our support and help: they cannot do everything and we cannot burn them out. It is our duty to respond to their commitment with our own.

RETIRED LIFE IS FULL *Vol. 17, No. 3 - Jan/Feb 2007*

There are many New Years in the Jewish calendar, the best known being *Rosh ha Shanah* and the New Year for Trees on Shevat 15. The secular society around us also has many new years, including the academic year and the tax year. But the best known new year in our society is January 1, the New Year as such.

It is an occasion for partying, looking back over the past year and forward into the unknown year to come, sharing with family and friends the change in the calendar in the depths of winter, and making resolutions to change and amend our attitudes and behaviour for the future. It has much in common with our religious New Year, *Rosh ha Shanah*. On both occasions we look back over the past year and hope to learn from what we did and didn't do; and we look forward into the unknown year to come trying to equip ourselves for that future by resolving to be better than we were before.

Because of this, we can as Jews join our non-Jewish friends in celebrating this New Year with no fear of compromising our Jewish consciences. This is a special time for Patricia and me this year, as we shall be beginning a new phase of our relationship with the community. I shall still be a member of the community of Agudas Israel, and still attending Services, though I shall now be actually leading Shabbat morning worship and study on two Saturdays a month. I shall still be available for special occasions and for teaching the Lunch and Learn group, and for guiding and helping potential Jews by choice. And I shall always be around to share with members their times of sorrow and times of joy.

This year is the 40th year of my receiving *semihah* from the Leo Baeck College in London. Ending one chapter of my life as a Rabbi and beginning another in January is therefore an experience that is appropriately Janus-like. I have to cope with slowing down while also feeling that I have much yet to give. Over those years I have accumulated experience and learning and I hope that I still have contributions to make and that they will be welcomed. I look forward to doing some travelling and completing (finally!) my translation of the *Hizzuk Emunah*, a 17th century study of the New Testament by a Karaite Rabbi in Poland. Perhaps, too, I will rework my study of Jewish values. And I have some plans for a study of modern religion as a source of both blessing and curse in human affairs. And Patricia is busy, too. Life is full, even when you are retired.

I hope that our members will keep in touch and continue to swap ideas and thoughts and want to have lunch with me from time to time. I am always available and I shall continue to be in and around the Synagogue.

So, Patricia and I wish all members of our Jewish community here and everywhere a year of health and fulfillment, of happiness and peace. May 2007 be a year of good for us all.

OUR TOUR BEGINS *Vol. 17, No. 4 - Mar/April 2007*

When you read this, Patricia and I will be getting ready to embark on our cruise. As a retirement present to ourselves we decided to take a long cruise, a once-in-a-lifetime experience, and now after a year of planning and anticipation, the time has come to begin our adventure. We sail through the West Indies to Barbados, and from there strike out due east to Africa. We travel up the west coast from Gambia to Senegal and Morocco, and then through to the Mediterranean. We sail around the Mediterranean, calling at Turkey, Greece, Italy, the south of France, Spain and Portugal; we also call in at Cape Verde and the Canary and Azores islands.

We call in at ports en route for excursions ashore, and we look forward to some souvenir shopping, a lot of photography, some gourmet food and a great deal of 'R and R'.

Among the new experiences for us will be a *Pesah Seder* at sea. Most of all for us this will be 56 days of renewal, a sort of extended honeymoon. And for me personally will be the novel experience of leaving it to others to lead *Shabbat* Services and that *Seder*: it is a rare thing for Patricia and me to sit together at these times. I shall have to restrain myself from jumping in and helping the Cantor who will be acting as the Jewish Chaplain on board!

In the meantime, of course, Services in the Synagogue will continue, thanks to the wonderful willingness and ability of so many of our members to act as *shelihe tsibbur* and lead community worship. I hope that the members will support them and ensure a healthy *minyan* at all times.

After all, this period does include Pesah, the birthday of the Jewish people, beginning the seven weeks leading through the desert to *Shavuot* and the birthday of Judaism that makes our Jewish identity so important, not just for Jews but for the whole world.

Our thoughts are with you all as we sail around half the world (the other half maybe next year!) Truly we do wish you were here! But from both of us may everyone have a joyous and meaningful *Pesah*, and we look forward to being back with you all in May.

SIX CORE JEWISH VALUES *Vol. 17, No. 5 - May/June 2007*

Each of us focuses our understanding of our Jewishness on a major Jewish value that becomes the core that holds together all the other aspects of Jewish identity as we understand it for ourselves.

There are, I think, six of these major core values: study, social justice, spirituality, ethnicity and culture, Israel, and the Holocaust and anti-Semitism. I want to look at each.

1. **Study, Talmud Torah.** For some of us the primary value, the core that holds the rest of our Jewishness together, is study of the sources of Judaism, both in the traditional sense, *lernen*, and in the modern way, *wissenschaft*. Academic study is not, of course, an end in itself, but a means of building a coherent way of being Jewish today. Study is a mitsvah, a privilege and a pleasure. But to be Jewish study specifically, it must result in action: Jewish learning leads to Jewish living, and so it must. Without this study there can be no Jewish living at all; unless we know what God requires of us, specifically and in practical detail, how can we respond in an authentically Jewish way?

2. **Social Justice, Tikkun Olam.** We are called upon as Jews to be a blessing to all humanity. We have to strive to comfort the mourner, heal the sick, clothe the naked and be a friend to the friendless. Unless we reach out to others and work with them to create a society of justice, and a world in which all can live in peace and

fellowship, we are not living Jewishly. We can never walk away from our destiny to be co-workers to make a world fit for the presence of God.

3. **Spirituality, _Tefilah_.** For some Jews the primary core value is the spiritual life, the encounter with God. We are children of Abraham, called by God to strike out into the unknown. Unless our covenant with the divine mystery is lived every moment of every day, how can we be meaningful Jews? Whatever we do as Jews, whatever we are, without encounter with God, we have no Jewish heart and soul.

4. **Ethnicity and culture, Yiddishkeit.** For many Jews, especially in modern times when faith may be at a low ebb, the core of Jewishness lies in identity and ethnicity, living a life filled with Jewish culture, making decisions derived from traditional values. We may no longer be linked with prayer, with study or with the urge to better our world morally; but we can live Jewishly from birth to death, celebrating by the rhythm of the calendar, finding pride and courage in Jewish music, literature, art and the creativity that brings beauty to the Jewish and human soul.

5. **Israel.** Many of us define our Jewishness in terms of the rebirth of Jewish life in modern Israel. We are determined that the people of Israel and the State of Israel shall live and flourish, regardless of spirituality as such: it is Israel that gives meaning to being Jewish in a world increasingly without religion and faith.

6. **Anti-Semitism and the _Shoah_.** For some of us being Jewish is a refusal to let Hitler have the last word. We may not be altogether sure why we want to remain Jews or what that actually means in terms of what we shall do or how we shall behave, but we are absolutely sure that we shall remain Jews. Those who have hated us shall not have the last word; they shall not define us; they shall not succeed in destroying us. The ship of Judaism may sink because we can no longer know what to do to keep it afloat, but we shall not abandon that ship.

It seems to me that each of these primary values is of overriding importance for many members of the Jewish people. It also seems to me that for any one of us to have a really coherent reason for being Jewish and wanting to hand our Judaism on to the future, all of those core values have to play a part for each of us. Each of us will stress one above the others, but to be complete each of us must find real meaning in all of them: we just weight them differently. The fundamental core value for me must be study — that is my personality. But I cannot and must not ignore social justice: nor, rationalist though I am, can I be unaware of the importance of spirituality. And the other values, less important in my personal mosaic of Jewishness though they may be, I cannot ignore: they are all essential to my constructing my Jewish identity. Which of these values are important pieces for you in making the jigsaw of your Jewish identity?

I have just been rereading Richard Dawkins' latest book, *The God Delusion*. I have to say that it is an excellent book, cogently argued and engagingly written. The case he presents against religion is often hard to debate, and I found myself again and again having to say, Touche!

There are many comments I would like to make on this book and indeed on Dr. Dawkins' work in general (I have read much of what he has written!) For the moment I want to make only one comment that I think is essential to any critique of the book.

There is a general feeling, shared by Dawkins, that religion is to be identified with beliefs that purport to be statements about the nature of ultimate reality: in other words, religion is a list of answers to the ultimate questions. In believing in those answers, we become privy to and guardians of ultimate truth. It is against this view of religion that Dawkins delivers his devastating broadsides of reason.

But I wonder if that is really what religion is about. Certainly my religious position is not. To me the concern of religion is entirely in the opposite direction: not to give me answers that, *mirabile dictu*, happen to coincide with what I would like ultimate truth to be. Religion to me is rather the questions that impel me into an unending struggle with what is in the light of what could (should?) be. The fundamental attitude of a religious person seems to me not to be belief but faith; and there is an enormous difference. Belief is assuming the truth claims of propositions that, by definition, are incapable of proof; faith is an attitude of being that makes no claims to know but impels an eternal quest to discover. The only assumption that faith requires is the axiom on which mathematics and science have to work, that there is something "out there" independent of us that exists and that we can investigate. That is not a rational assumption, but it is not irrational either, for, without it, we are condemned to flounder in a solipsist nightmare.

Faith involves trust: the trust that real meaning may be unattainable in practice but that human beings must persue to fulfill their humanness. Trust does tend to assume answers; it assumes that the search for answers is what life is for. Studying Jewish texts, living Jewish tradition, is something that a Jew does, not because it gives comforting answers to the meaning of life, but because, quite the contrary, it is uncomfortable: living with Heisenbergian indeterminacy. Trust means being aware that we are incomplete and always will be, but the search for completeness gives richness, meaning and ever-renewed hope to life.

And that, I would suggest, is precisely what Professor Dawkins has dedicated his life to, as has every scientist, every artist. And it is what religion is also dedicated to.

In future issues of *The Bulletin* I would like to continue my comments on this fascinating and well-worth-reading book.

LESS TALK – MORE ACTION *Vol. 18, No. 1 - Sept/Oct 2007*

This year, *Rosh ha Shanah* is early. We shall barely be back to work or classroom, just organizing our schedules after summer holiday mode, when the Holy Days will be upon us. We need to prepare ourselves for the profound experience of the annual spiritual and moral audit that our calendar imposes on us.

There is a fine story told by the Nobel Prize winner Shai Agnon in his wonderful compilation from the classical Jewish sources on the Holy Days, and it bears retelling, year by year, especially perhaps when, as this year, those Days of Awe come upon us so suddenly in September.

There was an old lady, a widow, with a large number of children to provide for, and they lived in dire poverty. One day, when out trying to find some food for her family, she chanced on an egg, a large, perfect egg. She brought it home and gathered the children. "See," she said, "I have found an egg. But, being a provident woman who plans for the future, we won't eat the egg. I'll put it under the neighbour's hen, and it will hatch and grow up and lay more eggs. But we won't eat those eggs, either: I'll take them to market and sell them, and with the money I'll buy a cow. And we won't eat the cow, but milk it, and I'll take the milk to market and sell it. And with the money I'll buy more cows and more chickens. And we'll have cows and chickens and eggs, and we'll be rich and never have to go without and be poor again." And all the time while she was explaining her plans for the future to the children, she was playing with the egg, hand to hand. And she dropped it!

The moral of the tale? Perhaps, "There's many a slip between the cup and the lip." Perhaps, less talk, more action. Perhaps, it's all well and good to lay out plans for the future; but while people propose, God disposes. In other words, it's not enough to talk about examining where we stand in life on these Holy Days, what we have done and what we should do, what we are and what we should be, but we must actually do something about it. Ideals may be silver, but action is golden.

Patricia and I wish you all a *Shanah tovah umetukah*, a good and sweet year, a year in which all your honeyed words become fulfilled in sweet deeds for good.

THE GOD DELUSION – PART II *Vol. 18, No. 3 - Jan/Feb 2008*

In my thinking about the issues for religious faith that Professor Dawkins raises, I want to concentrate on two areas. I want, first, to consider what is called the Anthropic Principle (in its "strong" form), and, second, the implications for belief in God of quantum physics.

The Anthropic Principle in its "weak" form states that the universe seems to be structured to produce intelligent and purposive consciousness, the proof being that if it weren't we wouldn't be here to observe it, and we patently are. This is not quite a redundant statement of the obvious — we are here because we are here! — but it really does not get us much further. However, the "stronger" form of the Principle is more interesting.

The basic forces of the universe that hold everything together and enable it to work are gravity (by far the weakest!), electro-magnetism, the strong and the weak. The last two apply on the sub-atomic level, but are tremendously important. The values of all of them are very precisely calibrated, so that a very tiny variance would have catastrophic consequences. Indeed, in the case of the strong force that holds the atomic nucleus together, the calibration is so precise that no variation occurs in two hundred decimal places! It is true enough, as Dawkins correctly says, that change occurs in biological evolution by sheer chance, the immensity of time ensuring a benign result. But in the case of the strong force the assumption of chance is so mind boggling as to require a deeply "religious" faith! It begins to look suspiciously as though someone or something were "cooking the books" and deliberately setting the coordinates precisely to produce what we have; a universe seemingly directed to producing us. The bad word "teleology" or purpose, forces itself back into the equation.

Quantum physics also has an intriguing part to play in our thinking. Light is carried by photons. But photons oddly function as either a wave or a coherent particle, or, astonishingly, as both. And we cannot predict which way it will go. What we have is potential which at some specific time concretizes or "collapses" into an event. It follows that there must be an infinity of possibilities in an infinity of parallel universes; and if an event accords with the laws of physics, what can happen will happen somewhere: if not in our universe, in another one. Not all those universes will be welcoming to life or consciousness; most will not. However, in a set of infinity there will be a sub-set of an infinity of universes that are welcoming. Again, is somebody, somewhere, cooking the books? And, again, as to chance, consider the old conundrum of monkeys hammering away at the keys of their word processors: would they purely by chance, replicate the works of Shakespeare? Of course they would, but the time required is a lot longer than the universe will survive before the proton disintegrates, taking everything else with it.

Let us consider, too, Heisenberg's indeterminacy. This is the reason we cannot predict the "collapse": of the photon as a wave or a particle. There are states that are incompatible, that is, the more accurately we know one of them, for example, position, the less accurately we can know the other, say velocity. It is also true that, at the microcosmic level, things can come into being out of nothing and nowhere, provided that they cease to exist immediately. Energy can be "borrowed" so long as it is paid back. At the Planck level all sorts of weird things can happen. It follows that a totally abstract God concept such as that of Mordechai Kaplan, where we are using the word to refer to a force that tends toward salvation, is perfectly compatible with

Buber's personal God of relationship that we experience when we honestly encounter others as I-Thou, in a mutually transformative experience. So a sophisticated God can also be a God we can meet, and in the meeting be transformed.

One thing I agree with Dr. Dawkins on: agnosticism is not an honest response, however tempting and seemingly rational it may be. Aristotle's law of the excluded middle applies. Either there is a God or there is not. Dawkins can demolish the anthropomorphic image easily enough. But popular though it may be (and it is), it is not the concept that we need have. And granted that, it is perfectly rational to believe in God (it all comes down to what you mean by the word!) and not in the least rational not to or to waffle in suspense.

I would recommend this book hugely. It is entertaining and provocative in the best sense. But it is not the last word. A more humble author might perhaps have put a question mark in his title. And to that question, The God Delusion?, I would answer, No. And even if God were a delusion, maybe we need the opiate. Marx may have been more right and more compassionate than he thought.

ON THE HALAKHAH — PART I Vol. 18, No. 4 - Mar/Apr 2008

Increasingly over the last few years, non-Orthodox Rabbis have been asked questions by their congregants along the lines of "What is the halakhah on...?" With the continuing move to the right of the Reform movement and its renewed openness to tradition, the halakhah seems to be becoming more and more important; and Conservative Jews have always been interested because, at least in principle, Conservative Judaism has always regarded the halakhah, even if open to continuous reinterpretation, as binding in serious Jewish life.

What, then, is the halakhah?

The single greatest creation of the Rabbis is what Jacob Neusner has dubbed the Dual Torah system. In addition to the written Torah, there is the ongoing oral tradition based on interpretation of the text of the Hebrew Bible so as to bring it into continuing dialogue with the changing circumstances of time and place. Hence, the Rabbis could avoid the danger of textual fundamentalism: they always read the *Tanakh* very seriously, but never literally.

They read the text using agreed-upon hermeneutic methods. They also accepted that there are dimensions of meaning, so that a text could be read on four levels. This they referred to by the mnemonic PaRDeS, the Hebrew word, from Persian, meaning garden or orchard. This means that you read a text first literally, the *Peshat*; then you read the *Remez*, meaning the hints that the text gives to a deeper significance; then the *Derash*, the application of the text to the specific situation, from a root that means investigate; and finally you read in that text the Sod, the underlying, often mystic, meaning. At all times they used the agreed hermeneutic principles, of which the 13 attributed to Rabbi Ishmael are the main examples.

The Oral tradition, including the hermeneutic methods, was assumed to have been revealed at Sinai, together with the written text. It is, therefore, authoritative. The written Torah together with the oral tradition as defined above constitute the Torah as such, and that, the Dual Torah system, is what has made Rabbinic Judaism for the last 2000 years. This, the Judaism that we know, is a system that depends on the scholarly elite, Rabbis, who continually interpret and apply the Torah to the intricacies and minutiae of Jewish life. The elite is also intensely democratic, in that any competent person, nearly always male, could aspire to join the club through merit.

Torah exists in two forms: *Halakhah* and *Aggadah*. The *aggadah* is material that is concerned with ethics and theology. The *halakhah*, the legal system, that has been unique to this Rabbinic style of Judaism. A Jew is basically concerned with the answers to questions such as What does God want me to do? How does God want me to do it? When does God want me to do it? That God does indeed require a Jew to live in specific and practical ways in response to every possible eventuality in life, is taken for granted. *Halakhah* is the answer to those questions, the way in which a Jew shall "walk" through life, from the root hlkh meaning walk, go.

In modern times, this consensual understanding of what Judaism is has come under stress. There has always been an underground opposition to the *halakhic* system, usually the mystic tradition that has always existed throughout Jewish history. But increasingly there has grown a feeling that the content of the system, and, more important, the very concept that underlies it, is no longer the reality of Jewish life, nor indeed should it be. Huge areas of *halakhah*, such as criminal and civil law, now fall under the law of the land and *dina de malkhuta dina*; the law of the land is law for Jews, too. Fewer and fewer Jews are willing to live by the *halakhah*, even that which remains possible for them; and most Jews do not accept that the *halakhic* system is even a theoretical ideal for them. In short, we live increasingly in a post halakhic world, and for most Jews concern with *halakhah* as binding law is purely academic. We look to *halakhah* as an interesting part of our Jewish history that most of us do not accept, even in theory, as being the will of God, and most of us have no interest whatever in being commanded by.

So, where do we go, and what can we make of *halakhah* for us today?

ON THE HALAKHAH — PART II *Vol. 18, No. 5 - May/Jun 2008*

There is no question that the *halakhic* system is flexible enough to be interpreted to apply to many modern situations, using the traditional hermeneutic methods.

Certainly, both Reform and Conservative Judaism have been able to use the halakhah with some success. However, it is not infinitely flexible; there are certain issues arising in modern society that cannot be accommodated entirely, or even at all, within the system, however ingeniously interpreted.

Consider, for example, the status of women and gender roles in modern Jewish life; sexuality in general and specifically the status and role of gay and lesbian Jews; and Jews and non-Jewish partners. In these cases there is no doubt where the halakhah comes down, and there is little or no wiggle room to accommodate the more liberal attitude that most Jews would take arising from what they would consider a more humane conscience. Where the halakhah can take us only so far we must surely, however reluctantly, go on into unexplored territory without it. And the attempts that have been made to introduce into the halakhic system entirely new and totally external factors such as environmental considerations, the spirit of the times, the developing conscience, bend the whole system to breaking point. To call some modern responsa part of the halakhic process as traditionally understood, rather than a search for some sort of supporting texts for an already-decided liberal decision, would be sleight of hand and not entirely honest. We can always play the game, but when we have to change the rules to do so, it becomes no more than a game that is now no more than a display of Rabbinic expertise without serious reference to reality.

Further, while many human beings do need a definite structure of law to determine their decision making in moral and religious terms, many do not. It is a moot point whether the halakhah as divinely mandated law is really something that most modern Jews feel ready to abdicate responsibility to. When the majority of Jews no longer believe literally in Revelation and see it as a poetic metaphor, to speak of halakhah as law that a Jew must obey, at least in principle, because it is ordained by God — and that is the traditional understanding of the word — no longer is at all meaningful. We really do live in a post-halakhic situation.

And throughout Jewish history there has always been an undercurrent of opposition to halakhah as the defining understanding of Judaism. What, after all, can the Hasidic movement, at least in its early phases, be understood as, other than a rebellion against the definition of Judaism as a halakhic system interpreted by the scholarly elite of Rabbis?

How then can we non-Orthodox Jews see the halakhah? Although we cannot regard it as normative and certainly not as mandatory in our Judaism, we cannot ignore it. It is an essential part of Jewish history, and played a role in defining Judaism and preserving it through the centuries. It seems to me that the Conservative movement is wrong in regarding halakhah as in any sense mandatory for modern Jews. Few Jews actually live a halakhic life, and not many more accept that they ought to, even in principle. On the other hand, the Reform movement, while denying, I think rightly, that halakhah is mandatory for a modern Jew, still takes it seriously as part of the process of making decisions that are authentic. Where we can use it, well and good;

where we cannot or have to make a dog's dinner of the process in order to make it fit, then we must have the courage to say that we are going beyond it. We should not get stuck with a word that no longer makes sense merely because we want to appear traditional; even when that is the last thing we actually are. Hypocrisy must not be the real game that we are playing. *Halakhah* is one tool among many that we can use in developing Judaism for our time. Another major tool, probably even more useful, available to us is *Midrash*, the *aggadah*, as our feminist thinkers are teaching us. We can no longer see Judaism as a pan-halakhic system.

JEWISH MARRIAGE *Vol. 18, No. 6 - July/Aug 2008*

From a Sermon at the Aufruf of Simonne Horowitz and Dwight Newman.

It is a long-standing Jewish tradition for a couple about to be married to come to the Synagogue on the preceding Shabbat and take part in the Service, particularly to be called to the reading of the Torah for an *aliyah*. They are declaring to the community their commitment to each other and asking for God's blessing on their forthcoming marriage; they are associating their future life together with Judaism, proclaiming that they will create a Jewish home filled with Jewish observance, dedicated to Jewish religious values. It is a practice that all Jewish couples, of whatever denomination, associate themselves with.

Increasingly in modern times, Jews tend to marry non-Jewish partners, and in North America it could be more than 50% who do so. Much of Jewish leadership, Rabbinic and lay, sees this as a threat to Jewish survival and urge Jews to avoid even dating non-Jews because they fear marriage between Jews and non-Jews. Although increasing numbers of non-Orthodox Rabbis, Reform, Reconstructionist, even some Conservative, are beginning to question this assumption, it is still regarded as almost axiomatic that Jews who marry non-Jewish partners are weakening Jewish identity and threatening the ultimate survival of Jews and Judaism.

We are celebrating today the marriage of Dwight and Simonne that will take place tomorrow, so it is right that we confront this issue head on.

Marriage in general is under great and increasing stress in our day: *qal va homer* (all the more so) marriage that brings together partners who are different, who cross lines that threaten identity. Of course the normal problems of any marriage are probably increased when partners do not share what society tends to see as common identity. Marriage between partners who come from different backgrounds of ethnicity, religion and culture raise misgivings, and it is clear to see the reasons for that.

However, we have to be very clear what we are talking about. We live in a world in which boundaries formerly seen as normal are being seen as no longer relevant. Thank God, few of us now would with a clear conscience condemn marriages between black and white, even, let us hope, gay and lesbian marriages. We live in an open society in which people from widely different origins come together with increased tolerance and find the boundaries of the past irrelevant and cruel.

We have assumed that Jews who marry non-Jews have deserted Judaism and no longer care about their Jewish identity and heritage. In many cases that is true: many Jews are apathetic about Judaism. But, it is not necessarily true. Many Jews who are totally committed to their Jewishness still find that they fall in love with non-Jews. Of course, you could say the same from the other side: good Christian boys fall in love with Jewish girls! Why then, do the non-Jews not convert? Sometimes they do: often they don't; and even when they don't, they often support their Jewish spouses in their Jewishness and have their children raised as Jews.

When both partners retain their identity it is still not a disaster, unless we, in our intolerance and lack of understanding and acceptance, make it so. As it is going to happen, why not try to make it work?

Surely, Jews treasure the liberal democracy of our society that grants us freedom and acceptance and honours our difference from the majority. By the same token, we must sincerely accept and honour the collection of minorities in our society that, together, make up that non-Jewish majority. It is for us to support people who marry and sincerely try to maintain the identity from which they come as they work together to create a new identity that encompasses both and enriches both.

In marriage we share many values and ideals and without that sharing we could not even understand each other and the marriage would be doomed. Today in our society Jews and Christians and Muslims share many values and ideals precisely because we have together contributed to the making of that society. We are all trying to be tolerant and knowledgeable citizens of a liberal democracy that is a work in progress, trying to overcome the ignorance-based bigotry of the past. At the same time, we know that we do not want to marry our mirror image: difference is an essential ingredient in a relationship. Life is filled with challenges; and it is the working together to meet those challenges that deepens our humanness and our partnership.

Religion honours above all else the human capacity to love. Without love we know that we cannot survive, as a species obviously, but even more so as individuals. Without love we shrivel and ultimately we die. It is love that gives us the courage to hope, the inspiration to dream. And love is not constrained by the boundaries of religion and race and ethnicity. Partners who are determined to create a marriage based on difference, to make things work, to look for what they share already and beyond that to what they will create together, will enrich their own relationship, and can be a blessing to all humankind. Our world needs a vision of a unity that transcends difference and that is prepared to take risk. The serious commitment, the whole-hearted giving, that is based on love, is what we are celebrating today. Let none of us today think in terms of Jewish loss or Christian loss but look forward to partnership together and try to compromise while retaining integrity. Let us all rejoice with them in that love and pray that they will enjoy a life together of ever deepening love and blessing.

There is a prayer from the new British Reform Siddur due to be published later this year that is very appropriate to this.

"God of all creation, we stand in awe before You, impelled by visions of human harmony. We are children of many traditions — inheritors of shared wisdom and tragic misunderstandings, of proud hopes and humble successes. Now it is time for us to meet in memory and truth, in courage and trust, in love and promise. In that which we share, let us see the common prayer of humanity; in that where we differ, let us wonder at human freedom; in our unity and in our differences, let us know the uniqueness that is God. May our courage match our convictions, and our integrity match our hope. May our faith in You bring us closer to each other. May our meeting with past and present bring blessing for the future. Amen."

SIMHAT TORAH *Vol. 19, No. 1 - Sept/Oct 2008*

As is our custom, we shall again be following the calendar as in Israel, and observing *Simhat Torah* and *Shemini Atseret* combined. We shall be holding *hakafort* (processions) with the carrying of and dancing with the *Sifre Torah* in both the evening and the morning, when we offer all members of the congregation an *aliyah* as we finish reading the Torah and begin immediately our reading of Torah. In accordance with Israeli *minhag* (custom), we shall be combining this in the morning with *Yizkor* prayers.

This is a very important occasion in our Synagogue life. We urge you to make every effort to join us. WE NEED YOU TO CARRY A TORAH AND TO MAKE UP A *MINYAN* so that we can read Torah and say *Kaddish*.

It is a long-standing tradition to honour members of our community who have worked hard in the community by appointing them *Hatanim* (literally Bridegrooms) who will be called to the reading of the last verses of the last book of the Torah (*Devarim*), and then to the reading of the first verses of the first book (*Bereshit*), so ending and straightaway beginning the reading of Torah to symbolise its eternity. They are called *Hatan Torah* for Deuteronomy and *Hatann Bereshit* for Genesis.

Our *Hatanim* this year are very special people in our congregation. *Hatan Torah* (or, rather, this year *Kalat Torah*, Bride of the Torah) will be Heather Fenyes, Chair of Ritual. Hatan Bereshit will be Nim, together with Kalat Bereshit, Shirly, whom we honour both in their own right and also as representing the Schlichim program, and so honouring all our young Israelis who have worked so hard for our community through the years.

Patricia and I wish everyone a good, healthy and peaceful New Year, and look forward to seeing you during the Holy Day Services, during Sukkot and for *Simhat Torah/Shemini Atseret.*

MAKING PRAYER BOOKS – PART I *Vol. 19, No. 2 - Nov/Dec 2008*

There has been a plethora of new Prayer Books published in the last generation. As the Jewish world has had to confront brand new challenges, it has become necessary to update the siddur to respond to them. This is mainly a phenomenon of the non-Orthodox communities, but is by no means confined to them; even the Orthodox have produced new editions of the siddur for their constituencies.

The new challenges have included, for example, the experiences of the Shoah and the State of Israel; issues of gender equality; human sexuality and specifically the place in the community of gay and lesbian Jews; the changing demographic structures of Jews, with the increasing valency of one-parent families and the impact of Jews by choice; ecology and our relation with our environment; and increasing dialogue with other religious and spiritual experience. All have necessitated a response in the prayer book: after all, the prayer book is the only specifically Jewish source that most Jews make contact with, and it therefore increasingly has to be what Franz Rosenzweig said it was, a textbook of Jewish thought and belief, as well as the expression of Jewish spirituality.

This year has seen the publication of new Prayer Books by two Reform communities: *Mishkan Tefillah*, published by the North American Reform movement, the Union for Reform Judaism; and *Seder ha Tefillot*, published by the British Reform community, the Movement for Reform Judaism. They both seek to respond to the challenges that confront Jews today. They represent two differing approaches and are therefore interesting for us to consider.

Mishkan Tefillah went through a difficult gestation, including the pulping of the whole of the first edition, before it finally arrived. It replaces the *Gates of Prayer*, and was edited by Rabbi Elyse Frishman. It is published in three volumes; a complete book of 694 pages that was evidently felt to be too big for easy congregational use, and two smaller volumes, one for Shabbat, the other for Festivals and Weekdays, that are indeed easier to handle.

The text is set out in a unique way. Each page normally has the traditional Hebrew text on the right-hand side, and a selection of mainly English readings on the left-hand side. It is intended that the *Sheliah Tsibbur* leading the Service choose one prayer from either side, and then continue by turning the page, so as to eliminate page announcements. Sometimes, the Service is continuous and includes both pages. Undoubtedly, it isn't as complicated as it sounds when in use. Pretty well everything in Hebrew is transliterated, to facilitate congregational involvement.

The book includes Services for Shabbat, evening, morning and afternoon; Festivals likewise; and weekdays. In addition, there are prayers for special occasions, such as *Kiddush, Havdalah, Hannukah, Purim* and *Birkat ha Mazon*. There are songs, but, oddly, no glossary or notes.

Seder ha Tefillot is the eighth edition of the British Reform Prayer Book, the first dating back to 1841. British Reform has a strong Sefardi base, and still retains much Sefardi *minhag*. This edition is edited by Rabbi Dr. Jonathan Magonet (who is both a Rabbi and a qualified physician.) It runs to 750 pages, but is actually considerably smaller than *Mishkan Tefillah* and easier to handle. Two place markers are included with the book.

Seder ha Tefillot does not include Festival prayers; they were published separately in 1995. But it does include an enormous amount of material. The Services for Shabbat and weekdays are an abbreviated traditional siddur, basically Sefardic style, with a straightforward translation and a huge amount of commentary explaining both custom and the meaning and significance of the prayers. There are meditations on the liturgy with detailed analysis of the prayers and suggested alternatives for variety. There is a full glossary of sources; there is a collection of prayers for all possible occasions (including what I think must be unique, prayers for welcoming into the family a new pet and a meditation on the loss of a pet!); a full listing of Psalms, with guidance for use; and, above all, a vast anthology of readings from Jewish sources, arranged by theme, that can be used privately for meditation and study, or in the Service as *divre Torah*, especially in communities without a Rabbi. It is intended to educate Jews and to stimulate a modern Jewish spirituality. There are alternatives for the Torah Service and the *Alenu* that represent differing theological perspectives. And there are two versions of a *Musaf* service, a traditional one or a modern and shorter version so as not to lengthen the Service unduly.

MAKING PRAYER BOOKS – PART II *Vol. 19, No. 23- Jan/Feb 2009*

I have to admit a possible bias. I grew up with British Reform and personally know many of those involved in the making of this volume, so when I say that I am impressed by and enthusiastic about it, you should make the appropriate adjustments!

Mishkan Tefillah is a tremendous improvement on the *Gates of Prayer*: how could it not be! But, bearing in mind the enormous investment in its production, there are nagging questions and an uneasy sense that perhaps an opportunity was missed. I suspect that individual Temples will be producing their own supplements fairly soon, as they did with *Gates of Prayer*. I find, for example that the print is sometimes difficult for those of us who are visually challenged; and perhaps the English alternatives on the left hand side of the page were not as judiciously chosen for the purpose as they might have been. And considering that it covers a basically restricted liturgy, it is a bit long. There are few notes and little guidance to custom. I suspect that it is basically a text for professional Rabbis and Cantors and that lay leaders of Services could get easily lost.

Seder ha Tefillot is a remarkable product: it is not going to need a supplement for many years to come . The attempt to respond to the modern challenges to Judaism and Jews is well done and honest. The anthology will be a never-ending source of inspiration and enlightenment to the book's users. The production and the use of two colours (blue for material that is used only on special occasions) are exemplary. However, the paper used will surely not stand up to regular congregational use. And perhaps in a second edition, Rabbi Magonet, the editor, might consider integrating into the book the volume including the Festival Services. Too many volumes of prayer makes life difficult (and expensive) for congregations. And this one, in common with everything British today, is a mite pricey!

I have to ask myself, what do I want from a modern Prayer Book? It is a question that examination of these *siddurim* makes very pointed. I am looking for many things, and it is impossible to be completely satisfied. I want a Book that I can use in my own prayer life with integrity and honesty; and I want a Book that is a guide to the wisdom of our Jewish tradition, an educational resource; and I want a book that opens up the possibilities of Jewish teaching to speak inspiration and comfort to a modern and sensitive Jew. I would also like a book that is well produced, user friendly, handsomely printed, a pleasure to handle and reasonably priced. I must also admit that I love the idea of encouraging modern Jewish art as an essential aspect of Jewish spirituality, and therefore I respond very positively to the art work that decorates the British book throughout.

If I consider carefully the options we now have for non-Orthodox Prayer Books, I have to say that I think that the British Reform siddur, even though produced by such a small group, is possibly the best available from the point of view of inspiring both spirituality and *talmud torah*. I also like the Reconstructionist *Kol ha Neshamah*, mainly for its selections of English readings and its artwork. I have a liking for *Sim Shalom*, despite its obvious imperfections, mainly I admit because I have a deep respect for its editor, Rabbi Jules Harlow. I have to admit that the liturgical work of the American Reform movement somehow does not speak to me, and I am not altogether sure why that is so: the new material just seems to me rather thin gruel, and it is rather loosely ensconced in the traditional text, the whole somewhat disarticulated. As I am a member of the Central Conference of American Rabbis, I find that this makes me a little uncomfortable The old Reform siddur *Gates of Prayer* never really got off the ground. *Mishkan Tefillah* is very much better as a book to daven with, but doesn't even start as an educational tool.

We are so used to reading the *T'nakh* as the *parashah* of the week supplemented by the *Haftarah* during every Shabbat morning service, that we probably don't stop to consider whether we really understand what is being read. Surely, the translations we have, plus the notes in the translations, mean that we are actually coming to grips with the text.

Actually, no!

There are some real problems with reading the Hebrew Bible and understanding what it means. It is not for nothing that many scholars suspect that the Hebrew text as we have it is (a) "corrupt" and (b) represents an artificial language created by the writers for religious purposes. By "corrupt" I mean that the scribes involved have made mistakes in transmission which make it hard to read the text with much understanding. It is the glibness of the translators, based on commentators who make educated guesses as to meaning, and are often more concerned with finding homiletic meaning than the real meaning, that give us this mistaken picture.

There are words that are used only once, in scholarly jargon *hapax legomena*; what they mean is guesswork derived from the context, or we hopefully find similar words in other languages that might fit. The verbal tense system in Biblical Hebrew has no relationship at all to time, so when things happen derives from what might be the context. And in Biblical style there is a device called "conversive vav" (*vav ha hippukh*), which means that in a narrative if you start with a verb in the perfect tense, then the next verb if prefixed by a *vav* (meaning "and" or "but") must be in the imperfect tense, and vice versa. The actual timing of the events derives from what makes sense in the context according to the reader.

Take, for example, the list of forbidden animals and birds in Leviticus. If you read an English translation every creature is clearly identified. Most of them are guesses. And to see just how weird some guesses must be, consider an animal mentioned in Exodus whose skin was used to decorate the portable Ark in which the tablets of the Ten Commandments were carried, the tahash. We have no idea what a tahash was. In the English it is translated as a dugong or a sea otter (in the Sinai desert?!) The best translation of tahash, surely, is tahash! And some of the Prophetic material, Amos in particular, is so "corrupt" that the Hebrew is literally incomprehensible.

We don't even know what the Hebrew of the Bible sounded like. It is convenient to read it as modern Hebrew, but we know that that is wrong. We also use modern Hebrew when reading Ugaritic (early Canaanite) texts and even Akkadian (Babylonian/Assyrian cuneiform) texts.

We also read ancient Egyptian hieroglyphs as though they were Greek or Coptic. To retroject modern pronunciation of a language 2500–3000 years into the past is exceedingly rash.

The problem is the vowels. We don't know what vowels are there because the language wrote only consonants. Only later did ancient languages begin to use some of the less used consonant signs to hint at the vowels; and not until the early Middle Ages did the Massoretes devise the system of writing vowels that we now have in Hebrew. And we know that the Massoretic vowelling and punctuation was invented to force us to read the Bible in a certain way, which we know from the Dead Sea Scrolls and the quotations recorded in *Talmud* was not necessarily the way earlier generations read the *T'nakh*. And anyway, these early languages only used three vowel sounds, a as in "father," i as in "pin," and u as in "brute."

So, how, then, are we to read our Bible and understand what the original writers wanted us to understand?

So Now I Am Seventy *Vol. 19, No. 5 - May/June 2009*

Was sich ueberhapt sagen lasst sich klar sagen; und wovon man nicht reden kann, darueber muss man schweigen.

What can be said can be said clearly; and whatever one cannot speak about, one must be silent about.

So now I am seventy, three score years and ten, time of the hoary head. Of course eighty is the age of strength, and anyway, in the long run we are all dead. In the meantime, all the world's a stage... and one man in his time plays many parts. Looking back, *ou sont les neiges d'antan?* Anyway, "when I was one-and-twenty I heard a wise man say, Give crowns and pounds and guineas but not your heart away". And for the time to come I am comforted for, Mithridates, he died old. And power corrupts.

Looking back over seventy years, I have seen much violence in our world, a lot of disappointed hopes, and yet also renewal of faith and hope.

I have seen violence, *ubi solitudinem faciunt pacem appelant*, they make a desert and call it peace, for war makes rattling good history; but peace is poor reading. But the aim of Judaism is the creation of a human being unable to shed blood. Indeed, I have learned that patriotism is the last refuge of the scoundrel. And disappointed hopes because "He that goeth about to persuade a multitude that they are not so well governed as they ought to be, shall never want attentive and favourable hearers" (which may not actually be a bad thing for it is always true enough); but primarily because tradition is the living faith of the dead; traditionalism is the dead faith of the living. And if, in the last resort, the world rests on three things: Justice, Truth and Peace, then I have well learned to have nothing to do with the powers that be. Power corrupts.

Yet, there has always been a renewal of faith and hope. After all, it is not up to you to finish the work, though you may never give up trying. There are things that

I have learned. Never wear a tie: it cuts off the flow of blood to the brain. Read a lot of detective stories, the more violence you read about, the less time you have to add to the sum of violence. It may be that we creatures are bearers of little brain, and it is certainly true that the best laid plans of mice and men gang aft agley.

But, no matter how much God laughs at human folly, God also has given us Torah and it is we, not God, who must live it. Remember that God also says that we, God's children, have overcome God. We must not abandon the vision that all will be Eden once again. Yet, power corrupts.

But, do we indeed have reason to believe? Is there really a country far beyond the stars? Or should we see reality, the God delusion? A little sincerity is a dangerous thing. And it is very easy to hold beliefs which would make life more interesting, if true, and have an engaging air of plausibility. But, while it is astonishing what a bundle of obsolete habiliments one's mind drags around even after the centre of consciousness has been shifted, do we have any choice? I think not. The opposite of faith is superstition. For nature abhors a vacuum. The courage to hope is all that is left; it is the entrance to hell that is inscribed "abandon hope all who enter here". Only in Judaism do we pray each day giving thanks that we human beings have knowledge, reason and rational discernment. The serenity of age is when one can look at life and say all is well and all shall be well.

There is nothing so stupid that some wise man has not said it. Much of life is sound and fury. Remember, do not on any account attempt to write on both sides of the paper at once; but do, however, remember also that life is like a book, write in it what you want to be remembered. For, if I am not for myself, who will be? But if I am for myself alone, what am I? And if not now, when?

What, then have I learned? Jaw jaw is always better than war war. God created human beings in God's own image, male and female. Shall not the judge of the whole earth do what is right?

Love your neighbour as yourself. I have lived through the best of times and the worst of times, but there is comfort that even when I walk through the valley of the shadow I need fear no evil, for if I should travel into the heights or the lowest depths, there is still the Presence. Even at seventy years, it remains for me to dream dreams and in dreaming to know that yes, we can. For it is forbidden to grow old. Yes, it is true that the one whom God wishes to destroy God first makes mad, but it is also true that life is for living and not dying.

So, *l'hayim*, to life. *Sh'ma*... Listen! Oh, and by the way, power corrupts.

(Note: There is no prize for identifying the quotes. I should be rather surprised if anyone can get them all!)

We have seen the difficulties there are when we try to make sense of the text of our Hebrew Bible. If nothing else, perhaps that will warn us not to assume too easily that when we read an English version we are actually coming to terms with the original. As with all translations of texts in early languages, translations of the Bible are just that: translations.

Does this, therefore, mean that we really cannot know what the Bible is saying to us? Sometimes, unfortunately, that really is the case: we are guessing based on the best information to hand. But, fortunately, this is not always so.

Much of the Bible, especially stories and the "historical" texts, is basically understandable. The Massoretes in the early part of the Middle Ages, punctuated and voweled the Hebrew, which enables us to read with understanding, bearing in mind, of course, that we are understanding the text as the Massoretes wanted us to understand it, which is not necessarily what the original authors and editors may have wanted. It is always possible to punctuate and vowel the text differently, provided that we observe the rules of Hebrew grammar. It is clear from the way in which the Talmud reads verses that the earlier Rabbis were doing this differently from the Massoretes.

It is often useful to read the standard Medieval commentaries on the Bible — Rashi, Ibn Ezra, Ramban, the R'dak. They often illustrate the text for us and open up possibilities of other meanings and readings. Again, though, they have their own agenda as to how they want the Hebrew Bible to be read.

A good rule of thumb in reading the Hebrew Bible is to eliminate the punctuation and vowels, by using, for instance, a *tikkun soferim*, which is the text used by people preparing to read from the *sefer Torah*. Then, read the Hebrew as straight forwardly as possible. The problem is not in Hebrew grammar which is fairly simple, but in understanding the vocabulary.

But obviously, one does not embark on reading the Hebrew Bible without knowledge. What will you need, at least ideally? You will need a reasonable acquaintance with the grammatical structure of the language. You will need the ability to read the commentaries, normally printed in "Rashi" script, which is different to normal printed Hebrew. It is helpful to know the cognate languages, Aramaic for the Targum (normally printed with the text in Hebrew Bibles, the Mikraot G'dolot); Akkadian (the language of Babylonia and Assyria, in cuneiform script); Egyptian hieroglyphs; and probably Syriac (a form of Aramaic written in a script that indicates the vowels); Ugaritic (a Cannanite language similar to Hebrew).

We have an advantage with Hebrew as against many other early languages, in that we have a continuing use of the language throughout history. This will help with some words, though we have to remember that some words have changed their meaning in the course of time. Israelis can help us to some degree here, though sometimes no more than expecting a modern English speaker to be able to read Chaucer fluently, even if it is the same language!

All this explains why translating the Bible is a continuing industry. As scholarship develops — and it does — we can hope for greater accuracy, though not necessarily greater poetic ability. In the meantime we must be guided by the scholars in the on-going attempt to understand our Hebrew Bible. Two recent versions that modern readers may find useful are those by Fox and Alter.

Rabbi Roger Pavey's Essays
from *The Bulletin*

RESPONSE TO KEYNOTE ADDRESS AT
HOLOCAUST MEMORIAL SERVICE *Vol. 2, No. 1 - July/Aug 1992*

The Holocaust is an experience that we look back on with a numbness of mind and spirit. Such gross evil overwhelms. Even to try to make sense of it is somehow beyond us. Yet we have to try to grapple with it; it is a part of us, the greatest evil of our history.

For us Jews, this is an occasion to mourn, to cry out in our agony. This was done to us, not only by men and women dedicated to evil, but, worse — much worse — by ordinary men and women, not evil but insensitive to the wrong they did, unaware and afraid. There is a pain too deep for tears; there is an anger, against humankind and against God. *Ha-shofet kol ha-arets lo ya-aseh mishpat?* Shall the judge of the whole earth not do justly?

For, as our people were murdered, both human being and God hid their faces from the tears, closed their ears to the cries, did not allow themselves to smell the stench of death. So few spoke of justice, knew what it was to be just, did justly.

And now, even now, there are many who deny the reality of the best documented crime in the whole of human history. Not only were their lives taken, their very memory is to be blotted out!

For us Jews, this is a time for memory; for mourning; to rage against what was done, and the evil people who did it and the ordinary people who allowed it to be done; to rage against what is still being done by those who would deny or trivialize what happened. So, we now remember. We say *Kaddish* for our lost sisters and brothers; and we join our cry to theirs; for justice, for memory, for compassion.

As human beings, of all faiths and none, we cry out for justice. We Jews were not the only ones to suffer. There were people of all religious and ethnic groups who were murdered by the Nazis. We especially remember Gypsies and homosexuals. All the outcasts of society martyred by prejudice and hatred. With few to help them then or mourn them now.

And we learn. We cannot understand, but we can learn — we must learn. The path of hatred, for homosexuals, Gypsies, Jews — the list is endless — leads only to Auschwitz. And until our hearts and souls are purged of that and our lives dedicated to making a society of justice and love, we shall not have learned.

So it is that, at this time of specially Jewish anguish, we invite all people to join us. Especially we invite Christian friends to share our sorrow and pain, and to join us in our common heritage of faith to seek healing together. For, I *amfot ha kol*, despite everything, there is good; and we shall not despair.

Thank you, Joanne, for being with us today, for speaking words of comfort, for extending hands of friendship and love. To you, we say *Barookh atah Adonai, eloheinu melekh ha olam, she-halak mei hokhmato lireiar*. Praised are you, Eternal our God, who has apportioned something of the divine wisdom to those who revere God.

May we learn to say, despite everything and with a full heart and soul *Ani ma-amin*, I believe:

I believe in the sun even when it is not shining.
I believe in love even when I do not feel it.
I believe in God even when he is silent.
Amen.

A Rabbi's Reflection on the 25th
Anniversary of His Ordination *Vol. 3, No. 2 - Nov/Dec 1992*

Any anniversary is important, but we especially want to mark silver and golden anniversaries. Twenty five years, a quarter of a century, in earlier time marked the passage of a generation; even today when life spans are so much more, it is still a sobering length of time. A psychiatrist once told me that the average length of time in a career before clergy became burned out was, in his professional experience about 15 years; he did not tell me the magic number for psychiatrist survival! Any way, I now contemplate a full 25 years in full-time pastoral ministry without a break. My first reaction is one of sheer incredulity: how on earth did I manage it? My second is to say that mere survival becomes after a certain number of years — and surely 25 qualifies! — no mean thing in itself, a symbol of a certain amount of spiritual, mental and even physical toughness, and also some sheer bloody-mindedness, worth of some sort of putty medal. It is no wonder that many Seminaries give their graduates who survive in the field that long honourary degrees, a doctorate in divinity seen like the British MBE, as a sort of long-service candy. And my final reaction is to look back and wonder what I have learned to equip me for the future.

What led me to the Rabbinate? That I know clearly. My family were not in any way religious. So I was not led to the Rabbinate by family tradition. Far from it; my mother's Marxist commitment, though a little compromised, was still alive enough to have regarded my ordination as not entirely a happy event. She did not live to see me ordained. She occasionally attended services in the Birmingham Liberal

Synagogue, though I suspect more because she loved to hate the Rabbi than out of any devotion. Rabbi bashing is a long-standing Jewish tradition.

There are two things that led me to the Rabbinate. First, and foremost, was my mother's illness. I was confronted with the problem of theodicy as it is called in the jargon of the trade, that is, why do people suffer if God is both good and all-powerful? Simple humanism seemed to me to be not good enough. As a result, I worked out a religious faith that may be a little idiosyncratic and is certainly heretical, but that has served me well. It has survived the slings and arrows of outrageous fortune and nourishes me still, despite further tragedy in my life. And in order to live that faith, I had to become a professional. I had to learn, to know, to teach. And that is with me still.

Second, though this was a rationalization *ex post facto*, there was the necessity of Jewish survival at all. After the Holocaust, to give up on Judaism seemed so cowardly. Were I not to be a Jew, and more, a professional Jew, a Rabbi, would make me an accomplice in genocide, an accessory to evil.

But it was not right for me to stand on the side lines as a dispassionate scholar. It was essential to me to be involved with people, to be part of their joys and sorrows, their pettiness and greatness, for life is with people. I have tried for 30 years, as student and as, I hope, Rabbi, to keep a foot in both camps, scholarship and practical ministry, but where I have failed, it has been to be with people rather than books. I have often wondered whether I was wrong to make that decision, for I have a good mind and the temperament of the scholar and I am a good teacher; but, on balance, I think that I chose well, at least in terms that I could live with. Of course, like nostalgia, congregational life often isn't all it's cracked up to be: there have been a lot of heartaches and failures. But I have learned to function within my limitations. It doesn't so much hurt me as confuse me that people have genuinely disliked, even hated, me: after all, I'm doing my best so don't shoot the pianist. But I have survived, I have had some effect in people's lives. There have been some people who have responded with genuine affection to me; so I can't have done everything wrong.

What have I learned in 25 years?

1. The older I get the more I realize, with increasing surprise, too, that I was very well trained at the Leo Baeck College. I remember the shoe-string facilities and the eccentricities of my teachers. But all of them somehow overcame all the difficulties and transmitted both a deeply based technical expertise and, over and above that, a remarkable love of learning. My respect for them has grown with the years, as has my respect for my colleagues who studied with me at their feet.

2. The most important thing I have learned is to retain one's own integrity. After all, we have nothing else; if we lose integrity, we lose ourselves. Everything, therefore, that I do or say, I must do or say knowing that I shall not have to defend it: for it is the right thing for me. So, I have made many mistakes and done many things wrong, I am only human; but I have never done anything truly immoral, and there

is a difference. I have not been mean-spirited, spiteful or malevolent. Have kept my own two prime commands: first, do no harm; second, do not violate my own or anyone else's integrity, physically, intellectually, morally or spiritually.

3. I have tried also to hold on to principle while remaining flexible. I will look for compromise at all times and will not look for a fight. Shalom is a major value of Jewish tradition. But I have not abandoned principle. I tolerate the decisions of others, but, where I sincerely disagree, I am not under any constraint to support rather than tolerate. The other's conscience — and mine — may not be forced. I am Rabbi of a whole community and must maintain the standards of community rather than any part of community, but the conscience may not be forced, theirs or mine.

4. I retain an open mind. Often, of course, an open mind can appear to be a blank; often, the civilized liberalism that tolerates difference can appear to be spineless and mush-minded: sometimes it is. But genuine tolerance is a humble acceptance of human finiteness. It says that this is where I am and I can do no other; but is prepared willingly to accept that others may say the same and end up in a different place. In a spirit of live and let live, I accept pluralism as essential to the human religious quest. And if I am to relate to others as I-Thou, which I profoundly believe, then I cannot live or think or act morally and responsibly for others, even when I am convinced without a shadow of a doubt that I am right and they are wrong. Because I am not God. Therefore, any system that imposes on the infiniteness of human relations in the presence of God, laws and regulations that are to be applied blindly and without consideration of circumstance, must, to me, be wrong morally and intellectually. Therefore, people are more important than principles. One must always bend rules to accommodate people. There may be absolutes, but I for one am not prepared to make a Procrustean bed of them. I suppose that this is one reason why I am dedicated to congregational life rather than pure scholarship, much as I love the exercise of the mind: I have a chance to be with people. There is the danger that I am tempted to play God; but I honestly don't think I am doing that. I really do respect people and want to empower them to live their lives more richly. A wise teacher once said to me that you can make many technical mistakes but you will do no harm if you really respect and love the people you are dealing with. And that is right. And that imposes tolerance, open mindedness, the acceptance of difference as a blessing.

5. I have learned, too, that the core of life is family. Both the larger family of the community, but more basically, the family of husband and wife, parents and children. Family to me is the love and learning of husband and wife, parents and children, as friends. Relationship is learned in family. Any relationship that grows out of a loving respect for the other, is true family. Respect for family values is not the monopoly of the narrow-minded and mean-spirited right wing, it is the core of being human. So long, that is, that we can define family in terms of loving partnership and mutually empowering friendship. I have learned that love reflects the divine love in our lives; it is the closest we can know of eternity on earth. Without it we shrivel and die and

become hurtful and mean. With it, with all our faults, we have the joy of life within us and we spread that joy around us.

Based on these learnings, where do I stand now in my religious faith as a Jew? I am now proposing to share some of my insights learned, sometimes painfully, over 25 years.

1. Religion is the questions not the answers. Because our being human imposes the duty to question — the meaning of things, the values by which we shall live. Answers, even if they were available, would close off the questioning. And life would be ended except as mere existence.

2. I believe that we are a unity of body, mind and soul, corresponding to the unity that we proclaim as Jews in the *Sh'ma*. We are impelled to honesty. Hypocrisy is the unacceptable face of religion. What we do, say, believe, must cohere. A little hypocrisy is a social lubricant; as the Talmud tells us, every woman is beautiful on her wedding day. But when we pray, when we talk about our religious experience, when we act, we must be honest. Our faith is a trialog between tradition, community and personal experience. If it is to be ours, it must be honest and sincere. *Eloheynu*, our God, must become *elohe avoteynu*, the God of our forebears. But, in the last instance, it must be 'eloheynu' first; to worship the *elohe avoteynu* that is not yet *eloheynu*, would be idolatrous worship of the past, stagnant and dishonest.

3. I have come to believe that my identity as a Jew is religious and religious alone. Of course it has cultural aspects that derive from the experience of a community in history: all religions do. But being Jewish as an ethnic identity divorced from the covenant with God is a dead end. We can grapple with the meaning of God to us — we must, we should — but ignore God we cannot. At the same time, while in all the historical ways of being Jewish we seek guidance, not a single one of those ways is, in itself, absolutely valid for us. Specifically, the Rabbinic way of being Jewish, allegiance to halakhah, is dead to the overwhelming majority. The option to live a halakhic lifestyle or nothing, is denying our future. In rejecting the halakhic lifestyle Jews will then be rejecting Jewishness entirely. We have to find other options, other ways. And for me the way to be a religious Jew in the modern world is the way of dialogue. Buber's 'I-Thou', that, too, is not an either/or. It is an option. And Judaism that is not centred on justice is for me no Judaism at all. *Tsedek tsedek tirdof.* And what does the Lord require of you, *Ahavat hesed, asot mishpat, matsnea lekhet im Adonai elohekha*, (love, compassion, do what is right, walk humbly with God). And the Torah is the guideline developed by the Jewish people in history by which this may be done. That is all. The rest is commentary: *zil g'mur*, go and learn!

So looking back over 25 years — is it really a quarter of a century? — there are two more things to do. I must think of all those who made me and moulded me, parents, family, teachers, friends, colleagues, Jews, non-Jews, and thank them and thank God for them. Many have gone on into the life of eternity: for them I will say a *Kaddish*. Those who are still alive have my personal thanks. All of them will live always in my heart. I have known love and pain, inspiration and goodness; I have been blessed with much friendship. I hope to have done them some credit in my life and career.

And I must summarize: to me, to be a Jew today requires of me scholarship and study; commitment; honesty and integrity; great sensitivity to the human story; openness to all human beings in their pain and sorrow, their joy and triumph; dedication to that which is right and just; courage; the ability to dream dreams and see visions; the ability to be alone and yet with others; the willingness to be vulnerable; the desire to heal the world, *tikkun olam.*

My ordination certificate reads, in part, "May God be with him and establish what he does, to strengthen and to beautify Torah. May he advance the Jewish people and increase peace in the world." Have I done well? I do not know. But with the help of God, Patricia, Jonathan and Danny, I will keep on trying.

THE LORD'S PRAYER *Vol. 3, No. 5 - May/June 1993*

A group of local parents of varied religious backgrounds have presented a brief to the Saskatoon School Board requesting the prohibition of all prayers and religious readings from Saskatoon schools. At present, it is permissible under the Education Act of the Province of Saskatchewan to begin each school day with such prayers and readings, which, if done, must be the Lord's Prayer and from the Bible. The School Board recommended in 1987 to its school Principals that this option should be exorcised.

The Jewish community has presented a brief to the Board in support of this request. The Jewish community has been urging this policy for many years.

I do not wish to rehearse the arguments being advanced by the parents or the reasons that the community has to support them. I do, however, want to consider the question of the Lord's Prayer.

There is no doubt that the Lord's Prayer comes from Jewish roots. It probably is a version of the *Kaddish*. There is also no doubt that its content is universal and not offensive to Jews, though its language is archaic and sexist. This does not, however, make its use in schools, or elsewhere, as, for example, in AA meetings, acceptable to Jews.

It is historically embedded in Christianity. It is specifically the prayer taught to Christians by Jesus himself according to Christian tradition. To argue that its content is inoffensive is blithely to ignore its context, and 2000 years of history cannot be so easily cast aside. One could just as well argue that Christians should recite the *Shma* on the grounds that its content is acceptable to any monotheist: it would ignore the historical reality.

Further, for people to use such an argument is itself disturbing. It continues the long-standing insensitivity of so many Christians to non-Christians. It presupposes something like, "We are all really the same, aren't we," and sees Jews as merely Christians — i.e. moral people — but without Jesus. To insist on the Lord's Prayer runs a spectrum from insensitivity at best to outright triumphalist bigotry ("We're a Christian country after all, so you— and others — had better conform") at worst.

There really is no such thing as a universal prayer, one whose content and historical context would both be inoffensive to all, Christians, Jews, Muslims, Hindus, Buddhists, Bahais, Unitarians, Humanists, Atheists. And if there were, such a prayer would be so meaningless as to be worthless anyway.

THE RESOURCES AND STRATEGIES
FOR JEWISH LIFE IN SASKATOON *Vol. 4, No. 2 - Nov/Dec 1993*

We must work within the constraints of our situation, and an honest appraisal of our resources must include a courageous acceptance of the realities of our demography. For, granted that we are dedicated to the maintenance and enrichment of Jewish life, and that, therefore, our fundamental resource is Judaism itself, this has to be placed within the reality of our present situation and a realistic assessment of the future trends of that situation.

Within a picture of basic stability, there will be changes in the make up of the Jewish families, we must realistically look to a greying of our community. The rate of out-marriage will continue to be high, and if we follow the general trends in North America, the numbers of non-Jewish spouses who seek conversion will decline. We shall have to confront the questions raised by out-marriage and the confused status of children without benefit of simplistic answers.

We shall, of course, be affected by long term trends within North American Jewry, both as they relate to the whole of Jewry and also those specific to the Conservative movement. With, for example, the loss of the right wing of the Conservative movement to the Union of Traditional Judaism, and the fact that Conservative Judaism is no longer the choice of the plurality of North American Jews, there are signs of two disturbing factors: a general loss of confidence in the United Synagogue as it struggles for ideological coherence; and a troubling loss of flexibility in dealing with the issues that arise from out-marriage and conversion. If we come to see conversion to Judaism as a part of the problem of Jews marrying non-Jews, instead of as a blessing to the long term survival of Jews and Judaism, we shall be more and more tempted to retreat into a fearful introversion. Any official policy and program directed to trying to discourage Jews marrying non-Jews is, in itself, in the long run ultimately futile.

To turn to our own community, it is true to say that, at the moment, we are fairly healthy. We are stable demographically and financially, we have a choice of hard working volunteers, we have educational and social programs that are working well, we hold services that are satisfactory to a large majority of our members.

Having said which, it would be idle to ignore the danger signs. I want to focus on two:

1. Our core of workers is diminishing. It is difficult to look to the replacement of our present lay leadership. With the pressures, for instance, of double-career families, there are fewer volunteers available to us. We shall have to assess our leadership needs: (a) we can look to more professional help, which will impose a strain on our finances; (b) we can cut back on our programming; (c) we can continue with the status quo and hope, but also risk a crisis.

2. Our religious life, and especially our Services, are satisfactory to our members almost by default. Those who feel strongly either for or against our present format are few. We are working, religiously, in terms of a lowest common denominator: few are offended, but even fewer are stimulated.

There are several issues involved here. As we are an "einheitsgemeinde," we are always painfully searching for common ground in the negative sense of being least offensive. We are inclined, therefore, to fudge issues so as to carry a majority with us, and inevitably, thereby confer a veto on minorities, even individuals, regardless of the will of the majority. We embrace an ideological incoherence that has both good and bad aspects, but, in the long run, means a slow decline into chaos. We ignore the needs of our members for spiritual relevance in their lives, in the name of a consensus to avoid divisiveness and preserve a nominal unity. In order to be all things to all people, our religious services are satisfactory but not satisfying. There will come a time, and soon, when, if we do not confront issues head on rather than ignore them in the name of unity, we shall disintegrate into meaningless incoherence. We are discovering, in common with the conservative movement as a whole, that eventually problems have to be faced and hard decisions made.

Our fundamental resource is Judaism. That is what our Synagogue is for: the preservation and enrichment of Judaism as a religiously based way of living. We look to our classical sources for spiritual and moral guidance. Jewish faith and practice, prayer and study, moral and ethical precepts — these are the *raison d'etre* of our community. Everything is subordinate to that end. Our allocation of our scarce resources in our programming must, therefore, be directed to that purpose in the most efficient way possible. We need to get the most Torah we can for our buck.

A word is needed here about the Rabbi as a resource. Ultimately, the Rabbi is the resource person for the community. There are two caveats to bear in mind when using the Rabbi: (a) any Rabbi is human and does some things well, some things not so well, some things not at all; therefore the Rabbi must be used efficiently as part of an ongoing process of prioritizing resources in a specific context; (b) the Rabbi in Saskatoon is sui generis, in demand by Jews and non-Jews alike, and therefore the

Rabbi's talents and energies have to be rationed.

We must plan for the future. This is what this whole exercise is about. There are rules for this process: 1) honesty and a willingness to face unpleasant facts and needs; 2) total commitment to the purpose for which we exist, Judaism; 3) acceptance of each other as equal partners in a process; 4) tolerance and compromise, a willingness to subordinate a personal agenda to the needs of the whole community. Without these rules, we are engaged in nothing more than a dialogue of the deaf. *Al tifrosh min ha tsibbur*, our tradition says, "Do not cut yourself off from the community."

Our community is heterogeneous. There are a few who come from an intensely Jewish and traditional background; most do not. There are Jews who were born in Judaism, there are Jews who have entered Judaism. There are religious Jews and there are more ethnically focused Jews. Each brings his or her own bias. It is a fact, for example, that Jews by choice are more religiously focused and less concerned about the ethnic aspects of Jewishness than are born Jews: it is also a fact Jews by choice are highly committed to their Jewish identity. Their concerns have become an essential part of the whole Jewish experience.

I want to pick out two areas that I would suggest are concerns that our members should be addressing today so that we can come away from our *Kallah* with positive ideas for action in our future programming.

1. Synagogue Services need to be looked at with honesty. What are we trying to do? I would suggest the answer to that is that we are trying to make the spiritual lessons of Jewish tradition resonate in the lives and hearts of our members. We are trying to: put Jews in contact with, in dialogue with, the sources of faith; to awaken Jewish spirituality that will inform life; help Jews to live better and more fully; give them guidance in the making of choices; comfort them in sorrow; help them to celebrate their joys; and bring them together in a community that lives for itself, but also for all humankind. Are we doing this? I would suggest we are, in the main, not. Why not? Because our services are arcane, a private world into which our members, in common with most Jews, have no real access. They sit respectfully through services, enjoy the nostalgia of melodies but are not really involved.

What can we do? Try to open up the contact between Jew and prayer. How can we do this? We need more and better music in our services. We need more congregational participation. This implies: setting up training programs for members who are willing to learn how to act as *sheliah tsibbur* and the use of more English in our Services. We need to shorten our Services, while retaining the halakhic integrity of the liturgy. We need to be willing to experiment with the format of the Service, especially to increase the educational content: it is more important to know what our Services are about than to daven without understanding. All this presupposes a fundamental attitude in mind: that we are willing to work together to open up access to our tradition to the whole of our membership, without being too much concerned with pre-existing agendas or party labels. It is the needs of our specific situation that we must satisfy.

2. The educational program of our community must become an integrated whole. The whole process of education must seen as a continuous one, from kindergarten to adult. We must, therefore, discuss together what we are aiming for, again in our own specific situation, and the resources we have to get there. It is for the membership to decide what is important in Jewish education, but I would suggest that we need to develop a base purpose, which I would term Jewish literacy. Jewish education is not intended to function in a vacuum, but to be an equipping of Jews to make choices in their lives, moral and spiritual, that are both authentically Jewish and also authentic to the person. It is dialogue with the classical sources that we need, not the imparting of information that will not be relevant to the life of Jews in Saskatoon. The core of such a program must be Hebrew, without which such a dialogue cannot take place. The end of our education program must be to enrich the lives of our members with the maximum relevant Jewish content. Again, the most Torah for our buck.

We have, I believe, reached the stage in our congregational life when we trust each other: each of us is committed to the advancement of Judaism. The status quo is one option that we can choose, to continue along the present pattern of congregational life. The signs are that this is an option that will result in a slow but steady decline: our communal stability will merely disguise an internal decay. We must change. We have no choice if we are to be a vibrant Jewish community. The direction of that change and its pace will be decided by the members. There are guidelines for us, and there are long-term goals that we are aiming for: basically the production of a community that is Torah-centred and knowledgeable. We will work within the parameters of the Conservative movement; that is the choice of the membership. The Conservative movement is a very broad church: it does not preclude our doing what we need to do in our situation to make Judaism live in the lives of our members. But we must also bear in mind that Conservative Judaism has definite ideological commitment: it is not a licence to do what we want without limit. Nor is it some no-man's land vaguely stuck between Orthodox and Reform. There are rules of the game. We must place ourselves in relation to those rules. If we are prepared to abide by them, let us honestly do so without equivocation; if we are not, let us also be honest and unequivocal.

I hope that from today's process of dialogue and searching will come specific and practical programs that will enable us to go forward as a united community with a more viable Jewish commitment in our Synagogue life, specifically in our services and our educational program, that will radiate into our personal lives, so that we Jews in Saskatoon will really be, as God has called us to be, "a light to the peoples." But I repeat: we must change. There is no going back, only forward.

Jews join the Synagogue for all sorts of reasons, and sometimes it is useful to think a little about why they choose to join, what they choose to contribute to the Synagogue that they join, and what they get out of it.

On one level, joining a Synagogue is a statement that "I am a Jew and I choose to be publicly known as a Jew." It is a badge of identity. It may be a feeling of loyalty to the nostalgia about the past, not necessarily as it really was but as it is perceived. "Not yet, therefore, am I willing to abandon ship and give up all links with the past of parents and grandparents and what it was that made them and helped them live in a harsh world." This Jewish identity, whatever it was, and however less significant it may have become to this generation, is still something that a Jew wants to preserve, at least to the extent of publicly acknowledging it to himself or herself and to the world outside.

And joining a Synagogue is also in a real sense an insurance policy. Any sensible person knows that life is interwoven with the good and the bad, joys and sorrows; any sensible person knows that there will be times in life when they will need help in all sorts of ways, and that none of us is Superman. We shall have times when we are ill and unhappy, defeated and disempowered; times when we are shattered by the deaths of those we love; times when we are unable to cope with the stresses and traumas of life; the loss of job, home, relationship. We shall also have times of great joy, when children are born, when sons and daughters reach Bar and Bat Mitzvah, when we celebrate marriage, when we rejoice in achievement. And then we shall want to share that joy with the community, just as we needed to share our sorrow and our grief.

We may also want to use the Synagogue we join to deepen understanding of that identity that we affirmed by the act of joining. Through the programs available in any Synagogue, we have the chance to enrich our Jewish identity through education for ourselves and for our children. Indeed, precisely because we live in an open world in close touch with non-Jews, we are impelled to learn something about what our Jewish heritage means, if only because we need to describe it and defend it, to explain to ourselves and to others, this Jewish identity that we have affirmed through belonging.

Yet others will join a Synagogue for social contact with fellow Jews, to find an oasis of Jewishness in a non-Jewish desert. For them, being Jewish is not a full-time commitment, but neither are they entirely full-time non-Jews.

And of course there will also be a few who join a Synagogue for religious reasons. They feel a need to try to understand Torah, to pray, to observe Shabbat and Festivals. For them, fulfillment involves close identification with the Synagogue as the core of their religious needs and striving.

So a Jew joins a Synagogue for all sorts of reasons: as a badge of identity, to say to the world and to themselves "I am a Jew," because they want to associate with other Jews; because they want to learn something of what the label might mean to them in their ordinary lives; to pray and observe Torah; to take out insurance for the indeterminacy of life; to re-create something of the world of our ancestors.

At the core of these lies an understanding perhaps explicit but more likely implicit and unverbalized — perhaps even unverbalizable — that there are values in the Jewish tradition that are worth preserving, and that the Synagogue is the only real way that they can be preserved.

And when the Jew joins a Synagogue, he or she can do so with a sense of pride and a determination to survive as a Jew, or with reluctance and always looking for rationalizations to slide away. As always, attitudes can be positive or negative. Any member of any Synagogue can remain merely a name on a list, often only accepting with great reluctance even the minimal responsibility of membership — to pay the membership dues. Or the member can be committed to the Synagogue and try to find through it meaning in being a Jew, in short, to give and receive the maximum through membership.

And those who go on from just joining and accepting that minimal commitment actually to pay the dues, will discover that involvement can be exciting and fulfilling. It can bring blessing to those who are involved and also to the community that they choose to be involved in, for there are so many aspects of Synagogue and communal life that all interests can find satisfaction.

Consider the breadth of the activities in this particular Synagogue, for example. There are the religious Services and the educational program which are, after all, the *raison d'etre* of any Jewish community. Education permeates every part of Synagogal life, as indeed it should.

But there are so many other things that go on in the Synagogue, and every one of them is totally dependent on members volunteering their time and energy and talents to ensure the Synagogue's continuance. Service on the Board and on committees is something that members do because it is important to them that the Synagogue and all it stands for should continue. Our women work through Sisterhood and through *Hadassah*, our men through *B'nai Brith*. Every Jew knows that a healthy Judaism and a prospering Jewish community requires that both the local community and also the broader Jewish world shall flourish. Jews need to assess both their Synagogue and what the membership means in their acceptance of personal responsibility for its well-being; and so their role and the role of their Synagogue in the well-being of the Jewish people throughout the world.

Each member has his/her own talents and abilities, interests and energies. No one's contribution, whether to the Synagogue in particular or to the Jewish community in general, is better or worse than anyone else's: all are essential. The professional person who volunteers expertise for the Synagogue, and the ordinary member who by regular attendance at Services ensures the maintenance of a minyan; both play their part in ensuring Jewish survival and, more important, survival in good health.

A Synagogue is a community of individuals and families. And it then becomes a building block in the making of the House of Israel. Its dimensions are horizontal through space and vertical through time. The Jewish people will not survive unless the Synagogue is healthy, nor the Synagogue unless ordinary Jews ensure its health by their commitment. But equally, nor can the individual Jew survive unless the Synagogue is healthy. The well-being of the Synagogue is the core of Jewish survival.

EROS AND THE JEWS *Vol. 5, No. 2 - Nov/Dec 1994*

Our study group meets each Monday lunch time from noon to about 1:30. Everyone is encouraged to bring lunch — *milkhig* only, please! — and tea and coffee is provided. Each year we study a text. I encourage participants to read the text chapter by chapter as the basis for our study and discussion. However, while doing the "homework" would enrich the experience, it isn't absolutely necessary. Nor is regular attendance absolutely necessary either; while it would be desirable to ensure continuity and the discipline of study, attendance from time to time whenever possible will also be beneficial.

The intention is to encourage participation by everyone. No previous knowledge is required, there are no exams and no grades. Although it is hoped that people will take the study seriously as a deepening of their Jewish lives, I appreciate that it is important to allow everyone to contribute. So, whatever concerns and questions people may have, we want them to feel free to contribute them to the group. No one should feel that they can't take a full part because of lack of previous knowledge or because their questions or comments might seem to them to be too basic.

In past years we have discussed the book *Standing at Sinai* by the Jewish feminist theologian, Judith Plaskow; this year our text is *Eros and the Jews* by David Biale, a study of human sexuality in the Jewish tradition.

I hope that every member would feels free to attend and take part, and therefore extend an open invitation. We have copies of the book available. This year the cost is $20, and even if you don't or can't come regularly to our sessions, it will still be an interesting addition to your personal Jewish library.

HANUKKAH *Vol. 5, No. 2 - Nov/Dec 1994*

The minor holiday of Hanukkah that we celebrate in mid-winter is the occasion when we recall and give thanks for the survival of Judaism in Jewish history and its resistance to the siren calls of assimilation to the religious faith and way of life of the majority around us. As it comes at the same time of the year as Christmas, it is an important reminder for us that we as Jews are different, that our difference has a reason and a purpose, that we have survived all sorts of threats to our identity throughout our history and will continue to do so.

When we are surrounded by the busyness of the Christmas celebrations of our neighbours with its all pervading atmosphere, we return to our own homes to light the little candles on the *hanukkiyah* and we are reminded by the contrast of the importance of the still, small voice in the overwhelming noise about us. The moral and spiritual values of our tradition do not depend on being a majority. The tiny group of Jews has been a source of blessing to the whole world, our few numbers have enriched the many, and, through our loyalty, will continue to enrich humanity.

On Sunday, November 27 at sunset we light the first candle in the *hanukkiyah*. The *berakhot* and the order of service, together with the traditional song *Maoz Tsur*, are in our *siddur Sim Shalom* on p. 243. We add a candle each evening. The Festival lasts eight days. In addition to the eight candles there is a ninth, *shamash* candle, with which the others are lit. The candles are placed in the *hanukkiyah* from right to left and lit from left to right. Obviously they are not lit on Shabbat, so on the Friday evening in Hanukkah, December 2, the candles for Hanukkah are lit before the Shabbat candles, and on the Saturday evening they are lit after *havdalah* and *motsa-ey Shabbat*. If the Synagogue holds *minhah* prayers on Shabbat afternoon, the *havdalah* includes Hanukkah in the weekday evening service that follows.

Because the Festival derives from the events recorded in the Book of Maccabees and celebrates the rededication of the Temple in Jerusalem through the miracle of the small amount of oil lasting throughout the eight days, the traditional foods associated with Hanukkah are oily ones. Ashkenazi tradition has *latkes*, Sefardi and Israeli tradition has doughnuts, *sufganiot*. The giving of a present is permissible, but we should avoid trying to expand Hanukkah into what it isn't, a Jewish Christmas. Its smallness, the littleness of the flickering lights in the dark of winter, is precisely what it is all about.

A happy Hanukkah to all. And do remember that it is not a "*Hag!*"

A JEWISH COMMENTARY
ON THE LATIMER CASE *Vol. 5, No. 3 - Jan/Feb 1995*

It is clear from the Ten Commandments that directly causing death is murder and prohibited *mi e Oraita*, from the Torah. Nor is it permissible to hasten death in any way, even when it becomes obvious someone is dying. See *Mishnah Shabb.* 23,5: TB Shabb. 151b, and the Shulchan Arukh YD 339,1. However, there is also no requirement halakhically to keep someone living at all costs. The illustration is of R.

Judah the Prince who was dying and his students continued to pray for his recovery until his servant smashed a pot to prevent the prayers being heard and so ensure his death, TV Ket. 104a. There are other accounts of silencing, by wood chopping outside so that the dying man should not hear the noise which was concentrating his attention and preventing his death, so as to allow him to die. There is even a duty to cease prayers for recovery, Sefer Has. 315-318. In commenting on the above passage in the *Shulchan Arukh*, Moses Isserles makes it clear that one may remove obstacles to death, and this reflects TB AV.Zar181. The general principle would seem to be based on TB Eruv. 100a, *Shev ve lo taseh adif,* i.e. benign neglect: it is not permissible to hasten death, but nor should one lengthen it unnecessarily, in other words, removal of obstacles to death.

There are two other relevant principles involved. There is a distinction between *le khathilah,* what should be done ideally, and *be diavad,* what is the consequences of acting first without consideration of the ideal. This is then associated with the concept of *anus,* that is a person in great agony who acts out of the emergency of what, for him, is an intolerable situation. So, for instance, while is prohibited to commit suicide, from the Ten Commandments, one who does commit suicide is assumed to be an *anus* and therefore all the implications of the sin are no longer applicable.

With reference to this specific case, there can be no doubt that Mr. Latimer is guilty of murder in terms of Jewish teaching. However, what should have been done and what actually happened are different in terms of halkhic consequence. Considering the question of *anus,* we should ask whether Mr. Latimer was under such agonizing stress as to make his action, while prohibited *le khathilah, ab initio,* understandable within the terms of *be diavad,* I suspect probably not. However, there is certainly room for halakhic doubt. Consequently, I would suggest that the sentence was not proportionate to the crime.

ON FORGIVENESS *Vol. 5, No. 4 - March/April 1995*

During the Holy Days we are concerned with the moral quality of our lives and we pray for forgiveness from God, from others and from ourselves for what we have done that we should not have done and for what we have not done that we should have done. We should note that when we do this, we speak in the context of the overall theme of *teshuvah,* repentance, or, better, "return." If we return to God, then God will turn to us, and healing can start.

In January, we remembered the 50th anniversary of the liberation of Auschwitz. Thoughts of the Holocaust dominated our minds and we struggled again with our attitudes to those events. What should be our response to those who carried out the crimes of genocide? Many in our society would answer that we should forgive the Nazis and their collaborators for what they did to Jews and to other human beings whom they wrote out of the human community. Especially as time passes, there is strong temptation to say forgive; perhaps, even forget. Indeed, the Jewish refusal to forget, to forgive; to continue to seek justice against those who carried out these crimes, seems to be an increasingly narrow-minded and mean-spirited search for vengeance. Forgiveness would be the higher morality.

It is essential that we say clearly that this is not so.

We must continue to remember. That does not mean that we should build our Jewishness around the Holocaust as the sole *raison d'être* for our continuance as Jews. Judaism exists not as a response to Hitler, but as a positive source of values and hopes for us to live by and for. But to forget is to murder the innocent dead yet again. Their memory is their guarantee of life, and ours also.

And we must not forgive.

In the first place, it is not for us, the survivors, to forgive. Only the dead can forgive what was done to them.

But, more important, to forgive would be morally wrong. If we forgive it is because the one who sins turns to the victim and seeks to make recompense. The sinner must confess and then turn to the victim to seek to undo what was done; only then can the sinner ask for forgiveness, and only then may the victim forgive. For then there is *teshuvah*, turning, and with turning there is the beginning of healing. First, there must be justice: then there may be forgiveness, and then, and only then, can there be healing.

Consider the implications of too-easy forgiveness. If I, the victim, forgive the one who sins against me without the sinner making the first move to repair the consequences of the act, then whatever one does results in automatic forgiveness. Then there is no accounting, no responsibility, and no possibility of a moral system. Forgiveness without accountability would destroy civilization.

The very essence of Judaism as a moral code is the assumption that we human beings are responsible for what we do. When we do wrong, therefore, we must repair the wrong before we can ask for forgiveness. The demand for justice must be satisfied first. And on this issue we cannot and dare not compromise.

Until the Nazi repents by confessing sin and then turning to the victim in the honest desire to make reparation, to ask us to forgive is to demolish the whole moral basis of civilization. The demand for justice is not vengeance; it is justice. It is non-negotiable.

Therefore when Eli Wiesel prayed to God not to forgive those who murdered the children he expresses traditional Jewish teaching. "The blood of your brother calls out to me from the earth." Until the Nazi makes *teshuvah*, justice is not satisfied. If and when the *teshuvah* occurs justice is done, the circle is complete, forgiveness is sought and given, healing can start. To forgive now would make us accomplices in the crime. It would destroy all hope for the future.

ON THE USE OF MUSICAL INSTRUMENTS
IN THE SHABBAT SERVICES Vol. 5, No. 5 - May/June 1995

From the account of the work that the people did in making and decorating the Tabernacle in the desert, as recorded in Exodus 35-39, the Rabbis deduce a list of 39 categories of work. None of these categories include the playing of musical instruments. Indeed, we know that musical instruments were played in the Temple in Jerusalem, as shown, by example, by Psalm 150, and that the *shofar* was blown even when *Rosh ha Shanah* fell on Shabbat.

What, then, is the objection to playing musical instruments as part of the Shabbat service? It is certainly not halakhic objection, but entirely one of custom, *minhag*.

First, there is a category in the *halakhah* of *shevut*. This is an extension of prohibitions so as to avoid breaking a clear Torah prohibition by adding a Rabbinic "fence." An example is the prohibition of handling money on Shabbat. This is not a halakhic prohibition: it is the Rabbinic *shevut*. Adding the injunction not even to handle money on the Shabbat. The *minhag* of not playing instruments in the Shabbat service is another example of *shevut*.

There are two elements involved. There is *zekher le huban*, remembering the destruction of the Temple. As we are in mourning for the Temple, music is forbidden, not halakhically and *mid de Oraita*, that is from the Torah, but as a Rabbinic enactment in the category of *shevut*. It should be noted that the objection is to any and all music, including vocal music. However, Jews have always, apparently, been attached to music, and just refused to accept the Rabbis' view: they insisted on having music in the Synagogue on Shabbat, the singing of the *hazzan*, accompanied often by choirs and even a tuning fork.

The second element is the concept of *makeh be patish*, literally "hitting with a hammer", that is doing repairs. It was possible, it was argued, that if an instrument broke, one would be tempted to make a repair. Playing the instrument is not what is forbidden halakhically, but making a repair certainly would be. Therefore, by the principle of *shevut*, playing was not done in case the player should forget that it would be forbidden to repair it. On the other hand, of course, if the player was not an expert in repairing musical instruments, it would be difficult to see any relevance in this extension of *halakhah mi de rabbanan*, basically a Rabbinic "just in case." The hypothesis becomes so remote as to create an absurdity.

In short, playing musical instruments on Shabbat in the services in the Synagogue is not halakhically prohibited. Further, the Rabbinic extensions of halakhah hover on the absurd. Therefore, the Conservative movement has ruled that it is a question of local opinion in the congregation. Many Conservative Synagogues use musical instruments, many do not.

Clearly from our survey there is a majority in our congregation who are willing to experiment with the use of musical instruments in our Shabbat services. The enhancement of the Service and the encouragement and enrichment of the members' depth of spirituality becomes the issue.

This, then, is the background to the decision of the board to try the experiment of using musical instruments for some of the Shabbat services over the next year.

It must be our hope that all our members will approach this issue with open minds and generous spirit, and a basic trust in the fundamental good taste and discretion of the Ritual committee and those who will operate this experiment. The concern of all of us must be the best interests of our community at large, and we must put aside our own emotions and feelings, however deeply held. Granted that there is no halakhic objection, which is the case; granted that the United Synagogue permits the use of musical instruments to enhance the Shabbat service, which is the case; and granted that the majority of our members feel that music is an enrichment of their spirituality, which is also the case, let us all determine to make this experiment work.

BOUNDARIES *Vol. 6, No. 6 - July/August 1996*

Judaism makes boundaries, divisions, between what is permissible and what is not, in ethical matters, in terms of ritual. *Havdalah*, the boundary, is essential to Judaism.

There are two kinds of boundary. There are boundaries that are walls that divide, that lay down clearly what is inside and what is outside, what defines *us* and what defines *them*. And there are boundaries that are permeable membranes. They still lay down what is inside and what is outside, but these boundaries are fluid and changeable. Walls either stay where they are or are torn down; they cannot be moved around easily. Membranes on the other hand, move and flow to encompass entirely new territory and to abandon old territory.

There is therefore a basic boundary between Jew and non-Jew. Of course Jews and non-Jews share far more than our boundaries define. We are all human, with the same human needs, hopes, fears, dreams, capacity for love and for pain. And we know perfectly well that this commonality of being transcends the boundaries that we construct that will define our differences. Yet we also know that the differences that we insist on laying down and defining are also important. While they are merely nuances on the theme of being human, the nuances are very important to us. We need to define who we are, both in the positive and also in the negative, who we are not.

If the boundaries really are walls that exclude others who are outside and *therefore* confer on those inside a special status, the differences become counter productive and the boundaries cease to have a real purpose other than to divide as an end in itself.

If on the other hand, the boundaries are permeable; like membranes, then they still define and give a clear identity, but they do not exclude, nor do they confer a feeling of specialness and privilege on those inside as opposed to those outside.

Jews marry non-Jewish partners. The response most of us have elected for, and I believe correctly, is to welcome the non-Jewish partner to the community and try to influence them either to convert to Judaism or to bring up their children of the marriage as Jews. In other words, we retain the defining boundary between Jew and non-Jew but we say that the boundary is permeable and that the non-Jew can and should have the option to be absorbed into Judaism, because we see Judaism as preserving and protecting and teaching moral and spiritual values that are immensely significant to the whole world, and therefore the nuance of being human that is being Jewish is valuable in itself and worthwhile to all.

Even if a conversion is purely formal and does not result in the living of a totally committed Torah-centred life, we still accept it: having the person in the community means that they are always open to the influence of Judaism, and the acceptance of the community and by the community ensures the continued openness of the situation.

What, then, of a situation where the non-Jewish partner has not converted to Judaism? Should we bury that non-Jew in the Jewish cemetery? The halakhah doesn't help us here in that there is really no halakhic objection to burying Jews and non-Jews together and in fact, it has been done and will be done, as, for example, in military cemeteries. However, outside the emergency situation, should we now do this as a matter of minhag?

There are two factors that I think are important here.

1. The Jewish cemetery was created by early members of the community for whom it was a halakhic and religious imperative to ensure the existence of a place for *Jews* to be buried. Traditionally, acquiring land for a cemetery and building a mikvah and a school, all must be done before building a Synagogue. Now, generations later, to change what the creators wanted and to permit non-Jewish burial in the Jewish cemetery would be a moral breach of faith.

2. But there is more important consideration, deriving from what I have been saying. The boundaries we set up between Jew and non-Jew are not an unscalable wall, they are permeable: the entry to Judaism for a non-Jew is always open. But there are boundaries: Jews need to affirm their identity, to know who they are, and this implies both the positive and, to some degree at least, even the negative: a Jew both is and also is not, a Jew is a Jew and is not a non-Jew, and by the same token, a non-Jew is not a Jew unless he or she wishes to become a Jew through the formality of conversion. That boundary is important. However liberal we want to be, indeed I think, should be, the boundary remains. Jews and non-Jews should work together, share life together in friendship and co-operation, should seek to advance common ideals and values. But, in the last resort, Jews and non-Jews should cherish and respect the different spin they have on being human. It is not

a barrier, but it is a boundary that marks the difference. Difference, not in terms of hierarchy and privilege, but difference in the sense of being diverse elements in the mosaic that makes up our common humanness. And the maintenance of difference of this kind is essential to the rich pluralism of human experience.

Therefore, I do not accept the propriety of burying a non-Jewish spouse in the Jewish cemetery with his or her Jewish partner. Indeed, to do so would actually demean the cherished different identity of the non-Jew. If his or her choice in life has been to support the Jewish partner but not, in all sincerity, to join that partner by merging his or her identity with that of the Jewish people, then surely, we should respect the integrity of that choice in death.

So long as the boundaries we draw are permeable, flexible, open, and do not become walls and barriers that are closed and hostile, those boundaries are good and useful tools in the creation of a rich diversity of human experience and being.

IMPRESSIONS OF SOUTH AFRICA *Vol. 7, No. 5 - May/June 1997*

South Africa is potentially an enormously rich country, both in terms of natural resources and of its people. After a generation of apartheid, which even the most bigoted whites are now coming to see was a colossal historical blunder, changes have occurred that have been revolutionary and that are still underway. It was an enormous opportunity to visit South Africa at this time and to assess those changes and to see the country itself and the people.

I have to say at the outset that I always regarded apartheid as immoral and inhumane, a moral absurdity; as unscientific in its racist premises, a biological absurdity; and as bad for business, an economic absurdity. The ease and the peacefulness of the transition from apartheid to democracy has demonstrated the correctness of my opinion. This was therefore the right time to visit the country and to experience a vibrant and vital society experiencing racial change, with its opportunities and its dangers.

The people — Black, White, Coloured, Asian, English speaking and Afrikaans speaking — were welcoming, friendly, cheerful and enormously helpful. I know that there are immense problems with crime and violence, it's just that we didn't personally meet them. We felt safe. As an example of their willingness to help, we booked a tour and the tour driver and guide noticed that I was having some difficulty getting on and off her van. At one of the stops she went out of her way to find some steps to help me. She stowed them in the van for future use. She just had not had an experience with disabled people before and was anxious to help as soon as the situation arose.

There are enormous disparities in wealth. Side by side with condominiums selling at R8m and two Rolls Royces in the same street was poverty on a scale that we could not have visualized. As an example, we went to a meeting of the Sisterhoods of the South African Reform Temples which happened to be held in Cape Town while we were there, and we learned that the women were helping with projects in the Black Townships which were of great interest to us. One was working with people to help them set up gardens to grow vegetables and become to some degree at least self-sufficient. This is important because the diet of so many is so inadequate. The other was working with a school and specifically to help provide the children with 3 meals a day as they might not otherwise eat at all — the unemployment rate is 30-40%. For this the school, even with Sisterhoods' support, had a budget of 8c per child a day, for 3 meals! Another indication of the poverty was clear to us when we visited a township, Guguletu. We were invited into a home there, basically a two-room shack — and shared African beer with the people; the reason they drink the beer is not to get drunk (the western beers are more effective for that) but to eat. The beer is made of fermented corn meal. There are worse conditions. People are flooding into the country from the rest of Africa — South Africa, after all, accounts for more than half of the whole economy of the continent. There is nowhere for them to work or to live, and they set up shanty towns which are basically cardboard boxes scattered higgledy piggledy along the highway, kilometre after kilometre of them, with no facilities, just thousands of people and their animals crowded together.

Not surprisingly, the number of Blacks who vote for the National Party is negligible. On the other hand, the old white liberals in the Democratic Party are insignificant and will probably be swallowed up by the African National Congress. The only other major group represents the forces of Zulu nationalism that wants to break up the country anyway. Without a coherent opposition, how can the ANC not become corrupt? But for as long as coloured voters in the Western Cape support the NP and keep the Provincial Premier, Mr. Kirel, in office the NP will not dissolve and a new centrist party appear to challenge the ANC nationally.

What of Jews? Jews in South Africa have been important for a century. Without Jews, South Africa would not have developed as it has in economic terms. Jews have also been in the forefront of the opposition to apartheid. To mention but one, the heroic battle of Helen Suzman who for years was the sole opposition MP, will remain something to be proud of. However, events have overtaken Jews. The transition has not in the main damaged the position of privilege that whites held and still hold. The need for radical change, however, has left behind the civilized but rather ineffectual liberalism that most Jews espoused and probably still do: the leader of the Democratic Party is a Jew, but he and his party are trapped. My impression is that this style, while maybe respected, really doesn't count for much any more.

Large numbers of Jews have left, particularly the young, not because of anti-Semitism, but mainly because of the perception that crime is out of control, that the economy cannot be saved, that problems are basically insoluble, and perhaps because they do not feel that Jews have a future because they are such a tiny proportion of the total population that now has power, whereas they were a major part of the minority white population that used to have power. So, the Jewish population has dropped from 120,000 to about 89,000. In the future, Jews will probably be confined to the major cities and will be an aging group. The long-term prognosis for Jewish life in South Africa cannot be optimistic.

As an example, a young Orthodox Cantor provided the entertainment at the wedding reception. He invited us out to dinner at one of the two kosher restaurants in Cape Town — both, incidentally, run by Israelis. His concern was to find out how he could get to Canada as a Cantor in a Conservative Synagogue.

That is not to say that the Jewish community is in imminent danger of disappearing. There are many large Synagogues that are still functioning. The oldest Synagogue in Cape Town, indeed the oldest in the country, is still very much in use. The old building is now a very fine Jewish museum, while the new building, a fine example of late 19th century Moorish style Synagogue architecture, is home to an active congregation. Similarly, the Reform Temple still has a membership of 1,200 families. Its Rabbi is an American Conservative, and its Rabbi Emeritus, the highly respected David Sherman, is still active at the age of 88. However, the old established communities in the small towns are disappearing; the Synagogue buildings in, for example Stellenbosch and Paarl are still there, but they are not in use except for the Holy Days. In Cape Town there are still adequate facilities for Jewish life — Synagogues, book stores, kosher restaurants, for instance. But there is a sense of a community that is aging and perhaps withdrawing from itself.

There are problems for the future. South Africa has the inestimable good fortune that its President is Nelson Mandela. He is a man universally respected, even by the most verkrampte Afrikaaner, and his charismatic appeal transcends all the racial and ethnic boundaries. He has a vision for South Africa that is a pluralistic democracy, a rainbow society, and that vision and the man who articulates it are holding the country together in a hope and a dream. It is, however, a fragile hope and dream. The challenges are immense: an exploding population; the need to provide the people with medical care, education and meaningful work; the long-term healing of the wounds of apartheid, providing justice for the victims and at the same time maintaining unity and the commitment to work together. The President's successor, Deputy President Thabo Mbeki, is a competent man, but he is not Mandela. Can he, can anyone other than Mandela, keep this country together, and overcome the destructive challenges of Inkatha and the recalcitrant whites in the Freedom Front, for example!

South Africa is the only functioning democracy in the whole of Africa. Mandela's vision of that democracy is also ours in Canada, a broad, tolerant and pluralistic vision. It is also the economic giant of Africa. Its well being, the success of this democratic experiment, is in our interests and in the interests of the whole world. That is why this country is so important, and its transition from apartheid to freedom has to succeed.

What, then, can we do?

We can, as Canadians, pressure our government to support South Africa morally and with financial aid. We can urge Canadian business people to invest in a country that is after all potentially one of the richest in the world. As Jews, we can support the efforts of the South African Sisterhoods: $100 can feed a lot of children at 8c per child per day; another $100 can buy a lot of seeds and tools to be used in the garden project to grow vegetables and enable people to feed themselves and attain human dignity in doing so.

As Jews, we are always concerned, rightly, with the fate of our fellow Jews anywhere and everywhere in the world. But as Jews we are called by our moral tradition to work for the healing of the world, non-Jewish as well as Jewish. When human beings call to us for help we cannot refuse, regardless of their identity. *Ve ashavta le rakha kamokha* is a demand that does not distinguish Jew and non-Jew. Of course we cannot solve the problems of the world. But we can do our part. *Tikkun olam* is the raising of people, one by one, from despair to hope.

My mind treasures most of all impressions I have — the wonderful beauty of the country, the promise and the challenge — the image of the people. The Xhosa people I met, adults and children, are people of immense dignity and irrepressible humour; even in their poverty they have not lost that. They deserve their dreams and hopes to come true.

JEWISH CUSTOMS RELATING TO
FUNERALS AND UNVEILINGS *Vol. 8, No. 1 - Sept/October 1997*

In the passage from Talmud that is quoted in our Prayer Book (p. 18) we are enjoined to bury the dead: "The Holy One buried the dead; you should bury the dead."

This is one of three fundamental *mitsvot* — dowering a bride, visiting the sick, and burying the dead. And burying the dead is the most significant because it is an act of total altruism: the recipient of the good deed cannot thank the one who fulfills the mitsvah.

Burying the dead, *halvayat ha met*, is a mitsvah that encompasses a range of acts. It includes the work of the *hevra kadisha* in preparing the dead for the funeral; it includes those who are involved in the actual funeral service; and it includes everyone who attends the funeral. Their presence guarantees a minyan so enabling the mourners to fulfill the mitsvah of saying the *Kaddish de Yatom*, the mourner's Kaddish. But more than that, the mitsvah is *halvayat ha met*, and the literal meaning of the Hebrew is "accompanying the dead." The mere fact of being present and accompanying the dead to the last resting place is itself an act that fulfills a mitsvah.

It does not matter whether one knows the one who has died or not. Indeed, all the more should one accompany the dead when one does not know the person. Obviously, the death of a relative or friend means that anyone will be forced to fulfill the mitsvah because they are so personally involved. To attend the funeral of a Jew one did not know is to fulfill a mitsvah for its own sake, purely and without necessity. Indeed, on the grounds of *mipne tikkun ha olam*, to attend the funeral of a non-Jewish person is also meritorious.

No one should be allowed to die alone or to be buried unmourned, Jew or non-Jew. We should mark our reluctance to let someone go. So we maintain human dignity even in death by not rushing the coffin to the grave, but rather setting it down seven times on the way. Even if there is no family, even if we ourselves did not personally know the deceased, we should regard it as a privilege, the last good deed that we can perform for a fellow human being, to be with him or her on their final journey and to part with them with reluctance.

Similarly, following the funeral, it is our duty to be with the family and friends of the dead, to comfort them and support them. It is often better just to be with them, to hold them, to hug them, rather than to try to find words. To pray with them in their bereavement is an essential part of this process.

The unveiling of the tombstone is also a mitsvah. The raising of a *matsevah*, tombstone, marks for most the ending of the stages of mourning that our tradition lays down. It may be done at any time after the *sheloshim*, the 30 days, but for many it is done sometime around the anniversary of the death. It does not mean that mourning ends, it never does, as is shown by the custom of *yahrtseit* and the holding of the *yizkor* services during the *regalim* and on the Day of Atonement. But it is a symbol of moving from mourning as such, the agony or irreparable loss, to mourning as healing, the celebration of the life that we shared together.

The ceremony surrounding the unveiling of the tombstone is quite modern. It is incumbent on family and friends to be present. But equally, it is a mitsvah for all members of the community to be with the family and their friends.

There are three reasons: to enable mourners to say Kaddish; to ensure that no one is left alone during the mourning and healing process; and to share together as a community with the symbolic enacting of Jewish faith in the eternity of the spirit. So we are mourning, with mourners, but we are also going through with them the rebuilding of life after death of one we have lost and the rejoicing in love and memory that triumphs over death.

Notice that on our tombstones we give the name of the dead in two forms: in the English by which he or she was known to the world when alive; and in the Hebrew by which he or she was known to the Jewish community when living as a mitsvah-fulfilling Jew. When we attend and we read both, we are remembering the dead as person and as Jew. We, and they, are becoming part of the *Kabbalat Torah*, the chain of tradition of Judaism.

For a Jew to attend a funeral or an unveiling is a fundamental *mitsvah*, whether they are known to us or not, whether they are Jewish or non-Jewish. Your presence is not an intrusion on private grief, it is a sharing of that grief and a statement of our common humanity and especially of our Jewish faith in the meaning and purpose and eternity of life.

THE KADDISH *Vol. 8, No. 1 - September/October 1997*

One of the most frequently used of all the prayers in our *siddur* is the *Kaddish*. The *Kaddish* is for most Jews associated with death and mourning. Few are aware that the mourner's *Kaddish, Kaddish de Yatom*, is only one form of the *Kaddish*. The fact that it is associated with occasions surround death – for funerals, during mourning, at *yahrtseits*, and for *yizkor* services at the ends of Festivals strengthens this connection.

Yet the Kaddish does not mention death and mourning. It is what the scholars call a doxology, i.e. a pure paean of praise of God. A literal translation of the words would read something like "May His great name be made great and holy in the world that He created by His will, and may His rulership be established in your lifetime and in your days and in the lifetime of the whole House of Israel, swiftly and soon, and say Amen. May His great name be praised, extolled, glorified, elevated and exalted, beautified, lifted higher than all blessings, praises and hymns that can be said in the world, and say Amen. May there be great heavenly peace and life for us and for all Israel, and say Amen. May the One who makes peace in the heights, make that peace for us and for all Israel, and say Amen."

This is as I said, only one version of the Kaddish prayer, the mourner's Kaddish. It is to be said by one who is halakhically required to mourn, that is someone whose parent, spouse, child or sibling has died. In addition, anyone may willingly accept an obligation to mourn — any other family member or a friend, Jewish or non-Jewish — and therefore say the mourner's Kaddish. It is then said daily throughout the eleven months of mourning and thereafter on the anniversary of the death, *yahrtseit*, and for *yizkor* Services at the end of the three Pilgrim Festivals, *Pesah, Shavuot* and *Sukkot*, and for the *Yizkor* Service on *Yom Kippur*.

The forms of the *Kaddish* are the *Hatsi Kaddish*, which omits the last two paragraphs and acts as a divider between parts of the Service; the *Kaddish Shalem*, which interpolates a paragraph before the last two — "May the prayers and requests of the whole House of Israel be acceptable to our Father in Heaven, and say Amen" — and which acts as a divider between major parts of the Service; the Rabbinic Kaddish, *kaddish de Rabbanan*, that is used after studying the Torah, and that also interpolates a paragraph before the last two, reading, "May there be great peace for Israel, for scholars, for students and for students of students, all who study Torah, here or in any other place, for them and for you, together with grace and love and compassion, long life, sustenance and well being and deliverance from trouble, from our Father in Heaven, and say Amen." Finally, there is a version that can only said by anyone at most twice in a lifetime, a form of *Kaddish* to be recited at the funeral of parents, the *Kaddish de Itkhadata*. It retains the last four paragraphs of the mourner's *Kaddish*, but re-phrases the opening paragraph to read, "May His great name be made great and holy in the world that He created by His will, that world that in the future will be renewed and where the dead will be raised to eternal life and the city of Jerusalem be rebuilt and the Temple re-established, when all idolatry will be uprooted from the world the worship of God be established. May the rulership of the Holy One, praised be He, be set up in glory, and your life and in your days and in the lifetime of all the House of Israel, swiftly and soon and say Amen."

All versions of the *Kaddish* require a *minyan*, and are not said without a *minyan*. Why? Because Judaism has always insisted in the importance of community. While personal spirituality is immensely important and to be encouraged, there are certain religious acts that need the community. Hence, the *Barekhu*, the call to worship, the reading and studying of Torah, and, importantly, the *Kaddish*, are done within the context of community. Death is of concern to the whole community as well as the individual. The pain of loss is, of course, intensely personal, but it is also pain that is shared by the whole community. No one dies alone or is mourned alone. All Jews are knotted together with other Jews. And that is partly our commonality of human experience, but it is also the special interconnectedness of Jews. Mourners are embraced by the caring of their community, and the love of others is there with them as they experience the agony of parting from ones whom they have especially loved. The same thing applies to studying Torah. Torah is the heritage of every Jew, but, more, it is the heritage and special possession of the whole community. Study, therefore, requires a minyan when the Torah is to be read. Every community of Jews anywhere in the world and throughout time is linked by Torah and the covenant that it makes between human and divine. Therefore, study is communal as well as individual, and the *Kaddish de rabbanan* must also require a *minyan* to be said.

What is the value of the *Kaddish*?

When a mourner or someone remembering love shared and lost at the time of *yahrtseit*, rises in the community to proclaim God in the words of the *Kaddish*, there are several things that happen.

The community acknowledges the death of a member of the House of Israel. It reaches out to share the pain of the mourner and to comfort and support the hurt of a fellow Jew. The one who says *Kaddish* declares the greatness and goodness of God even at the moment when he or she is most likely to deny that greatness and goodness and so begins the process of reaching out to the community. Both community and mourner begin the healing: life and beauty and blessing remain possible, and the shattered shards of death can and will become celebration of life. Any one of us who has gone through the process of mourning knows that there is a process and that the rituals of Jewish tradition work. And at the core of those rituals is the *Kaddish*. Rising to say *Kaddish* in the community is an essential part of healing. The *Kaddish* is deeply rooted in the historical experience of the people. We are weaving webs of connectedness with Jews throughout time and in all places and we are concentrating on the core that makes everything have meaning and purpose and sense, the empowering presence of God. Saying *Kaddish* is remarkably effective: it cleanses and stabilizes and heals. And for this, the experiencing and the knowing of the continuity of life, we don't need to know a word-for-word translation; we need only to open the heart and soul to the rhythms and the cadences of the prayer. The *Kaddish* is a creation of genius, filled with the faith and tears, the dreams and smiles, of ordinary people who have spoken those words through 20 centuries of time.

Thoughts on Thirty Years
in the Rabbinate *Vol. 8, No. 3 - January/February 1998*

At the beginning of December I celebrated 30 years as a Rabbi since receiving *semikhah* in 1967. It is a time for me for thought and reflection on what a Rabbi is and should be, what I started out wanting to do and what I now feel is the right thing to do.

The roles that a Rabbi fulfills in a modern community are many and so often irreconcilable. The expectations that communities have and that the Rabbi has often have only a tangential relationship.

A Rabbi is, of course, supposed to be a scholar. And, indeed, that is what a Rabbi sees himself or herself as being: a scholar and teacher. That is what a Rabbi, of any denominational group, is trained to be and do. A Rabbi's encounter with the Jewish sources is the very heart of his or her identity, and the essence of the role is to be the link between community and those sources. Alas, the job description is now filled with so many other things that no one human being could ever satisfy it, quite apart from no Rabbi being trained for most of it, while Jewish communities are so highly educated in secular areas and so under-educated Jewishly that they often feel threatened by Rabbinic scholarship.

Those other roles fall broadly into priestly, pastoral, pedagogic and ambassadorial aspects, both within and outside the Jewish community.

As a "priest," the Rabbi has to officiate at services, preach and lead life-cycle rituals. This is not the traditional role of the Rabbi, but created by the outside world that has thrust on the Rabbi the duties of Minister of Religion as defined by Protestant Christianity. Any Jew can act as *sheliah tsibbur*, but as fewer and fewer are knowledgeable enough to do so, the job falls on the professional in the community: the Rabbi.

As "pastor," the Rabbi is required to be sick visitor, counsellor, youth leader, psychiatric social worker. Modern Rabbinical training does include some of these skills, to some degree, though more to knowing what to do until help arrives, while in the meantime doing as little harm as possible. Rabbis have to learn their own capacities, what they can do and what they can't. After all, marital counselling, grief counselling, sick visiting and working with the young or the elderly, are all very different and require very different talents and training. The basic lesson that any Rabbi must learn is to know his/her own ability and stick to it, regardless of the demand of a congregation to do things that he or she just can't do and is not equipped to do. Much of this is specialist work, not for GPs, which is what a pulpit Rabbi is.

A Rabbi also teaches, formally and informally, adults and children, Jews and non-Jews, in preaching and discussion/study groups, by word and by example. Many Jewish communities assume all to readily that education is for children and that for adults whatever they have managed to pick up for Bar/Bat Mitzvah will equip them for the rest of life. Teaching adults and children is also different, needing different talents and techniques, and no one Rabbi does both equally well.

Rabbis are also ambassadors for Judaism to Jews and non-Jews. In the quality of their religious and moral life they are supposed to be examples of Jewish values at their best. As ambassadors, they are diplomats, trying to satisfy all. They must be traditional but modern, observant yet tolerant of deviation; kosher but willing to eat with anyone. They must preach and speak at all times with humour and good taste, with scholarship and yet down to earth and displaying simple piety and faith; political but non-partisan, brief but with spiritual depth, critical yet devout, inspiring yet emollient. Preferably all at the same time.

A Rabbi should also develop an elephantine memory for faces, names and the intricate genealogy of the membership of his or her community and the minutiae of their personal histories. And, of course, all Rabbis should remember that any and every community throughout the world, Jewish and non-Jewish, sees their congregation as uniquely desirable and that it is a privilege for their clergy person to serve them.

The one lesson that I think that I have learned about being a Rabbi is that it is essential to maintain human integrity and respect for that integrity, one's own and that of all others. In the last resort one has to do what one feels is right the best one can and then live with the consequences. It is helpful to accept the frailty and flawedness of being human, but not to tear oneself apart with guilt that one is not perfect.

On balance, looking back over 30 years as a Rabbi, I have not been too bad. I have helped some people and done some things well; I have failed and made mistakes and, unwittingly, perhaps hurt some people. But all things considered, I can live with myself. I have kept faith and the vision of the Rabbinate that I was taught: to be a scholar and a teacher, trying to relate Jews to their heritage. Perhaps I have failed because that wasn't what Jewish communities really wanted of me. But that is what I have tried to live by, and if I have failed, my failure is not mine alone, but, partly at least, that of the Jewish community, also.

HUMANKIND BEYOND THE YEAR 2000

Presented March 1, 1998 at an Interfaith Seminar   Vol. 8, No. 5 - March 1998

I am grateful to the Ahmadiya movement of Islam for organizing this Seminar and bringing together representatives from world religions to share their perspectives on the theme of humanity and the millennium.

While the year 2000 in itself is specifically a Christian chronology, the millennial fever and speculation is specific to the Christian world, it is true that a major factor in our lives is the coming together of a world perspective that means that non-Christians share concern for the year 2000 and its significance that they certainly did not for the year 1000. The year 2000 is for us all increasingly not only a mark of the Christian era, but also of the Common Era, not only AD but also CE!

If I were to try to identify central themes of the Jewish tradition I would pick up two Hebrew phrases: *Shema* and *Tikkum Olam*.

Shema is the first word of DT.6:4 which is the major prayer of Judaism, its declaration of faith. *Shema Yisrael, Adonai elohenu, Adonai ehad*, Listen Israel, the Eternal who is our God, the Eternal is One. It is said three times each day by an observant Jew, and is the final confession of faith when confronting death.

The *Shema* is not just a statement of mathematics, nor even of theological dogma. It is a statement about the nature of humankind, human relations, and the nature of ultimate reality. It is therefore as much a moral statement as anything else. Because God is One, therefore God's creation is One. There is an ultimate unity, of nature, of law, of human beings. Rabbinic tradition, for instance, stresses this unity when it says that human beings were created from one mould, the primal parents Adam and Eve, to show us that no human being is ultimately superior to any other; yet, even so, while a human being creates from one mould and all the coins are absolutely identical, the beings that God has created, even if from one mould, are nevertheless absolutely unique and different. The *Shema* is a denial of tribalism and racism, a celebration of human diversity within unity. Our differences as people are not hierarchical, they are beautiful pieces in a mosaic that is a paean of praise to the source of all.

Yet we live in an unredeemed and unfulfilled world. The vision of the Hebrew prophets, of a world of peace and justice and love, remains precisely that — a vision, a hope, a dream. It is for us human beings in our creaturely frailty to work with God as divine agents to make that dream a reality. And this is what the other Hebrew phrase, *Tikkun Olam*, means. We are responsible, morally autonomous agents, in the process of healing the dysfunctions of our present reality. In our work to bind up wounds, to wipe away tears, to make life whole, we are creating a new reality. This is our responsibility as human beings; and God is our guide and help along the way.

That our world is unredeemed goes almost without saying. Our problems must be confronted in their depth, in the human agony that they inflict. And we are responsible. There is war and violence, there is tribal conflict, there are false ideals and values, there is starvation and disease, there is injustice, there is pain and suffering, there is greed and selfishness, there is exploitation of human by human, of nature by human. We cannot solve all problems, but that does not mean that we can ever give up the task of trying to solve the problems that are within our grasp.

Let us consider just two major issues: the problem of social justice; the problem of tribalism. From these two arise much of our human travail as we enter the new century, the new millennium.

We are seeing the globalization and the privatization of our world marked by the acceptance of a free market system. The only model of human affairs that is not seemingly on offer is that of capitalism. As a result, not only economic affairs, but also human relations are marketized. Increasingly, we are looking to the bottom line interpreted in narrow terms of profit. Concerns of human emotions, human dreams and hopes, lose to the bottom line of making a profit. But can a society be built on mere human greed and selfishness? And what sort of society? A society in which people count only if they can exercise economic clout, only if they have money, only if they are consumers. How many human beings does this mean we must consign to the rubbish heap of economic irrelevance?

So, what happens, logically, to the poor, the sick, the orphan and the widow? Should we waste our resources keeping them alive even, the aged, the unproductive, the non-participants in the production of wealth? And if wealth is the be all and end all, the bottom line, does it matter how we make it? Currency speculation, the transfer of paper cash, cheating and hard dealing, all are as useful in this system as actually making something or working with people. It follows logically that health care and education should be available to those who can afford it, with the rest of us dependent on the vagaries of private charity. Universities, for example, should, on this understanding, eliminate from their course offerings non-marketable frills such as the arts, music and drama, poetry and literature, the classics, religious studies.

It is surely the moral imperative of religion to oppose this bleak view of society and human relations, and to speak out for the disempowered. Capitalism is an idol and we are in danger of sacrificing too much of our humanness, too many of our human brothers and sisters, to it. If it is true that Communism didn't work, can we really say that Capitalism works either? If we as religious people are to protect and enrich each other as fellow creatures of God, our lives must be filled with so much more than just greed. We have to have love, we must work for justice, or there is no point left in our being here.

In the last resort, human beings need the extension of the mind and soul in the creation of beauty, the search for truth, the experience of love and goodness. This is a moral and religious imperative.

The other area of religious concern from this Jewish perspective must be the question of tribalism. We have to break down the walls between human beings, so that our differences are enriching and empowering elements in the mosaic of humanness. We have to treasure human differences, they are part of the multi-faceted fabric of our experience. But those differences are not hierarchies of superior/inferior. We must learn to reach beyond race, nation, religious grouping, tribe, to speak to each other in our human community, while still valuing that which makes each one of us specific and unique. Remember that *Midrash* that I cited: each of us is unique, yet each of us shares in a common heritage.

Nationalism is a major shaper of recent human history. And so is religion. The two combined can be a dangerous mix. But there are two kinds of religion. There is a religious tradition that knows all the answers, that is exclusive and intolerant, that demands, not unity, but uniformity. There is a religious tradition that rejoices in the unending human pilgrimage, that asks questions, that is inclusive and tolerant, that values the human mind and conscience. It is the former, militant orthodox fundamentalism, that is a growing threat to us as we enter a new century, a new millennium. It is the latter, open-ended tolerant quest for truth, that is a potential unifying of humankind while preserving and welcoming pluralism within that unity.

When I speak of this fundamentalist orthodoxy that I see as a threat to the human future, I am not speaking of any one of the world's religious traditions. The defining line between my two types of religion is not between religious traditions; it runs across them. Within Judaism there is the closed orthodoxy that we see among the ultras, the haredim, in Israel. In Christianity there is a closed orthodoxy that sees no truth outside itself and seeks only to convert. In Islam there is a militant blindness that we see in the Iranian ayatollahs. In Hinduism there is the extremist wing of the BJP. There is too much intolerance, too many closed minds; and it links in with the mean-spiritedness of the free market fanatics.

Religion must surely invite us to a never-ending exploration of reality using all the resources of our minds and hearts and souls: an eternal process of growing. Religion must surely invite us to love, to see justice, to see in each other ultimate value, a spark of the eternal Thou.

As I look at this new millennium, as a Jew, I have hopes, I dream dreams. And I look for the fulfillment of the historic Jewish values: *Shema, Tikkun Olam*; Unity, Healing. I do not look for miracles. But I do have courage. And I reach out to all other women and men of vision. For we shall need to work together if we want all humankind to find blessing. For the threats are real and they are strong. But we can never give up working. And in God's good time, we have an assurance that we shall succeed. And for as long as one child lacks food, medical care, love, the job will not be done.

The issue of reciting the Lord's Prayer in some elementary schools in Saskatoon has been on the agenda of the Jewish community for many years. It now appears to have been resolved by the decision of the human rights tribunal to strike down the practice as discriminatory, though there is still some confusion as to the constitutionality of the practice: on the one hand, it seems to be mandated by the legislation that was incorporated into the British North America Act (which is part of the Constitution) on the creation of Saskatchewan and Alberta out of the old North West Territories in 1905; on the other hand, Calgary has interpreted the legislation to enable it to teach comparative religion.

I should make it clear that the objection is to indoctrination of young children in one particular religion by insisting on an act of specifically Christian worship. Teaching about religion as preparation of children to take their places as citizens of the pluralist society of modern Canada is something that I personally would strongly encourage.

BUT, IS THE LORD'S PRAYER ITSELF OBJECTIONABLE TO JEWS?

Regardless of the content, which I could criticize in detail from a Jewish perspective, what about the context? The Lord's Prayer carries with it a historical baggage of Christian faith. For many Christians, it has been a sort of summary of Christianity. In that light, to see it as a generic prayer is misguided. Surely, before Christians can claim that one of their prayers is acceptable to everyone, they need to consult the others. And, from a Jewish point of view, it isn't generic, and it comes with a specifically Christian label.

It is a prayer that Jesus taught to his followers when they asked him how they should pray. Luke 11:2-4. It is expanded in Matthew 6:9-13, the "sermon on the mount." Later, a concluding doxology (which Catholics do not incorporate), was added from the Didache 8:2, in the 2nd century CE. I find the attempts by Abraham Idelsohn in his study of the Jewish liturgy to find analogies with the paragraphs of the *Amidah* exceedingly forced.

Of course there are images and phrases that, on the face of it, are common to the Lord's Prayer and Rabbinic sources. An example is the use of the word Father for God. *Abba* is the Aramaic background to, for example, *Avinu*, in *Avinu Malkenu* which we recite in the liturgy for the *Noraim*. There is no reason to believe that the Aramaic is somehow more intimate than the Hebrew. But the idea of "deliver us from evil" is tied in to a concept of martyrdom that is not shared by Rabbinic thinking, and also negates the freedom of choice that is an essential part of the moral responsibility that is so important to Judaism. It introduces the possibility of an intermediary, and that is an alien concept.

IS THIS, AS SO MANY CALLERS HAVE INFORMED ME, A CHRISTIAN COUNTRY?

First, nowhere in Canadian law or in the Constitution is it said that this is a Christian country. Further, to accept this statement would mean that any immigrant would have to conform and therefore, logically, convert to Christianity. Yet the Constitution guarantees us freedom of religion. No, we do not have to conform. To insist is to indulge in bullying by the majority that may happen to be Christians. Canada is a pluralistic democracy, Saudi Arabia is not. All Canadian citizens have an equal right to free practice of religion, and not to be forced to practice someone else's religion. Minorities are just as much Canadians as the majority.

DOES THE RECITING OF THE LORD'S PRAYER DO HARM?

Assuredly it does. On the one hand, the school board insists that it wishes to build up the self-esteem and dignity of every child in its care. But by forcing every child either to take part in an act of worship (which reciting a prayer is) or to withdraw publicly, it runs roughshod over the dignity of the child who deviates from the Christian norm, or marks out that child as different, that is deviant. And different all too often means inferior.

Further, the recitation of words by rote without context or explanation makes a farce of the act of worship, and brings religion into dispute. What then is the purpose? To expose children to religion? Rather to expose them to boring irrelevance. How many generations of children have been raised to think that God's name is Harold? How evangelical Christians can imagine there is any value in this pointless exercise I cannot think.

In removing a future recitation of meaningless words from the classroom, the school board would be raising the standing of religion. It also clears the way for the teaching of religion in classes.

Of course, it is hard for some Christians to surrender their position of power and to accept that Christianity should be studied by students as one the world's religions rather than presented as the one and only truth. But that is the reality. Our children are growing up in a Canada and a world in which understanding the world's faiths is more and more important. We can no longer afford bigotry and ignorance: it is too dangerous.

A final word on tolerance. Religious traditions have a poor record of tolerating difference. As we look at the history of the Crusades and the Inquisition, though, we should remember as Jews that the only reason, as Ahad ha Am reminds us, that Jews didn't have the Inquisition was because we didn't have the power. We have to go beyond tolerance, that is, putting up with people whom we know are wrong! We have to accept each other as travellers on the human spiritual path. We have to accept human difference with joyous celebration.

Praised are You, Eternal God, source of life throughout space and time, who has such wonders in your world.

A JEWISH PERSPECTIVE
ON IMMORTALITY *Vol. 10, No. 2 - November/December 1999*

People are often surprised to realize that Judaism clearly teaches a belief in immortality. The second paragraph of the *Amidah*, the *Gevurot*, said three times each day, praises God who keeps faith with the dead and is *mekhaye ha metim*, the one who will restore life to the dead. Rabbinic literature makes clear that at the end of history there will be a resurrection of the dead. This is the source of the belief that there is one organ of the human body that is indestructible and that will be the base on which God will build the resurrected body. And this, incidentally, is the rationalization of the opposition of traditionalist Jews to cremation.

Many modern Jews find it difficult to believe in physical resurrection. They find the imagery of the dead rising from their graves bewildering, perhaps a little bizarre. Such difficulties are not only modern. Sophisticated Jewish thinkers always sought to reinterpret *mekhaye ha metim* in a metaphorical sense, as referring to survival of the spirit rather than as a reference to literal bodily resurrection. A belief in a spiritual essence of a human being that is released from the body at death and returns to God probably reflects the ideas of many sophisticated believers in the past and today.

Obviously, belief in immortality, however defined, is a logical implication of the Biblical statement that human beings are created in the divine image. If we have some spark of the divine within us, if we share with God the ability to create and to choose, we therefore in some way share in God's eternity. There is some part of us that is immortal. Equally logically, it is inconceivable that God could have created humankind with all that semi-divine capacity for creativity and choice, merely to blot us out after 70 years or so. That would imagine God as the ultimate sadist. The Jewish concept of God itself implies that immortality of human beings made in the divine image.

But what can we mean by "immortality"?

Obviously, we live on in the minds and hearts of those with whom we have shared life. The quality of our own living is a blessing to those we have loved and who have loved us. And we preserve that blessing both in memory and also in the way that we have been inspired by those we have loved to live a little better. We try to grow morally and spiritually as our tribute to them and to that love. That is why we refer to the memorial services in the Jewish year as *Yizkor*, "may he remember." It is not just that we pray that God shall remember. We pray, too, that we shall remember, and in remembering, become a little better because others have lived.

It is important both to mourn our dead and also to celebrate them. We acknowledge that living is not ended by dying. In doing so we learn that life and death are integral parts of the divine reality. Life continues. A pebble thrown into a pool causes ripples that go on forever, and so it is with life.

Unquestionably, the traditional sources teach that individuals survive death, though it is hard for modern Jews to understand what that could mean. The importance of memory, the lessons about the nature of ultimate reality and death teaches, these are important, but can we really go further and accept personal immortality?

There is a unanimity of the world's religious traditions: all teach that, in some way that we cannot understand, human beings survive death and their lives are eternal. In modern times, those who have survived clinical "death" and been resuscitated attest to the same universal insight. They appear to undergo some sort of rebirth experience into a state of light and joy. This is not proof that we survive death, but the unanimity of the reports is indicative that there is something more than mere hallucination going on. How the mind grapples with the implications of personal survival is another matter. Maybe the desire to survive is merely selfish. Maybe it is part of an infinite process of becoming something better.

Judaism has insisted that belief in immortality is part of its teaching. It has also insisted that in the end this is a matter that is beyond us and for God alone. We are best advised to learn how to live well with the time that we have and to leave the rest in trusting faith to God. What we can be sure of is that life is a gift of surpassing wonder, and that lived at its best, it affords us glimpses into eternity. The heart and mind of human beings who have known love and beauty and goodness together cannot accept that all is to be blotted out by death.

Our tradition speaks to us in the three Hebrew words: *ruakh, nefesh, neshamah*. All can be loosely translated as "spirit, soul." But there are profound differences. *Ruakh* is that spirit that animates all living creatures and distinguishes them from non-living things. *Nefesh* is that which marks off the human from the non-human life force. *Neshamah* is that which lifts human beings to reach for eternity and to reestablish our link with God. There is eternity in the human spirit. More we cannot say.

JEWISH MORAL AND SPIRITUAL VALUES

Vol. 11, No. 2 - November/December 2000

Jewish speakers, lay and Rabbinic, talk frequently about Jewish values. They hardly ever specify what they actually mean, and certainly never in detail.

It has been my concern to spell out what we mean by Jewish values and to show how they can be applied to the way in which Jews can live in the modern world. I hope to write a book entitled *Jewish Moral and Spiritual Values* for this purpose.

I have examined the Jewish sources, Bible, Rabbinic literature, and Prayer Book and derived a list of 200 core values. I have retained the Hebrew words and phrases in which Jewish tradition has couched these values for two reasons. First, because translation is necessarily lacking and often indeed totally misleading and second, because we should try to retain the flavour of the Hebrew in which our tradition is embedded.

In the next few *Bulletins* there will be a few short extracts from this work. Each value is defined and illustrated by stories from the sources, usually, but not always, *Midrash*. Often, the more important values are developed more fully to show their application to today's problems.

My reason for engaging in this research is two-fold.

I believe that Jews need a listing of the moral and spiritual values of Judaism, arranged encyclopedically, defined and illustrated — spelled out in detail — to deepen their own understanding of how to see the world and live in it Jewishly.

And I believe that the paradigms of how to be Jewish that are the norms for Jews to choose from today have problems. A theological interpretation of Judaism or a halakhic interpretation of Judaism, while acceptable to some, are both unlikely to commend themselves to most. On the other hand, an interpretation of Judaism in terms of the values intrinsic to the traditional sources could be a viable paradigm of Judaism for many Jews. Jews who cannot in conscience commit themselves to the *halakhic* life-style, nor accept traditional Jewish vocabulary and imagery of faith, may still find their link to Judaism through its system of values. And even those who can and do, halakhically or "religiously," will find their Jewish life deepened and strengthened by dialoguing with the values derived from the sources.

And that is why I have spent time and energy working those sources to derive this detailed listing of the moral and spiritual values of Judaism.

Edut

The core of Jewish faith is the *Shema*. Traditionally, this has been printed in Prayer Books so that the last letter of the first word and the last letter of the last word stand out extra large. This is because the two letters spell out the Hebrew word *ed*, meaning witness. When a Jew says *Shema* he or she has accepted the duty to be a witness to the world to the meaning of the *Shema* as expressing the Jewish historical experience of divinity. *Edut*, bearing witness, is important. Human beings are autonomous moral agents; their loyalty to God cannot be assumed or forced, it must be willing, as opposed to angels, who, according to Rabbinic tradition have no free will and worship God willy-nilly. Rabbinic tradition refers to *avodat ha lev*, the service of the heart. As it should be noted that the Hebrew word *lev*, usually Englished as "heart," actually seems in Biblical usage to mean the intellect, we should understand the phrase as referring to willing intellectual assent. And ideally, we should take it both ways as a total existential commitment. So the Jew willingly testifies to God — mind, body and soul — with everything that flows from that.

Testifying originally has a more legal then theological connotation, and this, too, is important.

There are halakhic requirements to be a *kasher* witness, one whose testimony may be accepted. Basically, there are certain categories of people whose testimony is invalid. Broadly speaking, halakhically, one who is not obligated to carry out a mitsvah, a religious commandment, is not a valid witness. So minors and slaves are excluded. And, because women are exempted from all positive commandments that have to be carried out at specified times (*mitsvot aseh sh ha zeman geramah*), they are also excluded as witnesses, except in a few limited areas that affect them directly. So are the mentally handicapped. An adult male slave could become acceptable through manumission. However, the exemption of women in the *halakhah* is not a prohibition. Any Jewish woman who voluntarily accepts responsibility for carrying out the positive commandments dependent on time may do so. In this she would seemingly have something of a higher status in that Jewish men do not have options: their observance is compulsory. The *halakhah* does not see it this way, and regards the fulfillment of a compulsory command of more significance than fulfilling something which is not mandatory by merely a voluntary act of spirituality. (Perhaps this is conspicuous piety!) As saying the statutory prayers has to be done at specified times, it is the major positive commandment from which women are exempt. Therefore, women are not regarded as witnesses to God by saying the *Shema*. (There has never been any objection to women saying prayers if they want to, and there is a huge amount of women's prayers preserved in, say, the Yiddish language *Tekhines* literature. Jewish women must have expressed their own spirituality in the statutory liturgy as well, for we know that many Jewish women are capable in Hebrew as well as the vernacular languages around them such as Yiddish.) But as they could not say the *Shema* in fulfillment of any obligation to do so, for they had none, obviously, they could not act as witnesses to God in saying the words of the prayer.

In modern times, most Jews accept total gender equality. Therefore, they would accept without question that Jewish women are as bound as Jewish men by traditional rules relating to prayer. If Jews are in covenant with God, and if that implies rules of relationship incumbent on all, and if Jews are called to witness to this before all humankind, both in word and in deed, then bearing witness is an essential part of being a Jew in the modern world, and giving an example in both spiritual precept and the moral quality of daily living. Some Jews are male, some, the majority, are female; all have equal obligation to do so.

JUDAISM AND EUTHANASIA Vol. 11, No. 5 - March/April 2001

The "Latimer Affair" has brought to the fore the question of euthanasia, mercy killing, and Jews are interested in what guidance our classical sources can offer to the conscience.

First and foremost, Judaism does not provide black and white solutions to our moral problems. It cannot. Every situation that we confront is unique. We cannot solve our ethical dilemmas by merely looking up a source. What Jewish tradition can provide for us is a sensitive series of guidelines as to the values that are involved and their relative weighting, and this can help us in making our moral decisions. But, in the last resort, those decisions are made by us, and not by tradition for us. Contrary positions can be equally valid in Jewish terms. *Elu ve elu divre elohim hayim*, both this and that are words of the living God.

It is clear that murder is forbidden in Judaism. *Lo tirtsah*, you shall not murder. However, that is deceptively simple. What is "murder?" Does the Commandment enjoin absolute pacifism? Vegetarianism? Does it forbid capital punishment? Does it forbid abortion? Interpretation of the Commandment in the Oral Torah makes it clear that the tradition appreciates the awesome complexity of applying the simple prohibition to the reality of the moral choices that confront us.

With regard to abortion and war, for example, the Rabbis bring forward the concept of the *rodef*, the "pursuer". If someone is being "pursued" by another person bent on harming him or her, it is incumbent on the bystander to intervene to protect the one being "pursued", using whatever force necessary, including, if necessary, killing the pursuer, the *rodef*.

What of "mercy killing," then; is it murder, or can we evoke the concept of the *rodef*?

It is halakhically forbidden to do anything to shorten natural life: that is indeed murder. However, it is not required to make heroic efforts "officiously to keep alive." Further, if a physician prescribes drugs to a dying patient, intended to relieve suffering and make the dying person more comfortable, knowing that those drugs will inevitably shorten life, this is permissible. Shortening life is not the intention, however certainly it is the consequence. And it is permissible to "pull the plug," that is, stop treatment, at the informed request of the patient, or to restrict care to the maintenance of the comfort and well being of the patient. When we pray for the ill, we pray for a perfect healing, but not a *refuat nefesh* as well as *refuat guf*, a healing of soul as well as body. That is, Judaism acknowledges that healing, *refuah*, is not the same as cure. The acceptance of death is a crucial reality in Judaism. Our concern is the quality of living and dying, and when cure is not possible we seek "healing" as spiritual reconciliation to and acceptance of death.

We cannot question Mr. Latimer's sincerity of motive. As a loving father, he was in despair at his daughter's suffering. Medical intervention seemed to him to exacerbate her situation. There was neither healing nor cure for her. So he ended her suffering.

On the other hand, his act was an act of taking life. The crux of the issue is: was it murder?

We are in the area of the insoluble. If we condemn his act as murder, then are we to condemn the physician who knowingly but not directly intentionally shortens the life of a suffering dying patient by prescribing a drug overdose out of compassion? Are we to condemn the solder who in war kills an "enemy" soldier, or the officer who orders the act? Are we to condemn the air force pilot who bombs a target and kills many undoubtedly innocent civilians? Are we to condemn the public hangman who executes a criminal?

Our tradition cannot answer these moral dilemmas for us. We must struggle with our own consciences. But there are values taught by tradition that must be taken into account when we make those decisions, so that moral decisions are firmly based and not just a matter of personal choice and opinion.

Life is a prime value for Judaism. *"Lehayim"* we say. To Life! Because without life there is no possibility of fulfilling the *mitsvot*. But life involves a certain minimal quality. The halakhah says that we cannot know what stress a person was in when they killed themselves, and is therefore loath to call it suicide. The act is not judged with full severity because we are not privy to the mind and soul of the actor.

But what of the possibility of creating a precedent? Does Mr. Latimer's act open up the possibility of so demeaning the value of the life of the handicapped as to declare it acceptable to kill the handicapped as a nuisance to society? We Jews are particularly sensitive to such considerations, bearing in mind the official euthanasia policies of the Nazis, where the mentally and physically handicapped were ruthlessly eliminated in the very hospitals and by the very physicians supposedly dedicated to their care. Of course we are civilized and would never do such things. But then so were the Germans, yet they did!

To sum up, I can only speak personally, though in consciousness of the Jewish sources and hopefully with sensitivity. Mr. Latimer was guilty of taking the life of his daughter, and we cannot condone any human being arrogating to themselves the right of life or death. However, I am very aware of his motives, and, as a father myself, I can sympathize deeply with him. I also know that to condemn him is implicitly to condemn many honest physicians of total integrity and deep human compassion who also shorten the lives of dying patients by trying to relieve their sufferings, yet knowing full well the indirect consequences of their act. I also know that to condemn the taking of life too simplistically will call into question the very existence of our armed forces.

Therefore, to sentence Mr. Latimer is necessary. But to sentence him as a murderer on the level of Olsen or Bernardo is brutal and unnecessary. The two-year non-custodial sentence seems to me to be a compromise that fits the ambiguity of the moral issue. The ten-year sentence decreed is barbarous. The Supreme Court of Canada has not, I think, served the cause of justice.

From time to time in *The Bulletin* I raise various moral issues, particularly those posed by the advance of modern technology, and consider possible Jewish responses. It may be of interest to members to know how Rabbis set about dealing with such issues so as to produce a Jewish perspective in responding to them.

Judaism is based on the concept of the Dual Torah, that is the written text of the Hebrew Bible, the *T'nakh*, *Torah she bikhtav*, and the Oral Torah, the Torah *she baal peh*. Traditionally, both are seen as revealed on Sinai, and therefore are equally authoritative. The one cannot be read without the other, and when we say "Torah" we should understand both written and oral as a joint text. Among the many implications of this approach is the rarely-spelled-out fact that traditional Judaism is not a fundamentalist approach to the Bible. It reads the text carefully but never literally. It assumes that God has foreseen human needs throughout time and has implanted in the "Text" of Torah guidance for all problems that will arise. The written word must be read with the lens of the oral.

Interpretive reading of Torah is further seen as being on four possible levels. There is the *peshat*, the obvious meaning; so the prohibition against eating rabbit is not to be read, at least initially, as a symbol, but as is. Then there is the *remez*, the hint that lies under the plain meaning; so rabbits are not just little furry symbols of behaviours that we are to avoid as well. Then there is *derash*, the midrashic and homelitic level of reading the Text; learning from story-telling. Finally there is *sod*, a mystic layer of meaning that the text may also be teaching. The layers of interpreting the Text are known by the acronym "Pardes," meaning an orchard, the Farsi word that comes into English as paradise.

So, when confronting a modern issue, a Rabbi will turn first to the Torah Text, in this Jewish sense, starting with the text of the Hebrew Bible, but reading that text through the oral tradition of the Rabbinic literature. He or she should also consult the records of *halakhic* case law in the search for analogous precedent. So the search will begin in the *Tenakh* and continue in *Mishnah* and *Gemara* and through the Responsa literature.

When there is an analogy that can be built, a reasonably clear-cut answer to the enquiry can be given from the sources and applied to the issue raised. Often this is not so easy. There may be halakhic principles involved that are contradictory. Then decisions have to be made as to comparative weighing of principles and values in a particular situation. Then of course the personality of the Rabbi and the context of the actual question being asked will come into play. A Rabbi will, for instance, have to judge the reason that lies behind the question, the covert need, the hidden agenda, and assess the relevance of that to the sources and values and principles being raised. One can answer either the question being asked, or more importantly, the question behind the question. Even in *halakhah*, an I-It response differs radically from an I-Thou one.

As an example of this, may I cite a Responsum that I was asked to produce when I was in England. Colleagues asked me for the Jewish attitude to vasectomy. It does not take much investigation of the Torah sources to know the answer. But that was not the issue. I had to remind myself of the question behind the question; why, indeed, was this question being asked? So I had to place the issue in context. And there are two contexts, the individual and the communal; whether a couple may Jewishly use vasectomy as a means of family planning, and the needs of the Jewish people concerned with both Jewish communal survival and also with the issue of world over-population. So the weighing that any Rabbi will give to the sources will vary according to personalities involved and context, according to a personal assessment of those needs in that situation. A Responsum is not an academic exercise, it is a real attempt to give help and guidance to the conscience of a specific Jew or specific Jewish community in the making of moral decisions that are authentically Jewish.

Conflict is the norm. There are no clear-cut answers. Nearly always, differences of opinion based on the same sources will be acceptable. It is always useful to know something of the bias of the Rabbi making the decision, the *posek*. My own bias is toward the most liberal and inclusive decision. I will also privilege the need of human beings over the letter of the law. And I will also take more of the traditional reminder that one should be *makhmir* (strict) with oneself, but *mekil* (lenient) with others. The differences are obvious when you compare two halakhic giants of our generation, Rabbi Yitshak Soloveichik and Rabbi Moshe Feinstein. The former took account of the environmental and historical situation when giving guidance and looked at the question from the perspective of non-legal factors such as ethical values, while the latter worked with the principle that halakhah is outside history and entirely independent of non-legal factors.

It is useful for people to know how Rabbis go about their research in making decisions. It is an analogous process to making jurisprudential ruling in English law, where both statute (written Torah) and precedent (oral Torah) are essential parts of the procedure.

Judaism and the Handicapped

Vol. 11, No. 6- July/August 2001

The famous Holiness Code in the Torah says, "*Lo tekalel heresh ve lifne iver lo titen mikhshol,*" "Don't curse the deaf, and don't put a stumbling block before the blind." (Lv. 19:14)

It is clear that the Torah is sensitive to the problems of the handicapped, and their right to be treated as competent human beings.

We could also cite the Midrash that compares the scholar who has become old and forgetful with the smashed shards of the first Tablets of the *ascret dibrot* that Moses broke in his anger when he saw the people worshipping the golden calf. Just as the shards were carefully preserved and carried with the people in the Ark because of what they represented, so also should the scholar who can no longer function be preserved and carried with the people in respect for what he used to represent.

The whole of Jewish tradition is sensitive to the physically and mentally handicapped alike.

However, it is also clear that this is somewhat simplistic. Halakhically, the handicapped have traditionally been very much disadvantaged. The physically handicapped, the *heresh* (deaf) and *iver* (blind), cannot carry out certain *mitsvot* that require hearing and seeing, such as saying the *Shema* or reading Torah. Nor can the mentally handicapped carry out *mitsvot* that require understanding and *kavvanah*, such as contracting a marriage. They are all halakhically *shoteh*, that is *katan* (minor), and therefore exempt from the *mistvot*. And as it is carrying out *mitsvot* that makes a Jew fully Jewish, any Jew who cannot carry out *mitsvot*, at least in principle, cannot be a full member of the *halakhic* community. In the Temple, a *Kohen* had to be without any physical or mental defect. And even today any man with defective genitals cannot contract a marriage and therefore cannot in principle fulfill many of the *mitsvot*.

The passage of time has brought many medical and technical means of diminishing the effect of handicaps, both mental and physical. Hearing aids have enabled the auditorily challenged to function; glasses have enabled the visually impaired to function. Various prostheses enable the physically challenged to gain some degree of control of their lives. Similarly, with the mentally handicapped, we have seen huge advances in education and care that can restore some degree of independence and human dignity. In many cases of handicap, the *halakhic* disability no longer applies.

In addition, we are more sensitive to the issues involved. As the human life span is lengthened, more and more of us attain the years when these disabilities affect us personally. We want to extend full membership to the *halakhic* community of mitsvah-fulfilling Jews to as many as possible, regardless of mental or physical handicap. And there are ways open to us to include even those who as yet cannot be helped by medicine and technology.

For example, we are allowed to count in the minyan, in emergency, anyone over the age of six. We may assume that a six year old can understand the meaning of Torah, *tefillah* and *kehillah*. Can we not extend this so that we can include in the minyan a mentally challenged adult and so confer on that person the full rights of Jewish status? We accept as a matter of course that a handicapped child may have a Bar/Bat Mitsvah that is geared to his/her abilities.

And where the handicap becomes so great as to preclude even this, will we not apply the same view as the *Midrash*? We cherish the person both for what they are, created in the image of God, and for what they represent, the potential of a Jewish soul, and include them in community today as our forebears included the shattered pieces of the Torah in the past. After all, if I as a diabetic can never fast on Yom Kippur, does this mean that because I cannot fulfill one mitsvah, even in principle, that I am to be excluded from the community of committed Jews? Obviously not.

In the Talmud, Rav Yosef, who was blind, demands to be included in the Torah community (TB Baba Kamma 87a). He speaks for all handicapped person.

Every effort should be made by all Jewish communities to include every Jew, however handicapped, in a spirit of *ahavat Yisrael* and to enable them to fulfill all *mitsvot* that they want to, so far as they possibly can. I am aware that the costs of providing access, signing or hearing devices for the deaf, braille siddurim for the blind, ramps for the disabled to have an *aliyah* and so on, are enormous. But if there is a need, all Synagogues must strive to provide such aids as to include all Jews in Judaism and Jewish life.

ON STRESSING THE POSITIVE

Vol. 12, No. 1- September/October 2001

We Jews are good at mourning. We have assimilated the view of Jewish history as being a chronicle of doom and gloom, unending persecution and suffering, perpetual victimhood. We need to remind ourselves of the other side of Jewish history.

We have been immensely creative. "We have moulded the outside world and made a contribution in all fields of human activity far disproportionate to our numbers." We have not been passive victims, so much as dynamic actors.

Just consider what we have given to the world!

To give just a brief list of the Jewish gifts to humanity.

We have given the world the Hebrew Bible, with the ardent spirituality of the Psalms; the stories of the Patriarchs and Matriarchs that are filled with unending depths of meaning and insights into what it means to be human; the very concept of history as purposeful; the image of Exodus and Liberation from slavery; the

Prophetic passion for justice and compassion for the poor, the orphan and the widow.

We have given the world the idea of worship that is now the norm everywhere: a worship focused on prayer and study, orchestrated by liturgical genius into a symphony of spiritual adventure. Everyone in the ancient world had a Temple and sacrificed animals to divinity. Only Israel created the Synagogue; and without the Synagogue there could be no Church or Mosque.

We have given the world the wisdom of the Rabbis, the insistence that religious life cannot be based on high ideals alone, but must be lived in detail, with every moment potentially filled with the presence of the Holy.

We have given the world the concept of religious law, of binding the passing moment to eternity by building into life the continuing awareness of the holy. We have created the concept of the *berakhah*, the concretization of "Know before Whom you are standing".

We have given the world the enormous gift of *Shabbat*, without which human beings are diminished. The idea that everyone, including servants and slaves and even animals, has the right to rest, a right built into the very fabric of creation, says that all life is ineffably worthwhile and that each of us is created in the divine image. That is what *Shabbat* is about, the ultimate denial of slavery. Ahad ha Am was right when he said that more than Israel keeping *Shabbat*, it is *Shabbat* that has kept Israel.

We have given the world the idea of the unity of God in the *Shma*. Without the *Shma* we could still believe in a multiplicity of sources of ultimate value. It is the *Shma* that denies any form of racism, for we are all created by the One God. And it is the *Shma* that is the source of science. Unless we could assume that all things are united and make ultimate sense, it would be impossible to think in terms of natural laws: polytheism means a chaos, both morally and intellectually, and a polytheistic system could not produce modern science. Science, the arts and religion are the three ways in which human spiritual and intellectual creativity works; there can be no conflict. This is a fundamental meaning of the *Shma*.

We have given the world the idea that religion is rational and not contrary to human reason. Judaism has had the courage to include in the daily prayers a grateful acknowledgment of God as the source of human knowledge and reason. Judaism is the path to faith without superstition. Jews have combined faith in God with a total willingness to question, even to defy, God. And all in the name of God!

"We have given the world the example of the courage to go out into the unknown." The image of the Jew is Abraham, willing to go out into the unknown when God calls, not knowing where the journey will end, but trusting.

Jews have given all these things, and more, to the world. It is time for us to rejoice and celebrate. True, there have been pain and sorrow in Jewish life: that is part of being alive in an unredeemed world. But just as true, there has been immense creativity, deep joy. As we approach the Holy Days we should remember these things as well, and rejoice that we have been part of them, and if we will it, will continue to be so.

NOTES ON WORDS Vol. 12, No. 2 - November/December 2001

Words are fascinating and important. Let us consider a few of the words that we use in the Synagogues to describe various people who help with the conduct of services.

The Hebrew word "*Hazzan*" does not mean the same as the English world "Cantor." *Hazzan* refers to someone who leads the Service in the Synagogue, and the range may be very wide indeed in terms of ability and knowledge. Cantor means someone who has completed post-graduate courses in music, liturgy and *halakhah*, culminating in a Master's degree in Jewish music. A cantor is a highly trained and qualified Jewish professional. A *Hazzan* may be a Cantor in this sense. Or a Hazzan may be better referred to as *Sheliah Tsibbur*, or a *Baal Tefilah*. A *Sheliah Tsibbur*, literally "congregational agent," represents the community at prayer by chanting the prayers as leader of worship. A *Baal Tefilah*, literally "someone who leads prayer," does much the same, but the amount of knowledge required is less. All who lead communal worship are required halakhically to know Hebrew, to be able to read the prayers fluently, and to be of good moral standing in the community. If in addition they happen to have a good voice and some musical ability, all the better! Any member of the community may in principle act as *Baal tefilah* or *Sheliah Tsibbur*, and indeed it is the custom to invite anyone observing a yahrtseit, for instance, to do so if they are able. A *Hazzan*, like the modern Cantor, has a slightly different status, as a semi or fully professionally trained person. To confuse the words is to loose some real if subtle differences.

Traditionally, the person who reads to Torah for the community is called *Baal Kore*, literally "one who can read," the text read being the Torah, also known as *Mikra*, "what is to be read". Torah should be read from the *sefer Torah* direct, where the text is written by hand without punctuation, vowelling or musical notation. In emergency, if there is no one in the community who can do this, the portion of the Torah to be read on the specific occasion, known as the *parashah* or *sidra* (depending on the custom of the community) may be read from a printed *humash*. The reading is actually to be chanted according to musical tradition known as *trop*: this is the musical interpretation of the accent signs, called *teamim*, written in the printed and fully vowelled text. This is done form memory and requires knowledge of Hebrew and training and practice. There are many differing musical interpretations of the *teamim*, Ashkenazic and Sefardic, with many sub variants.

The *Haftorah* is also chanted, but normally (though not always) from the printed text with the vowels, punctuation and *teamim* in full, which is why it is easier to do. One of the jobs of the *gabbai*, acting with the person receiving *aliyah*, is to follow the chanting from the *humash* and correct mistakes by the *Baal Kore* in the reading of the words, though not in the musical chant. The process of reading Torah in this sense is known as Ashkenazi tradition is *leyning* Torah. Any knowledgeable Jew may chant Torah, but in most modern communities the task will rest on the Cantor or Rabbi. All Cantors and Rabbis are able to do this, but in practice Rabbis tend not to like doing it, after all, Cantors are the ones who are musically trained!

Finally, the *Gabbai* is an officiant in the Synagogue whose job tends to overlap with the *shamash*. To *Sefardim*, the *Gabbai* is the community treasurer, to *Ashkenazim* the *Gabbai* helps with the conduct of the service, particularly in terms of the reading of Torah, *keriat Torah*. The *shamash*, often Englished as "beadle," may also do the same thing, as in a Sefardic Synagogue, or be more confined to the role of usher and keeper of decorum in the Synagogue, along the lines of the old joke that an usher is someone who goes around calling out "Ush!" (Hush!) (It is a very old joke!)

Modern Synagogues have tended to professionalize community personnel. Rabbis and Cantors are highly trained and well educated in both Jewish and non-Jewish areas. And they are supplemented by administrators and youth workers and social workers who are similarly qualified in their own fields of expertise. Only *gabbaim* tend to remain volunteers from the community. In small congregations like ours we have retained more traditional views out of financial necessity. For us, *shelihe tsibbur* and *baale kore* are also to a large degree members of the community who volunteer to help maintain Synagogue services. We are fortunate that we have members willing and able to discharge these *mitsvot*.

LEADERSHIP *Vol. 12, No. 3 - January/February 2002*

An edited version of address at the installation of the new Board, November 16, 2001

Leadership of the Jewish community has always been difficult. Even Moses was continually criticized, as we read in the Torah, and often, humble though he was, responded with exasperated temper tantrums. As a result, he was refused the right to enter the Land of Israel.

In many ways, difficult though it has been to exercise leadership of Jews throughout history, the reasons for that difficulty should be a source of pleasure for us. Jews have always been nonconformists, the conscience of humankind. We have always been unwilling to accept authority, always anxious to question rather than obey, always determined to insist on the principles of justice, always preferring reasoned argument to unquestioning acceptance. It is precisely because of this that we Jews have been the Prophetic people, a source of blessing to all humankind.

Nevertheless, accepting a position of leadership in the community has always been something of a thankless task. However, it is possible to give some advice to those who have the *hutspah* to attempt it.

First, there are some qualities that we definitely do not want in a community leader.

We do not want Jewish leaders to be charismatic. Charismatic leadership has been shown throughout history to be dangerous. And we Jews, more than most, have suffered much from such leaders. Leadership requires rational thought and reasoned planning and a search for consensus, definitely not charisma. As a consequence, nor do we want our leaders to be massaging their egos at the expense of community need, nor living a power trip, or seeking to impose themselves on the community. Nor indeed do we want our leaders to be imposing their own agendas regardless of the community. Even less do we need leaders who are engaged in a display of spiritual one-upmanship, with a "holier than thou" attitude toward their fellow Jews: Jews in history have suffered enough from such judgemental attitudes; we do not need homegrown practitioners! And we surely do not need leaders who do not listen to those they lead, and are consequently unwilling to change their minds, for flexibility is the touchstone of success.

What then do we need in our leaders?

We need leaders to lead, that is, to have clear commitment, but at the same time, be willing to listen and to learn, always open minded and generous spirited. Acceptance of personal integrity — without which no human being can possibly function — requires also acceptance of the integrity of others. It follows that leadership requires dialogue in a spirit of mutual tolerance, with a willingness to learn from and with each other. Without this there can be no leadership because there will be no one willing to be led.

Jewish leaders should also be people with a personal commitment to Judaism and to the living and enrichment of Jewish life for themselves and for the future. And leaders in the Jewish community should have their own personal spirituality. Note that I am careful to phrase it that way rather than to say that they should attend services regularly in the Synagogue or live a halakhically *frum* lifestyle; what I mean is that leaders should be aware of, committed to, and trying to live, the moral and spiritual values of Judaism, of which the halakhah is part but not the whole. Without that, why would people want to come forward to lead their fellow Jews?

Further, our leaders should be people who welcome dialogue with all members of the community, in total respect for the whole spectrum of Jewish opinion, even where they personally may choose a different option. The crucial point must always be the subordination of the individual agenda to the need of the community. Without the coherence and continuing identity of the community there can ultimately be no continuing identity of its members. Each of us can and should put forward our own opinion as best we can and live our own Judaism, but, in the last resort, without compromise from everyone, we will not survive at all. Not everything that we personally value is a principle that must not be compromised.

Anyone who seeks to be a leader in the Jewish community must love Jews and Judaism. If we speak to each other words of encouragement and gentleness we shall achieve so much more than if we shout hatred and criticize. *Ahavat Yisrael*, love of Jews and Judaism, will guarantee our survival; *sinat hinam*, mutual hatred and carping criticism, will guarantee our rapid demise.

And at the end, as we look back at the history of Jewish leadership and especially the career of Moses in the Torah, a career that is the paradigm of leadership, we learn that leaders need patience and, above all things, a sense of humour.

We welcome the new Board that will lead our Synagogue for the next year, and we pray for God's blessing on them. We will listen to them, support them and help them; and we will trust them to serve us to their best. In turn, we ask them to listen to us, guide us and support us and trust us to play our part. And let us both, leaders and led, pledge ourselves to the survival of our Synagogue as a focus of a rich Jewish life and identity for us all as we face the future with confidence and hope.

RELIGION AND VIOLENCE *Vol. 12, No. 4 - March/April 2002*

We have been made very aware by the events of the past few months of the significance of violence in world affairs. We seem to be a species very prone to violence against ourselves, against each other, and against our fellow life forms on this planet. And the association of violence with religion has been made clear in the terrorists attacks and distressing events in Israel.

Dr. Marc Ellis, a recent guest speaker on Campus, put it very bluntly in one of his lectures when he said that religion and violence are the same thing. The statement is shocking and perhaps extreme in its wording, but there is enough truth in it to make us uncomfortable.

History documents clearly the association of religious faith with violence. We can recall the Crusades, the Inquisition, and the Thirty Years War in 17th century Europe, all involving the infliction of brutal violence precisely in the name of religious faith. And let us not as Jews forget the events recorded in the Book of Joshua in the *T'nakh*. Add the violence inflicted on individuals in the name of God and unrecorded by historians, and the total of human suffering must be immense. We should not forget that we are not talking only of the public record, but also of the suffering caused to women and children by religious faith willing to sacrifice individual human beings to a God seen all too often as bad-tempered and sadistic human being writ large.

And that is the crux of the problem of religion and violence. It is very easy to absolutize one's own views and equate them with God's will, and then in the name of faith to enforce those views by any and all means needed, including extreme violence if all else fails. War; violence in human relations such as spousal abuse, hatred and contempt for others of different faiths, sadistic delight in the eternal punishment in hell of people we dislike — all are to often related to religious faith.

Of course, we can say that such misunderstanding of the basic teaching of all human religions — love of our fellow creatures — is an abuse of religious faith. And that is true. But such misunderstanding is quite normal. The question is how to work against such misunderstanding.

In the first place, we need to develop much more humility than perhaps we have thought proper in the religious context. If we appreciate that we may be too simplistic in our interpretation of our faith, even sometimes just downright wrong, and that our religious faith must always be in dialogue with change and with the outside world, then we have opened the possibility of limiting the violence we are prepared to inflict in the cause of that faith. When tempted to absolutize our own position so that it becomes the very word of God that we must impose on others, if we fall back on the possibility, even probability, that, being human and subject to error, we may be wrong, then we may realize that a truth that may be doubtful (at least from our human perspective), cannot validate or justify the infliction of violence causing suffering to a fellow being. And then our religious faith can become what it should be, a motivation for us to do good and to proclaim love and justice rather than violence.

There is always hope that we can help to make our world a little better. We must always remember that it is not our job to complete the work of *tikkun olam*, but it is our job to persist in working toward it.

A MESSAGE FOR THE B'NAI MITZVOT

Vol. 13, No. 1 - September/October 2003

I have a favourite poem written by a modern Rabbi, Alvin I. Fine, that sums up much of the Jewish attitude toward life.

"Birth is a beginning
And death a destination
And life is a journey;
From childhood to maturity
And youth to age;
From innocence to awareness
And ignorance to knowing;

From foolishness to discretion
and then perhaps to wisdom;
From weakness to strength
Or strength to weakness
And often back again;
From health to sickness
And back, we pray for health again;
From offence to forgiveness,
From loneliness to love,
From joy to gratitude,
From pain to compassion,
And grief to understanding,
From fear to faith;
From defeat to defeat to defeat
Until, looking backward or ahead,
We see that victory lies
Not at some high place along the way,
But in having made the journey, stage by stage,
A sacred pilgrimage."

It reminds us that change is essential in life. We change physically, intellectually, emotionally, spiritually. We must welcome that change. But in the midst of change we must also hold on to our central unchanging core of identity and integrity. We cannot define what we mean by this, but we know when we lose it, know that we have to hold on to it if we are to survive as us.

Change can be unnerving and frightening: it can be exciting: it is always challenging. What helps us along the path of life, guides us, signposts the way for us through continuing change, so that we hang on to that core of identity and integrity?

It is two things.

First, what we are, our willingness to explore, adventure and take risks. Our willingness to accept growth and change. Our willingness to learn, that is the capacity to integrate growth and change into our expanding understanding life. Our willingness to have confidence and to trust that ultimately life is rich and good and beautiful and full of joy.

But second, we are not alone: we have family and friends and community.

From our family we learn to accept who we are while striving to become better. From our family we learn to accept as well as give undemanding love. From our family we learn that we belong, we are home, we need no apology for being and being who we are.

From our friends we learn to take risks, to make life an adventure. From our friends we learn not only who we are but the infinite possibilities of who we can be. From our friends we learn responsibility for others as well as for ourselves. From our friends we learn to grow.

From our community we learn the riches of tradition, the rootedness of our past. From our community we learn to take as well as give. From our community we learn the beauty of ritual and discipline, the possibility to question and criticize. From our community we learn a vision of the future, rooted in and growing from the past.

You have begun this journey through life. Go on with courage and with hope and with love. Never compromise that core of your integrity, never deny your own experience, your own conscience. Accept what life brings, always be open and sensitive. Be proud enough to learn your own lessons, think your own thoughts, dream your own dreams. But be humble enough, too, to accept family, friends and community and learn form them. While the past certainly does not have a veto, it must certainly have a vote. And only a fool imagines that he is the genius who invented the wheel.

Bless life and be blessed by life.

KISLEV/DECEMBER Vol. 13, No. 2 - November/December 2002

On the 25th of Kislev, Jews begin Hanukkah: on the 25th of December Christians begin Christmas. Is there a connection?

There most definately is. they are both Festivals that celebrate light in the dark of mid winter. Forget winter beginning on December 21st with the solstice. On the ground, particularly in Canada, winter begins at least six weeks earlier! They are both Festivals and therefore teach a fundamental lesson of hope. They are both marked by eating, singing and celebration, albeit on different scales. And of course we should never forget that, had the Maccabees not won, which is what we remember at Hanukkah, there would have been no Christmas at all. Jesus would not have been a Jew because Judaism would have ceased to be; and without the Jew Jesus there would be not Christianity.

The Talmud also reminds us that we should wish our friends well on the Festivals, *mipne darkhe shalom*, for the sake of peace. And as Christians are not idolaters according to the halakah, even more so should we wish our Christian friends a merry Christmas.

However, Christmas is also the time of the year when businesses of all kinds do most of their trade. Inevitably, it has become more of a commercial celebration than a religious festival. Much of the ritual surrounding Christmas had been created in the 19th century, primarily by Charles Dickens. Christmas trees, Christmas cards, Santa Claus himself, are all that recent. The faith of Christians has been marginalized, even carols heard more in malls and the media than in churches. Our modern month-long celebration of over-eating, over-drinking, over-spending awash in fake sentimentality, bears little relationship to what was the second most important festival of Christianity, the birth of Jesus.

Even from the Jewish side, our Hanukkah has become what it was not originally, though we have managed to retain more of the essential meaning of the observance than our Christian friends have retained of theirs. Originally a quiet family time for lighting the menorah, singing songs such as Maoz Tsur, and eating oily foods such as sufganiot and latkes, Hanukkah has become a Jewish Christmas. We have to compete with Christmas. So we give large presents, have huge parties, and light public menorot. We have bought into the myth of Judeo-Christian heritage that makes Judaism public property side-by-side with Christianity. But the essence of Hanukkah is precisely its quietness, its private joy in survival. Maybe our Hanukkah should become what it used to be, and lose its shrill competitiveness with Christmas. Hanukkah is not the Jewish Christmas. Christmas is a delightful Festival for Christians, and we should wish our friends well. Hanukkah is a much lower-key Festival, a delight for Jews, but very different in style, even though there is much meaning in common.

Many Jews today are, of course, Jews by choice. They have Christian family and friends. How should they relate to Christmas? All Jews should respect the religious faith and practice of others and should avoid hurtful judgementalism, particularly with non-Jewish family members. Of course, a Jew by choice should wish Christian family members well for their Festival, join them for parties, even go to midnight mass with them as a sympathetic, if non-participating observer. By the same token, they should invite them to their own Jewish homes and share the lights of Hanukkah with them. There is no competition (whose lights are bigger and brighter!), just a small manual respect of human beings on their differing spiritual paths. Even the carols in the malls, obtrusive and irritating as they are, do point to a time of year when people seem to yearn for a gentler human relationship. Even talking about human fellowship and peace is an improvement on the rest of the year!

So, let us keep our own identity: Christmas is not for us Jews. But let us also learn from our celebration of our spiritual survival to honour all that we have given to the world. Jesus was a Jew, and Christianity is one way that God speaks to the human family. Our Christian friends are increasingly coming to know that, and consequently to honour us as Jews. And that is as it should be.

We shall shortly be reading Exodus Chapter 20, *Prashat Yitro*, which includes the *aseret ha dibrot*, literally the Ten Words, usually known in English as the Ten Commandments. It is often taken symbolically to represent the whole of the Revelation experience of the people at Mount Sinai and the Covenant made then between God and the People of Israel. In consequence, when it is read in the Service on that Shabbat, the whole community stands and so relives the experience of the past: the Covenant made at Sinai so long ago is confirmed again and again, year after year.

And yet, the *aseret ha dibrot* are not read in the Synagogue other than on the occasions when we read them in the Torah portions Yitro and Ethanan, and on the morning of Shavuot. They do not form a sort of Jewish creed. Their standing in Jewish tradition is nowhere near their standing for many Christians. They are not seen as the core of ideal moral life for the world.

Why is this?

The Talmud tells us that we do not use the *aseret ha dibrot* in the normal Service so that the *minim*, heretics literally, but in this case it means Christians, should not be able to claim that this is the whole Torah. To give them that status would be to deny the whole of the Oral Torah. There is much more to Judaism than the Ten commandments.

And we can go further. The *aseret ha dibrot* are actually so vague and general and therefore require such enormous amounts of commentary and interpretation as to be practically speaking quite useless as they stand. For example, *al tirtsakh*, don't murder, opens up huge questions of meaning and application. How does this apply to war or abortion, for instance? (We should note that there is no commandment not to kill. This is a gross mistranslation of the Hebrew that applies to wilful murder. Please make this clear to non-Jewish friends.) And what of not bearing false witness? Is this a blanket prohibition of lying? Evidently not. But would it prevent a Jew from working in an advertising agency? And that is more arguable.

Which is not to say that Jewish tradition does not take the *aseret ha dibrot* seriously. There is enormous discussion, halakhic and aggadic, about its meaning. And if we see the Words as precisely that, "Words," rather than as "Commandments" (which they are not), then we can learn many profound lessons.

Traditionally, the ten are divided into five on each of the two stones on which they are written. Many teachings are derived from this. That the first five relate to the duties *ben adam la Makkom*, between human and Divine, the second five relate to those *ben adam le adam*, between human beings, is well known.

Another lesson, not so well known perhaps, is that they are linked together, first to sixth, second to seventh, third to eighth, fourth to ninth, fifth to tenth. So, for example, the first which proclaims the existence of God, is supplemented by the sixth, the prohibition of murder. Why? Because murder is the destruction of God's Creation (The one who destroys a single soul is as if destroying a whole world). And that is the denial of God's existence and purpose. So it is number six that clarifies and gives practical resonance to number one, which would otherwise remain an abstract principle. And so on.

When we come to read the *Aseret ha Dibrot* let us therefore bear two things in mind.

First, it is not, as many think, some sort of essence of Judaism. It is too vague and indeterminate for that.

Second, if we read through the lens of Jewish tradition and enter the "text" in a sense of dialogic encounter, we shall uncover layers of meaning and richness, and begin to find practical application in the way that we live Jewishly.

SPIRITUALITY AND RELIGION *Vol. 13, No. 4 - March/April 2003*

The passages that we read from the Torah at this time of year raise some basic issues. They seem to be concerned essentially with various laws, sometimes moral sometimes not, and legislation relating to the building and decoration of the Tabernacle and the consecration of the priests and their function.

Many modern Jews might feel some discomfort with these passages. They might feel them to be irrelevant to modern religious life, anachronistic in their concern, and wholly ritualistic.

This fits some of the general attitudes among so many today about the relation between spirituality and religion. Spirituality is one of today's buzz words. It refers to personal encounters with the other dimension of possibility/reality, unmediated by the rules and regulations that are seen so often as restrictive. "Spirituality" is a positive word. On the other hand, religion is seen as precisely those seemingly pettifogging rules and regulations. It is the structure of organized religion, the constraining of free-flowing spiritual experience by the heavy hand of tradition. "Religion," and even more so "organised religion," is a negative term.

This is not a new dichotomy. The writer Ahad ha Am wrote an essay more than 80 years ago that contrasts the Prophet and the Priest. For him, Prophecy was the very essence of Judaism, and many of us might agree. What then was the role of the Priest, if any? For Ahad ha Am, it was necessary to have priests to preserve and protect the prophetic genius. The word is all too easily lost without the medium that enables it to remain accessible through the generations. As the *Pirke Avot* reminds us, *"siyag la Torah,"* build a fence around the Torah, for without the fence the Torah can so easily be lost. On the other hand, though, there is of course always the danger that we shall come to protect the fence and forget what is within it. Hence the pan-halakhism of some of our Orthodox spokespeople, in which the spirit is lost in the literalism of the word, the primary experience disappearing beneath the weight of commentary.

It must be said, though, that those who speak of their spirituality being choked by the formalism and legalism of the organized form of religion, should beware of two possibilities. First, that they do not really take their spirituality all that seriously so much as use it as a stick to beat forms of religion that they do not like. And second, that it can become itself superficial, a sort of fuzzy "feel good" that gives an excuse for not making decisions.

After all, Judaism is not really overly concerned with religious experience as such (spirituality), but is intensely concerned with religious action, both lifestyle and ethical deed. *Sh'ma*, Listen! and *Mitsvah*, Commandment! and *Kehilah*, Community! are the pillars of traditional Judaism. Spiritual experience, direct encounter with the Divine, *fascinans et tremendum*, is a bonus, but not essential to Jewish religious commitment.

What these Torah passages are really telling us is that Judaism is lived in community that spans the generations. It is concerned very much with maintenance of a covenant-based identity through time. It is not, in the first instance at least, bound to immediate spiritual encounter of the individual, but with the living of that encounter into the future. There are pros and cons, but Judaism has firmly opted for the disciplined life, the lived mitsvah, rather than the New Age fuzzy feel good of the immediate encounter with the Other. It is in that frame of mind that we can learn to appreciate *parshiyot* that, at first blush, seem totally irrelevant to us. Ultimately, of course, Judaism is a tradition that honours both spirituality and religion, both the Prophet and the Priest, but it has opted for communal living of the mitsvah, mundane as it often is, against the ecstatic storming of heaven of the mystic.

JUDAISM AND HISTORY *Vol. 13, No. 5 - May/June 2003*

We have often been taught that Judaism is a religious tradition that is interwoven with history. Many of us have learned the German term "heilsgeschichte", meaning sacred history, implying that Judaism teaches that God is an actor working out history as a drama with a plot written in; indeed, God has written the script, and is producer and director of the drama, and plays the leading role, though all human beings and societies have a role to play.

The question that arises from this is: Does this mean that the events of history as recorded in the text of the Hebrew Bible have to be read as history, that is, they happened when they are recorded? And does a Jew have to believe in the historicity of the text to express this faith that history is the stage for the divinely written drama? In other words, do we have to read the Bible literally?

The straightforward answer is no. But we need to go beyond that to understand why that is the answer.

The German historian of the 19th century, von Ranke, is famous for saying that history is what happened, and the task of the historian is therefore to deal with events as they happened and link them together into cause and effect. It is also possible actually to know what happened. But this is unduly simplistic. It would be more correct to say that history is what people think, believe, perceive happened rather than what actually did; perception, in sort, is more significant than reality. Consider, for example, the way the same event is seen by different peoples from their specific perspectives. This is so with the witnesses of ordinary everyday events. All the more *som kal ve homer*, with historical events. The reading of the Battle of the Little Big Horn by the Sioux is radically different from the reading of battle by white Americans.

Further, perception is a combination of many factors. People see what they expect to see which is what their own history and experiences will lead them to see. They weave together the events of their history into a pattern, and the events come to be seen through the lens of that pattern rather than as discrete happenings. They invent their history and reinvent it as needed in order to make sense of one thing after another: so, indeed, do we all as individual human beings. The events may or may not have happened, but they certainly didn't happen in exactly the way that we perceived them happening. Human beings create midrash all the time. The history that we remember is midrash; we remember it as part of a coherent pattern.

So it is with us Jews. We impose on history a pattern and a meaning. We see God working in history, which has a beginning, Creation, and an end, the *Olam ha Ba*. And the meaning is woven into that history by God's choice of the people Israel, and the Covenant of Torah which symbolizes that relationship. All the individual events are seen through that structure and not in their own right. The Bible is not, therefore, a history book, but a book that sees history as theology. History is "midrashised." That does not mean that the events didn't necessarily happen, even precisely as recorded; but it does mean that the events did not necessarily happen, certainly in the way they are recorded.

And events happen on many different levels, each important. An event can happen just as it is written: X did Y to Z. But it is more important to most chroniclers to find out why and what it means, rather than just establish that X did Y to Z. But an event can also have an existential reality. X may not have done Y to Z, but if people believe that it happened that way, because it should have happened that way to fit into the pattern by which we understand and make sense of history, then it did. Poetry and Midrash are just as important as "reality," whatever that reality may be, because human beings cannot live in a world where things just happen: they need to find meaning and purpose in what happened.

This is the way in which we can understand our Biblical text as history. It is a theological meditation on meaning in history, using events linked by midrash. It doesn't really matter whether they actually happened, even less, whether they happened as recorded; what really matters is that history has a meaning and a purpose. It is the stage on which God works out a divine plan using human actors and especially the people of Israel. So it is possible for us to accept the academic study of the text, which overwhelmingly tells us that the events recorded in the Bible did not necessarily happen, and certainly not as recorded; and also to accept the reading of Jewish tradition that these events are existentially true as a midrashic meditation on history that ties everything together into a pattern in which we see the hand of God injecting divine purpose into history.

So it is that I personally can function as a person of faith and also of scholarship, retaining integrity of both conscience and mind. And I would suggest that it is the approach most likely to commend itself to a modern Jew who wants to be loyal to the traditional midrashic understanding of history, and also to the honesty of modern research.

ON HOLIDAY *Vol. 13, No. 6 - July/August 2003*

Patricia and I were away in April and May. We went to England to help celebrate Patricia's mother's 90th birthday. It was also my brother's birthday, my cousin's birthday, and mine, so we were birthdayed out!

After that we went on a bus tour of western Europe. It was very intense, including eight countries and a total of 5000 kms. Our guide made every effort to ensure that Jewish sights were part of the tour, and our driver to ensure that we got to them. The experience led me to think about Jewish life in modern Europe. Jews in western Europe have a deep history, but we have to ask whether there is a long-term future for Jewish life in a continent awash with Jewish blood spilled over the centuries, and where a Muslim presence is now putting down roots.

The demographics are depressing. The Jewish population of western Europe is basically in decline, not — thank God — because of persecution, but because of migration and non-replacement of an ageing population. Only in Germany (of all places) is the Jewish population actually increasing. But Jews are secure and enjoy a high standard of living. The threat for the future is a strong tide of anti-Israel feeling throughout the area that could easily spill over into anti-Semitism, but for the moment that is containable, and there are strong barriers against anti-Semitism both in law and in the anti-racism of the young. Perhaps 800,000 Jews live in those eight countries we visited, and organizational life (though not Synagogal life) seems strong.

The largest Jewish community is in France, augmented by immigration from the former French colonies in North Africa. That immigration has also included large numbers of Muslims, and France's Muslim community is now about 10% of the French population. There have been anti-Semitic incidents in France and undoubtedly some of the hostility to Muslims has also affected Jews, and some of the Muslims are hostile to Jews. It is difficult to see what the future possibilities are, but it is reasonable to be a little apprehensive. On the other hand, large numbers of young French people do not share the racism of their elders and have marched in large numbers to protest against anti-Semitism and anti-Muslim feelings and acts.

Belgium has an established community of 40,000 or more Jews, including a large Hasidic group in Antwerp involved in the diamond business. The diamond business also provides a living for many Dutch Jews, 35,000 or so centred in Amsterdam, Rotterdam and den Hague. Amsterdam is one of the freest and most liberal cities in the world and Jews are probably as secure here as anywhere. Anne Frank's house, one of the many fine 17th and 18th-century houses fronting the beautiful canal system of Amsterdam, is an abiding symbol of the evils of the past, the large Sefardi Synagogue in the city centre an abiding symbol of the splendours of the past. The Netherlands produced the largest number of righteous gentiles who risked their own lives to save those of their Jewish neighbours during the Nazi years. I have a feeling that the Dutch community has a future: two of my fellow students from the Leo Baeck College are serving as Rabbis here, in Amsterdam and in den Hague, and another fellow graduate is involved in counselling Holocaust survivors and their children. Belgium, though, is not so secure. Antwerp is the stronghold of the Belgian Fascist movement , the Vlaamse Blok, and this is precisely where most Belgian Jews live: there is clearly some apprehension in order here, though, of course, mingled with hope.

JEWISH REFLECTIONS ON HOLIDAY II
Vol. 14, No. 2 - November/December 2003

A Jew visiting the German countries — Germany, Austria and Switzerland — is inevitably somewhat ambivalent about the experience. The memories of Nazism and the Holocaust and the "business as normal" attitudes of the Swiss, remain very much alive. I was distinctly uncomfortable with the thought of visiting those countries and also very concerned to analyse my feelings as I walked around and imbibed the atmosphere.

Germany has a fast-growing Jewish population, in itself ironic, given the history.

On the one side, no Jew can ever forget the *Shoah*; on the other side, the German government has behaved with exemplary correctness and assisted in many ways the re-establishment of Jewish life. Despite struggles with the integration of the former East Germany and of many immigrants from the Third World, resulting in many social problems and undeniable racism, Germany has established a firmly democratic, tolerant society, and has strongly resisted racist feeling. And it is true that no one born since 1945 — which is the majority of all Germans — bears any responsibility for those terrible Nazi years. Probably we Jews must in all fairness respect the democratic bona fides of modern Germans, and hope for some peaceful, secure, and productive modus vivendi between modern Germans and the reborn Jewish community. Certainly, the basis for Jewish and non-Jewish relations is honestly laid. Though I'm not completely confident, I am also, oddly, not unhopeful for the Jewish future in Germany.

But not in Austria! I cannot forget that the Austrian people elected a Nazi as their President, in full awareness of his past and that he seemed, to put it mildly, unrepentant about the past. Nor can I forget that Hitler was an Austrian, and that Austria has a history of "respectable" political anti-Semitism many years before Nazis. The 15,000 or so Jews in Austria today are certainly not under immediate threat. It may be, too, that the membership of the European Union makes anti-Semitism less of a real option. This however, relies to some degree on the fact that more than 10 million Muslims living in the EU provide a much more obvious target for bigotry.

Switzerland is not a member of the EU. It has a Jewish community of about 20,000, part of a very high proportion of its population that are resident aliens. We should not forget that Switzerland has had a Jewish president recently— and a woman at that! But the Swiss President is not that important. Does the acceptance of a few wealthy refugees from Nazi Germany — not enough to upset German authorities of the time — balance the turning back of so many more? And what of the fate of so much Jewish money in Swiss banks? The traditional Swiss neutrality can seem little more than a refusal to accept responsibility, a desire to carry on doing business without moral considerations. I doubt that Swiss Jews are in danger, but I am not altogether comfortable with Swiss hypocrisy. I also found them much more irritating than the members of the EU, who seem genuinely to want to build for a new future of co-operation.

In Germany, I was interested to journey down the Rhine and see the country that my mother's family came from in the middle of the 19th century. When we left Austria and moved to Italy, I was interested to see the northern Italian plains that my father's family had come from in the mid 17th century. And it was the Italian Jewish experience, and later that of Britain when we returned to Dover that I turn to next, with the conclusion of this summer holiday reflection.

I now come to the end of my reflections on my trip to Europe in May.

Jews have lived in Italy since the Roman Empire. Italy has been a model of Jewish-Christian relations because it, and specifically Rome, has been the centre of Christianity, obviously for Catholics, but also in many ways for non-Catholic Christians as well.

From the time of the formation of modern united Italy in 1871, relations between Jews and non-Jews have become very different from the Church-inspired anti-Semitism of the Middle Ages that continued until the middle of the 19th century in the Mortara affair. From then, Jews became an integrated part of the general population, producing academics, professional people, Cabinet Ministers and Generals, even, in 1910, the Prime Minister, Luigi Luzzatto. Even under the Fascist regime, Jews continued to be accepted, until closer alliance with Nazi Germany imposed official anti-Semitism, and even then nearly 60% of Jews survived the Holocaust years, supported and hidden by non-Jews.

But there is a price to pay for tolerance. A loving hug can be as dangerous to Jewish survival as a hateful blow. Jews in Italy are a declining factor in the population, so assimilation is the norm. Though Jewish life is stable and anti-Semitism at a low level, it is questionable how many Italian Jews will remain in another generation.

Similar considerations apply to Jews in Britain. Since the return of Jews to Britain in 1656, there has been little physical violence directed at them. There has been a miasma of social exclusion, stereotype-based prejudice, a general feeling that Jews are "not our sort," but Jews have still become economically, politically, and to some extent, even socially significant. No political or religious group has ever espoused anti-Semitism as a policy, and Jews were never officially excluded from the professions. In one of Lady Thatcher's Cabinets in the 1980s there were five Jews, and Jewish MPs are still out of all proportion to the number of Jews in the country, representing all three major parties. There are even few if any golf clubs left who would blackball a Jewish applicant.

However, British Jews are paying the same price for acceptance as Italian Jews have paid. The Jewish population is declining, from 450,000 just after WWII to about 300,000 or fewer now. While new small communities are being founded in parts of the country that have not seen organized Jewish life since the Middle Ages, at the same time, old established communities are dying. There is some growth among the ultra-Orthodox and among the Reform sections, but this is offset by a huge decline in the middle. The United Synagogue is rapidly reaching the need for some sort of kiss of life. There is much out-marriage, a low birth rate, an aging population, with little compensation from conversion or immigration. The picture is of a community well entrenched in the host society but in terminal decline.

What have I learned from my journey? Fundamentally, while we of course welcome the decline in anti-Semitism and the rise of tolerance and a sense of being at home, we increasingly are aware of the price that we have to pay in the decline in Jewish affiliation and commitment, coupled with a worrying polarization that arises from that. It isn't just that there are fewer Jews, it is that those Jews who remain are increasingly divided between right and left, and the majority are less inclined to be observant religiously.

There are lessons for us. The religiously affiliated are becoming a minority of Jews here as well, and, although most Jews will still claim their identity, there is less and less hope that this will continue into the future. We have to consider very seriously how we shall persuade Jews not only to keep claiming that label for themselves, but actually to want to fill the label with real meaning in terms of religious faith and commitment. Now, as throughout our history, the future of Judaism rests entirely with each one of us. If we are to survive, we shall have to do it ourselves. No one else will do it for us.

THE SIDDUR *Vol. 14, No. 3 - January/February 2004*

All too often people come to the Synagogue for the Service and soon get lost. The Service seems to be totally foreign, obviously in language, but also in structure. Indeed, it may seem that there is no structure at all, just one thing after another, one prayer and melody following another with seemingly no link. This is not true. The more we understand the structure of the Service, the more we shall get out of coming to the Synagogue; and the more we get out, the more we shall be able to put in.

There is a structure to our Services, hence the Hebrew name *siddur*, which means "order," that is, pattern. And the structure is in terms of meaning as well as emotion. The Service is not just a succession of pretty tunes, it is bound together by a coherent developmental process that is highly intellectual. The words convey ideas; tunes are merely the packaging of the words, and the words are considerably more important than the music.

Over the next few issues, therefore, I want to examine our siddur, in order to give you, the consumer, some idea of what is going on, what the words mean and what are the concepts being taught.

Let us start with Friday evening.

There are two distinct parts to the Friday evening Service: there is the *Kabbalat Shabbat*, welcoming and bringing in *Shabbat*, and then immediately the standard evening Service, *Arvit* or *Maariv*.

The *Kabbalat Shabbat* begins in our Prayer Book with the poem *Yedid Nefesh*, p.252. It could be many other things to introduce the mood of this part of the Service. The core of *Kabbalat Shabbat* is the six Psalms, 95-99 and 29. These are Psalms that celebrate the creativity of God during the 6 weekdays of creation. The culmination is Psalm 29, a remarkable paean of praise to God as Creator and Master of the Universe, p.254-260.

Then there is an interpolation before the theme continues. Our siddur has grown through the generations; communities in different times and places have contributed their own spirituality. And in the 16th century the mystic tradition focused on Sfat in Galilee produced the remarkable and beautiful poem *Lkha Dodi* in which the community together welcomes in Shabbat personified as Israel's bride. The poem has been set to many differing tunes in different communities. It ends with the whole community rising and facing the entrance to the Synagogue in formal welcome. It is at this time, traditionally, that mourners break their mourning and enter to join the community in joyous celebration of Shabbat.

We conclude this section of the Service with Psalm 92. This refers to God's resting from creating, and our joining with God in serene contemplation of that Creation, with its promise of ultimate healing when justice shall triumph in the re-making of a world without flaw. This segues into Psalm 93 which recapitulates the whole theme of Creation and Creation made perfect when God shall be enthroned as ruler, not only *de jure* but also *de facto*.

Kabbalat Shabbat ends, as does every section of prayer, with a *Kaddish*, in this case mourner's *kaddish*, *Kaddish Yatom*, marking the fact that we have just been joined by mourners, and so both we and they proclaim God's greatness as fulfillment of Creation and our hope of ultimate redemption and perfection that reflects that of the Creator.

This section of our Service is a coherent unity, intellectually, psychologically and emotionally. It teaches some of the profoundest concepts of Jewish tradition in words and music knit together in a satisfying whole. It prepares us for our encounter with Shabbat.

THOUGHTS ON THE HALAKHAH

Vol. 14, No. 4 - March/April 2004

The United Synagogue has raised the issue of the place of the halakhah in Conservative Judaism.

At the recent convention in Dallas, Rabbi Jerome Epstein urged ConservativeJews to recognise the primacy of *halakhah* in their lives. He was not saying anything new, in that Conservative Judaism has always stressed that *halakhah*, as interpreted by the Law and Standards Committee, is mandatory for its members. Now, however, with Conservative Judaism losing ground to Reform among North American Jews, Rabbi Epstein felt it important to remind all members of the United Synagogue that living a *halakhic* lifestyle is an essential mark in defining a Conservative Jew.

There are some issues that come to mind in the light of Rabbi Epstein's address in Dallas.

If Conservative Judaism defines itself as *halakhic*, but open to interpretation by its own Rabbinate, it seeks to demarcate its difference from Orthodoxy and Reform. In actual fact, Orthodox Rabbis are also open to possibilities of interpreting *halakhah* in specific situations; and Reform Rabbis, while not accepting *halakhah* as mandatory in practice or in principle, still interpret *halakhic* sources for their members. There is no clear position that Conservative Jews can regard as uniquely defining their approach to Judaism. There is a spectrum in Jewish life on *halakhah*, no clear-cut differences.

Further, we must accept that the majority of modern Jews have been educated in universities, and have integrated academic methods of study. They question, and are not, in, the main, willing merely to accept. They have to be convinced by rational argument. They are not unsympathetic to traditional thought and observance: many are looking for a more patterned life style. But Jews are democrats to the core: they want to be consulted and to have a say in what Jewish things they want to have in their lives. They are unwilling to master traditional *halakhic* sources and methodology, but are also unwilling to concede to the experts the sole decision making.

Nor are most Jews in the western world at all willing to accept that there is some sort of abstract standard out there of what it means to be Jewish and that their task is little by little to attain that standard. All too often, Conservative Judaism seems to many to stand in judgement on its members in a rather patronizing way. This is the way to go; we accept that you are not there yet, but in due time and with sincere effort you will reach the end of the *halakhic* lifestyle. In the meantime, we have to accept that those of us who are not there yet are inferior to those who are. But if the real Jew is the *halakhic* Jew, it must follow that we are being asked to grow toward a sort of modern Orthodoxy. And many of us who have voted against that path, not only in practice but also in principle, have no intention of going back there.

Of course, the *halakhah* is an important part of our history, the way that we have defined our Judaism. But it is not and never has been the only way that Jews have defined themselves. Judaism has always been a pluralist phenomenon with many strands. There have been mystical Jews, rational Jews, secular Jews, and those who have seen their Jewishness in terms of the search for justice. *Halakhah* has served Jews well in maintaining Jewish identity through the ages, but the other ways of being Jewish have to be honoured as well.

Why? Because the challenges of modernity have made it impossible for most of us to accept the *halakhic* way as the only way to be Jewish. Scholarly study of our sources, Biblical and Rabbinic, makes it impossible to continue to accept their absolute authority. They are an essential part of our Jewish identity and must be respected, but they cannot be for us today the only way. Our intellectual and moral integrity demands that our dialogue with the outside world be more complex. It is difficult, but retreat into the simplicity of the past cannot work.

There are broader implications of this approach. Perhaps Conservative Judaism, if it is to survive as one answer to our need to define ourselves as Jews, will have to find some other ground on which to stand. Perhaps we will have to live with the fact that, religiously, there are only two options: fundamentalist clinging to the past, or, for both good and ill, a liberal dialogue with the present and future. To quote Ibn Ezra, *ha meyvin yaskil.** I suspect, though, that the *halakhic* way, what Abraham Joshua Heschel called *pan halakhism* is not a firm rock on which we can stand so much as a morass. As Ahad ha Am says, "*lo zu ha derekh.*"**

*The intelligent person understands
**This is not the way

ON ANTI-SEMITISM *Vol. 14, No. 4 - May/June 2004*

In commenting on the impact of world events on Jews it is important to retain responsibility and avoid exaggeration and paranoia, however merited it might seem in the context of Jewish history. All the more important is this when we think about anti-Semitism. It appears to be commonly accepted that we are seeing a huge upsurge in anti-Semitism around the world, and understandably all Jews are very concerned.

But let us first consider what we mean by anti-Semitism. Dislike of Jews can run all the way from Jewish "jokes" that assume negative stereotyping, through offensive remarks and active discrimination against Jews socially and economically, to hostility expressed in acts against Jews, culminating in hatred expressed in genocide. Anti-Semitism is a spectrum. It can also be expressed by individuals or by groups, or, as in Nazi Germany, by governments and societies. It is also true that criticism of the actions and policies of the government of Israel can be a cover for hatred of Jews as such: in itself it is no such thing, but it can be used by anti-Semites as a fig leaf.

Is there a rise in anti-Semitism? It is difficult to say because we are not analysing phenomena properly. Are we talking about word or act, and what kind of act, and are we distinguishing between generic vandalism or specifically targeted vandalism? What we do know is that there is an enormous rise in criticism of the State of Israel and a concomitant rise in sympathy and support for Palestinians. Increasingly,

Palestinians are seen as victims, and Israel as the perpetrator of acts of violence against them. This is not only true among Muslims in the world, especially the militant youth, but it also affects non-Muslim young who identify with the political left: the old anti-Semitic right wing remains.

What is our role in this situation?

We must be careful in defining what we are talking about. Old fashioned anti-Semitism exists and will continue to exist. It is not the same phenomenon as new anti-Zionism and anti-Israel feelings, though it may have similar effects in terms of attacks, verbal and physical, on Jews and Jewish institutions. This requires a different approach from us.

Not all Muslims in the west agree with their radical young, certainly not in terms of physical attacks on Jews. Most Muslims are recent immigrants and are basically concerned to make their way in their new homes, which means keeping a low profile and being law abiding and avoiding potential troubles that could affect their integration. We should be looking to make informal alliances with responsible Muslim leadership to hold Islamic radicals in check: "informal" so as not to make their task more difficult within their own community.

It is important to be informed and to inform others, friends and neighbours. Defence of Israel is along two lines. First is to make sure that Israeli fears and needs are understood, by ourselves and others. Any country has a right to defend its integrity and security and the lives of its citizens. Second, more controversially, is to agree that there can be legitimate criticism of any democratic government, our own as well as Israel's, and that such criticism is not necessarily a sign of anti-Semitism. If it were, then we would have to say that half the Israeli population are anti-Semitic! Distinguishing between such legitimate criticism and that which really is anti-Semitism under a respectable flag, is not easy. But we have to make it clear that we are trying. Legitimate critics of Mr. Sharon are, after all, what we would know in a democracy as the loyal opposition, not traitors. There is an essential difference, and to blur that difference is to do no good to Jews and Judaism, or to Israel. And to say that we Jews who do not live in Israel must ipso facto not criticise what we feel is wrong or misguided government policy because we are not in the firing line, makes no sense. I did not live in the FSU, but never felt any constraint about criticising its policies. Nor does the fact that I am not a US citizen dampen my opposition to George Bush's Iraq policy. What Israel does and is affects all Jews, whether we live there or not; all Jews, therefore, have a legitimate voice. If Israel represents world Jewry, then world Jewry has a voice in Israel. After all, we non-Orthodox Jews felt no compunction is pressuring the Israeli government not to amend the Law of Return to take away the Jewish status of our converts!

Another issue that arises here is our credibility as Jews in the non-Jewish world. If we cry wolf too often, if we see every critique of Israel as anti-Semitism, every act of vandalism as an incipient *pogrom*, we lose our credibility, we look hysterical. We need to keep our powder dry for real anti-Semitism, the sort that threatens Jewish lives, not the sort that offends us; and we need to be absolutely certain that it is what we say it is, and not generic vandalism or a criticism of Israel that may be harsh but founded. In short, we must remain responsible and level headed.

Anti-Semitism is a fact and we must continually monitor it. We must always work for a society based on total acceptance of pluralism and the integrity of human dignity. But we live in a western world that, imperfectly, is working to that end. Governments and our educational systems are working for such a society. Our task as Jews is to work with everyone of good will patiently and to be aware that the path is long and there are barriers along the way. The order of the day is unceasing vigilance, but not panic or hysteria.

HALAKHAH AND PRAYER *Vol. 14, No. 5 - July/August 2004*

Halakhah is, to put it simplistically, doing things the right way, at the right time, in the right form. It applies to prayer, in that prayer has a right format to be done at the right time. Prayer, is also, of course, the subject of a great deal of non-halakhic thought in Jewish tradition: there is a certain amount of spontaneity in prayer, by definition.

Prayer is talking to God. Whether it be petition, praise, meditation, whether communal or individual, it is human expression of need, hope, fear or joy, to God.

An important consideration in Judaism is what is and what is not proper prayer. There is in our tradition the concept of *tefilat shav*, useless prayer. Prayer that is directed at harming another, or that asks for personal miracles, is *tefilat shav*. Morally and theologically, it is a waste of time and breath. Examples are given in the Talmud. If a man is returning from a journey and comes over a hill to look down on his home village, and he sees a fire, and then prays, Please God, let that fire not be in my house; if a man's wife becomes pregnant, and the man prays, Please God, let it be a boy: these are *tefilot shav*, worthless prayer. They are directed against someone else even if indirectly, or they ask for a specific miracle.

The Torah contains a prayer that is always regarded as an example of prayer at its purest. Moses marries a black girl, and Aaron and Miriam, his brother and sister, protest. As a result, Miriam (not Aaron, note!) is punished by God with some sort of skin disease (not Hansen's disease). Moses prays for his sister, using five Hebrew words, "*El na r'fa na lah,*" Please God, heal her, please.

That prayer comes from the heart. It also breaks all the rules that govern Jewish prayer. There is no *petihah* or *hatimah*, correct opening or concluding formulae. Prayer begins with a formula that refers to God as sovereign of space and time, and ends with another formula that sums up its content. In other words, prayer is a *berakhah*. The *halakhic* formulae control the way prayer is ordered and give it a pattern. There is no reference in these words to time or context. It is a prayer so spontaneous that is hangs without support.

Let me give an example. When I was in *yeshivah*, we naturally davened the statutory services during the day. The *Amidah* is the core of the daily liturgy. When preparing to read the words of the *Amidah*, one should stand straight, with feet together, head slightly bent, in the presence of God the King. This is so both for one's own silent prayer, and also respectfully, when the words are repeated.

On one occasion, the *rosh yeshivah* called me to him after the service and rebuked me for not standing correctly for the *Amidah*: I was perhaps a little slouched, and certainly my feet were not firmly together. Afterwards, I thought, though of course I did not say it, that he was completely in the wrong. If he was not himself concentrated on his prayer, but was looking around to note my "mistakes," he was the last person, surely, to be critical of me.

The point is that the *halakhic* framework is to give structure; it is not to destroy all personal initiative. Sometimes, one recites the words of prayer and they remain merely words on the page. Better that than they not be said at all. Sometimes, very rarely, but sometimes, the words come alive and carry the soul to the gates of eternity. In that case, the rules have done their job and should be left behind to leave the individual who prays alone with his or her God. To insist on the rules then is to be spiritually obtuse, to confuse the mundane prose of ordinary living with the ecstatic poetry of transcendence.

Now, let us return to Moses' prayer. Moses has to speak what is in his heart. His prayer is not really a prayer at all; it is a cry deep from the human soul. Moses is not asking God to do a miracle and heal his sister. His words are filled with tears because they are words of his love for his sister. And when we love, we speak what is in our heart. Whether it is love of a brother for his sister, of parents for children, of wife for husband, it is a prayer that goes far beyond the *halakhic* rules.

And the next stage beyond even that prayer which is a cry of human love, is the prayer of silence. For when we are alone in the divine presence, words are meaningless. We learn that we rise on a ladder, from words neatly ordered, to words that are an inchoate cry, to silence that lies beyond words at all. We can reach the encounter with the Thou that cannot and must not be spoken, only known.

The structure of prayer teaches us to pray, and it gives us words and forms for prayer that have been filled with the sanctity of the generations that have yearned for God. Beyond those words and forms are the words of the innermost being that speak of personal love. And beyond all words at all is the silence of the ultimate encounter. It is for us to use the *halakhic* tradition not to be used by it.

We are poised to begin another new year. It is a time for us to look back on the past year, to be thankful for our blessings and to be pained by our failures and the hurt we have caused to others, especially those we love. It is a time to look forward to the unknown year just about to begin, with determination to improve, to ask forgiveness for our faults, and pray that we have learned from our living. Let us do things better because we are better. May we increase the love in the world and decrease the pain, despair and hatred. And may we hang on to our Jewish hope that it is possible to do it: that what is, is not inexorably what must be.

Among the many confusions in our hearts at this time is our relationship to Judaism. To so many of our people Judaism has become a thin veneer. It is what we are, but we are not all that sure of what it means. All too often our Jewishness is more negative, dependant on others, than positive, something that we actively cherish and live by.

Many of us are Jews more by label than anything else. We are Jews because we are proud of Israel and Israel sort of guarantees that we and our children will continue to be Jews without our having to do anything about it. But romantic ideals cannot overcome real politik, the realities of being a small state in a naughty world. We are Jews because anti-Semitism forces us to be Jews; for as long as there is anti-Semitism we do not have to find positive reasons for being Jewish. We are Jews because of the Holocaust and our determination that it must not happen again. As Alan Dershowitz might put it, so long as we can stress the *oy* of being Jewish we don't have to think about the possible joy of being Jewish!

This isn't good enough. Unless we can find positive reasons for being Jews, then our children and grandchildren will have nothing to bother about: they will drift inexorably away. As J.M.Keynes once said, in the long run we are all dead. We need to find a need to be Jewish.

So my sermons this *Yom Kippur* will focus on this issue. I ask myself, What does being a Jew mean to me? Why should I bother? What is it in Judaism that is so important that I am prepared to gamble my life on it? These are the questions I want to struggle with. And I want to do it not just on *Yom Kippur* but throughout the coming year. Because if we can't come up with some constructive answers, we as Jews, as a community, as a people, are in serious trouble.

I want to order my thoughts using the traditional Jewish categories of God, Israel and Torah. But I want to remain open and therefore will not be constrained to those categories. The words may not really mean much to many, but our thinking, however honest, has to be guided, and the words of tradition, however possibly faulty, are all we have to discipline us and show us a path.

I assure you that I am not prepared to give up and just fall back on being Jewish because I piggyback on Israel, or because an anti-Semite tells me I am (what can she or he know!), or because a Jew is a Jew as a rose is a rose. I do happen to believe that there are positive values that not only make it important for me to remain a Jew, but are actually crucial to the moral and spiritual survival of the whole of human kind.

What I am asking of you all, perhaps having the hutspah to challenge you all, is to come and listen to me, and then let us discuss together, argue together, in love and respect, and perhaps learn from each other to fill our Jewishness with richness and hope and strength that will overflow and make us and our little Synagogue really be a blessing to all humankind. With those stakes to play for, what have you to lose? Let's make our experience together these Holy Days really special for our learning and our living.

Madonna (Esther) and the Kabbalah

Vol. 15, No. 2 - November/December 2004

Much interest of late has been shown in the *Kabbalah* by both Jews and non-Jews, especially by well-known show business people. A recent conference in Israel on *Kabbalah* was attended by Madonna, who now calls herself Esther and seems to regard herself as Jewish in some form. This has brought the whole issue to the fore.

First, let us be clear about terminology. The *Kabbalah* (literally "Tradition") refers to the whole of the Jewish mystic tradition. Specifically, it often relates to the *Zohar* (literally the Book of Splendour), which is a vast commentary on the Torah written in Aramaic.

Anyone interested in the Jewish mystic tradition can turn to the work of Gershon Sholem, and particularly his *Lectures on Jewish Mysticism*, the standard source on the subject, and still available. People should avoid a large number of more popular books that are proliferating on bookstore shelves these days: their common feature is lack of deep knowledge by the author.

The mystic tradition was traditionally not supposed to be available to students under the age of 40, to ensure mental and emotional maturity, so that people would not be carried away by the material that they were studying.

The mystic tradition goes back into the *Tnakh* and there are visions recorded in the Talmud and other Rabbinic literature; but it is especially to be found in books like *Sefer Yetsirah* (The Book of Creation), and the *Zohar*. The *Zohar* is attributed to the 2nd century Tannaitic tradition, but scholars agree that it actually comes from 14th century Spain and reflects the historical situation of the time. Mysticism is particularly significant during the periods of Jewish history marked by increasing persecution and a reaction to this of despair of ordinary religious life and a tendency to turn to mystic speculation and Messianic hope. Trying to bring about the coming of the messiah to relieve Jews of the burdens of history is a continuing theme in Jewish experience.

On the other hand, one could claim that mysticism is integral to any real religious faith. For most of us, religion is the acceptance of experience and faith mediated to us through the classical texts, *Tnakh*, *Talmud*, *Midrash* and *Siddur*. But for some spiritual geniuses, religious faith came through direct experience of God. The desire of many for that sort of immediate experience, unmediated through the text, informs the mystic quest. The mystic is the person who sees God directly and not through the lens of the experience of others.

Mysticism is to be found in every religious tradition. In times, like now, when religion is replaced for many by "spirituality," the way of the mystic becomes very appealing. For many Jews it has been the mystic experience of the Hasidic sages, conveyed to us in their stories as told to us by Martin Buber, that has been our contact with the mystic tradition. But increasingly today many are turning to *Kabbalah* and the *Zohar* for spiritual enlightenment.

Unfortunately, this "first hand" experience is mediated through unreliable translation by scholars whose scholarship may not be as sound as one would hope. It becomes as "second hand" as any faith based on Rabbinic texts that are more normative. We might remember the criticism of Buber's retelling of Hasidic tales by Sholem. As a scholar, Sholem felt strongly that Buber's work was not so much a retelling of the stories, as a re-creation reflecting Buber's own midrashic talents and needs; Buber conceded that his work was not entirely true to his sources.

It is also true that one's reaction to mysticism will depend on personality. The 60's search for spiritual enlightenment — that has gone through Hindu gurus of varying authenticity, Buddhism in its non-rational forms, and Sufism, all "retold" for a western audience with no direct knowledge of the original sources and a large amount of gullibility — has now focused on *Kabbalah*, the Jewish mystic tradition. Again, no real knowledge of the original is required, quite the contrary. It appears that with intellectuals disillusioned with western religion, the mystic path is irresistible.

It should be stressed that translation, while necessary, forces one to read a text through the eyes of the translator rather than the author. Further, religion requires a disciplined life, morally and intellectually, and that concentrated effort and discipline cannot be short-circuited by instant revelation by obscure text interpretation. Whatever quick fix Madonna (Esther) is looking for in her spiritual quest, she will more likely find it in her own tradition of Julian of Norwich and St. Theresa of Avila than in anthologized snippets purporting to be *Kabbalah*.

A final word: we must always beware the abandonment of human reason in religion. The very crux of Judaism is rational study of text. The mystic way has never been mainline Judaism and never could be. Judaism is the practical response to the question, What does God want from me? Mystic speculation has always been a side line, i.e. irrelevant to the Jewish path of life.

THE CHOICES THAT JEWS MAKE

Vol. 15, No. 3 - January/February 2005

The beginning of a new year is a good time for me to write a new series about the choices that Jews make.

We each define our Jewishness in differing ways: there are as many ways of being Jewish as there are Jews. Some are religious, some secular. The religious call themselves Orthodox, Conservative, Reform, Reconstructionist, Renewal. And within those labels there is a spectrum of intellectual commitment and observance. Each of us makes our own choice from the immensely rich buffet of Jewish tradition. And each choice is subtly different, with its own strengths and weaknesses.

It is essential to hold firmly to the view that these choices are valid; they are all parts of the mosaic of Jewish experience. Without each of them, and without the holding together of all of them in the fabric of Judaism, we should be immeasurably the poorer. Judaism is inherently pluralist, and that is its vibrancy and power, in that its continued survival.

Let us begin with the religious options, if only because it is the religious vocabulary of the Jewish experience that defines every Jew, and without that vocabulary we cannot talk about Judaism at all. A Jew is defined religiously, however secular his or her own identification, and lives by the rhythm of the Jewish year.

Orthodox Judaism is part of the multicoloured fabric of Jewish historical experience. It defines itself as the only authentic form of Judaism, based on loyalty to the Torah, written and oral, systematized in the *halakhic* way of life. At its best, it produces a disciplined life dedicated to study and observance. At its worst, it produces a sterility and stagnation, unwilling to dialogue with the real world outside. It can also often be unduly judgemental of the Jewish paths of others. The values it contributes to our Jewishness are discipline, the ideal of study, and the real possibility of walking with God through the practice of the presence of God through the halakhic lifestyle. It has much to teach us and Judaism as a whole would be poorer without the stubborn survival of Orthodoxy. But it cannot be the way for the majority of Jews to define their identity, not just because human beings, including Jews, are lazy, but for very good reasons of principle.

Intellectual and moral integrity will inevitably lead most Jews away from this expression of Judaism. Many have been drawn to call themselves Conservative. They find a home in what they feel to be a middle of the road liberalism. On the one hand, it enters into dialogue with the non-Jewish world; on the other, it tries to preserve the best of tradition from the past. "Tradition and Change" is a motto of great power and meaning. It seeks to retain the halakhic backbone, while being flexible in interpretation of halakhah. That is its strength. It, too, cannot however be the only way to be Jewish. It has problems, in principle and in practice. There is some degree of hypocrisy in the gap between what Jews do, and what, according to the rules, they ought to do. There is such a breadth of halakhic interpretation possible and acceptable that it is sometimes difficult even to define Conservative Judaism, except as what members of Conservative Synagogues do, and most of them do not live a halakhic lifestyle, however liberally interpreted, nor want to.

Reform, the oldest of the "denominational" options in being a religious Jews, also has its strength. It has always stressed the ethical teachings of Judaism, especially in terms of social justice. Though guided by the halakhic model, it has never defined itself in those terms. It speaks to the autonomous conscience of the individual Jew, and accepts informed choice. All too often, the choices that people make are not "informed" and do not arise from deep knowledge and sincere commitment. But we are talking of human beings with all their flaws, even Jews! At its best, it has challenged the Jewish conscience; at its worst it has been lazy, too willing to judge by non-Jewish standards.

The Jewish groups have been characterised, scathingly, but not too untruthfully, as crazy (Orthodox), hazy (Conservative) and lazy (Reform). But they are the choices that most of us have made; and in making them we have dialogued with the possibilities within them and come up with our own definitions of what we mean by "Jewish."

THE CHOICES JEWS MAKE - PART 2

Vol. 15, No. 4 - March/April 2005

The fourth religious choice that Jews make is the Reconstructionst movement founded by Mordechai Kaplan. Simplistically, this is a combination of radical theology and traditional liturgy and practice. It has been the branch of Judaism most open to experimentation in both belief and practice, the cutting edge of Judaism in the modern world. Its strength is its inclusiveness and open dialogue with modernity; its weakness for many Jews is its association with denial of Jewish chosenness, and its naturalistic God idea.

Generations ago, there was yet another option for many Jews: secular identity. This was the maintenance of Jewish culture and tradition, without reference to any form of supernatural origin. When Jews were concentrated in particular areas in large numbers, this option made sense and was popular. Nowadays, with the decline of the Yiddish language and the cultural experience bound up with it, this option has become far less viable. Indeed, as more and more minorities, including Jews, have had to identify themselves in "religious" terms within their host societies, a secular option of Jewishness becomes difficult even to define.

What determines which "denominational" choice Jews will make? There are many factors, some almost accidental. If, for example, as in Saskatoon, there is only one Synagogue, any identifying Jew will have to join, without reference to its membership of a denominational group. If we are affiliated with the United Synagogue, all of us are defined by that membership as Conservative Jews, which I would suggest is probably not the case for many. As we try to be inclusive and sensible, we are aware that we must serve Jews who in other circumstances would affiliate with one of the other groups.

If we have the opportunity to chose, what will determine that choice? Family tradition is one factor, regardless of personal commitment. A feeling of correctness is another factor.

That is, we may feel that the style of being Jewish represented by one or the other of the denominations represents what Jews ought to be, regardless of what they actually are. We might in some cases make a conscious decision that this is the way that we can honestly identify ourselves as Jews. We may also, perhaps, be rebelling against our family background or against the type of Synagogue we grew up in: so we may see it as hypocritical or out of date or too radical, to either left or right.

I personally have some problems, for example, with the identification of Judaism with the *halakhic* system that is the norm in Orthodox and Conservative Judaism. The *halakhah* is an essential part of the Jewish historical experience, and it can certainly be open to development to deal with many modern problems. However, there are fundamental weaknesses. There are built-in biases against non-Jews and women that are difficult to accommodate to a modern liberal approach; there are areas where there is no wriggle room whatever for a more liberal interpretation, the halakhah is fixed, such as with the issue of homosexuality; and, most important, regardless of the scholarship of non-Orthodox Rabbis—and many really are outstanding Talmudists and halakhists—the Orthodox Rabbinate claims a monopoly of the *halakhic* system and will not budge from the most rigorous interpretations. Orthodox Rabbis are, in general, just not interested in dialoguing with more liberal colleagues, indeed do not even see them as such.

As a result, respectful though I may be of the *halakhah* as part of Jewish experience, I cannot accept its binding authority. So, as observant as I may be personally, I am fundamentally a liberal Jew and cannot work within the framework of Orthodoxy or even Conservative. I respect the committed Orthodox or Conservative Jew and accept unequivocally that they are valid choices for any Jew to make, but I cannot conscientiously share that choice. I must in all integrity choose to be a Reform/Reconstructionist Jew. I expect my choice, made with knowledge and integrity, to be as respected by fellow Jews, as they are entitled to expect me to respect their choice.

What Jews Have Given To The World — Bar Mitzvah Sermon

Vol. 15, No. 5 - May/June 2005

During the past few weeks, we have seen the trial of David Ahenekew on the charge of incitement to racial hatred, specifically against Jews. The trial arose out of comments that Mr. Ahenakew made at a FSIN conference, and afterwards to a Star Phoenix reporter. Our community was represented during the trial by a lawyer from Montreal representing specifically B'nai Brith; many of our own members attended in the public gallery, and I was called as a witness.

The trial and the repetition by Mr. Ahenakew of his hateful comments in court and the attempted justification of his right to make those comments by his lawyer, all left a nasty taste in the mouth.

We were reminded that the evil anti-Semitism of the Nazis is alive and well, and that people of such similar experience of bigotry as we have suffered in history as the Native peoples, are as capable of holding such views as our — and their — persecutors. Mr. Ahenakew is so twisted by the history of his people's sufferings, that his whole being is eaten up by hatred, hatred for all others, especially white people, and particularly Jews.

We were reminded that our history as Jews has been marred by anti-Semitism, the irrational hatred of Jews, the creation of myths about us that feed that hatred, the deep suffering inflicted on us. We are aware that others have also suffered from similar hatred, similar myths; and because of our experience we are enjoined to reach out to others who have suffered, other victims of bigotry. All the more are we hurt when fellow victims of hate turn against, not their persecutors, but against fellow victims. There is no competition in victimhood.

We are reminded that our existence as Jews has been so fragile in history that our mere survival is a miracle. Next week, indeed, when we begin our Festival of Freedom, *Pesah*, when we celebrate being freed from slavery and injustice, we are reminded of what our existence as Jews means, and the enormous price we have had to pay, generation after generation, for that existence.

If we are honest, there are times when we ask whether it was worth it, whether it might not be better for us, and our children, to give up being different, being Jews, and join the majority. Yet, we know that if we were to disappear, we would be playing false to our forebears, we would be making ourselves into accessories of evil, we would be guaranteeing Hitler a posthumous victory. And all the suffering and the courage and the tenacity of the past would be made meaningless by our treason.

But we have to ask another question. Granted that we shall survive despite the anti-Semites, the Hitlers, the Ahenakews, is our survival only to spite them, only because we are ashamed to give in? There has to be more than that to being a Jew.

There is so much in our Jewish heritage that is worthwhile, that makes our lives rich and blessed, yes, but also can make the lives of all humankind rich and blessed as well. Let us count the ways in which it is good to be a Jew, rather than just the ways in which we are determined to spite those who hate us.

We Jews have given the world our Bible, the record of our people's wrestling with God. We have given the world a vision of justice and hope, and the means by which to bring that vision to reality in the guidance in how to live together in society. Others have spoken of spirituality and relations between human and God. We, our Prophets, have spoken of decency and how we are to live together as human beings in society.

We Jews have given our world the Sabbath, the idea that one day a week shall be given not to making a living but to learning how to live well. *Shabbat* declares that human beings are entitled to rest, to rediscover and renew the links of love between parents and children, partners in marriage, people in community. Human dignity does not arise from calculation or legislation, but from the fact that we are created in the divine image and have the right to rest and be human and find the humanness in others. On *Shabbat* we embed ourselves in eternity.

We Jews have given our world the *Shma*, the statement that, beneath all the seeming differences in our world there is an underlying unity. And that gives hope and courage. It says that we are united, that the whole of being is united. Without the *Shma* how could we know the foolishness of racism, how could we have pursued the vision of science?

We Jews have given our world the understanding of history as being a drama with a beginning in Creation and an end with the Messianic time when all the world shall know real peace, the peace that is firmly based in justice, the justice that is love in action. *Tsedakah*, the duty to strive for justice by helping others; *tikkun olam*, the duty to heal the world, to hear the pain and sorrow of Creation and to respond by speaking words of comfort and doing deeds of love, to bind up wounds, to clothe the naked and feed the hungry. This, too, we have given to the world.

Yes, we have suffered, and we are determined to survive despite those who have sought to destroy us. But, yes, even more are we determined to survive that these gifts shall continue, that we shall truly be a blessing to our world. We have given so much, and we have so much more to give.

And this is the message that I want you, Jared, to take with you as you grow up to take your place in our community as a loyal and committed Jew. We pray today with you and your family that you have begun your journey as an adult Jew so well. Step by step. We pray that you will go along the path of that journey with deepening knowledge. We pray that you will accept your duty to be proud of being a Jew and the determination to continue to be a Jew, honouring the past generations of our people who survived horrendous challenges, and taking pride in the gifts that we as a people, so small yet so rich morally and spiritually, have freely given to our world. It is for you to carry this on; it is for you to enrich this heritage even more in the quality of your life. As the Talmud says, It is not for you to finish the work, but neither may you ever stop working. *Hazzak, hazzak ve nit-hazzek.* Be strong, be strong, and let us strengthen each other.

Amen

ON TRAVELLING *Vol. 15, No. 6 - July/August 2005*

There are two things that rapidly become obvious when travelling in Europe. Europe has only just begun to discover the handicapped and disabled, and there are few real facilities anywhere to make life easier for them. And the Jewish presence in Europe is deep and all pervasive. There may be few Jews living now in many areas, but the historical connection of Jews with all parts of Europe is extraordinarily deep. Reminiscences of Synagogues and cemeteries and Jewish life abound, even where there are no Jews living today; and many communities that are now tiny and perhaps on the point of disappearing have been established in many places for centuries.

We were in Venice in late May. Venice is important in Jewish history for many reasons, but one above all. It had the first recognized ghetto in Jewish history, dating back to the beginning of the 16th century. The community at that time was officially confined to a small area near the arsenal, called getto, and that Italian word became Judaised as ghetto.

If you take the vaporetto from St. Mark's Square along the Grand Canal and get off at the St. Marcuola stop, it is a few blocks' walking north to the ghetto. Incidentally, this water bus system of public transport is remarkably efficient (no traffic jams!). You will know that you are in the ghetto because some of the street signs are in Hebrew.

The first thing that strikes you is how small this area is, basically a central square and a few small alleys leading off it. At the south end of the square is the community centre, which houses a museum, a book store and a small cafeteria. If you buy a ticket here, there are guided tours that are well worth taking (E10 each). There are five Synagogues, and the tour takes you to three of them. Because the community was confined within this small area, as it grew it had to build upward, and, as the Synagogue had to be on the top of the building, you have a lot of climbing to do. But it is worth it.

The three Synagogues that you go to are the German, the Ashkenazi and the Italian. The names refer to the areas that immigrant Jews to Venice came from and the style of liturgy that they brought with them. They are all small but beautiful.

Branching off from the main square is a short street, at the end of which there are the other two Synagogues, to the left the Syrian, and facing you the Sefardi. The Sephardi Synagogue, the largest, is the only one still in use, and serves the present community. The others are used only for weddings and special occasions, but are carefully maintained.

Coming back to the square, there are two shops where you can buy ritual objects and souvenirs. To the east of the square there is an old people's home, where nine people now live, and a memorial to the 250 Jews from Venice deported during the war — only nine came back. And that is it, all that remains of an historic Jewish community.

To mark my visit I brought back something that represents this special Jewish community, a *yad* (Torah pointer), made of Venetian glass, which I am delighted to use when reading Torah in our own Services.

I am sure that, wherever you travel, you will find some evidence of a Jewish presence, either now or in the past, and that you, too, will be able to bring back some memorial of that presence.

ON MAKING BOUNDARIES *Vol. 16, No. 3 - January/February 06*

For all the non-Orthodox Jews the major question must always be: How do we decide on boundaries? What are our criteria for deciding what we do and what we don't do?

First, and perhaps most obvious, there is a clear difference between the moral demands of Judaism and the ritual ceremonial traditions. It is the moral and ethical that takes priority, and no one really has any problem with that. Moral *mitsvot* are mandatory. However, there is a complication. Some of the *mitsvot* are a mixture: it is not clear whether they are moral or ritual/ceremonial. A major example is *Shabbat*, the only Festival included in the Ten Commandments, the *aseret ha dibrot*. *Shabbat* is both a ritual *mitsvah*, but also a moral *mitsvah*, in that it teaches the right of every human being to respect as an end in him or herself and not a means to an end.

With the ritual/ceremonial *mitsvot* we have to have criteria so that we can decide what to observe in our Jewish lives and what not. Even with agreed criteria, though, there will still be differences in individual human judgement in evaluating the application of the criteria to specific cases.

The criteria I would suggest are three: Is this *mitsvah* esthetic? Is this *mitsvah* moral? Is this *mitsvah* theologically sound? As a result of applying these criteria, we can then categorize the *mitsvot* into those we should observe, those we should not observe, and those that are totally neutral and we can observe or not depending on personal taste and desire. Consider a few examples. First, *halitsah*. A man is enjoined to marry his sister-in-law if she and his deceased brother did not have children. If he refuses, he must go through the ritual of *halitsah*, involving her taking off his shoe and spitting before him because he has refused his duty. The *halakhah* insists that he must do this and that if he did marry his sister-in-law he would commit *zenut*, sexual immorality. Is *halitsah* esthetic? I think no one would consider it so. Is *halitsah* moral: Even the *halakhah* doesn't think so because, insisting that a marriage would be *zenut*, it enforces a ritual that itself is immoral because it humiliates two human beings in the name of religion. But does *halitsah* teach sound religion? Again, no, because it is not moral; and also because it teaches us lessons about human relationships and marriage that are not in conformity with Judaism at its best. Marriage is not directed to reproduction as its major or even sole purpose, but includes friendship and companionship. Also, according to Judaism, human beings are not means to an end but ends in themselves, deserving of total respect and dignity.

Second, *kashrut*, Let us distinguish here between halakhically defined *kashrut* and the concept of laws regulating diet that lies behind the *halakhah*. Let us introduce the concept of eco-kashrut, that the dietary laws are basically concerned with how and what we eat as reflecting our relationships with fellow life forms on this planet. How do we regard animals? How do we treat them when we use them for food? Does the mitsvah of not inflicting unnecessary pain on an animal, even if slaughtering it for food reflect the way we should see it as a fellow creature? In other words, should we not be concerned to sensitize ourselves to pain and suffering, even of animals? The *halakhah* of *shehitah*, slaughtering for food, is intended to minimize pain for the animal. The *halakhah* also forbids hunting, certainly not for sport or pleasure, and a hunted animal is not *kasher* by definition.

If we look at dietary laws in this way, our criteria are all satisfied. We shall indeed probably end up by saying that they would lead us not to eat meat. There could not be anywhere less esthetic than an abattoir; killing, even an animal, offends many people's consciences; by not killing animals we learn about our relationship with fellow life forms and we re-assess the way in which we can feed our fellow human beings more fairly and equally. In a world in which a few gorge and have to diet, while many are always hungry, we can learn many lessons for eco-kashrut.

Similarly, we must ask questions about how food is produced, and about justice, not only for animals, but for farm workers, if we are concerned about what we eat and why. We will be sensitive to the issues of factory farming and alcohol, for example.

We can apply these criteria to all other mitsvot, and we shall find that many that seem to be purely ceremonial turn out, on analysis, to be essentially moral issues. And some, perhaps many, will be acceptable to us as modern Jews in all three dimensions. Lighting Shabbat and Festival candles, for instance, is clearly a mitsvah that is esthetic, for it taps into the universal symbol of light and spiritual warmth and is obviously beautiful; it is clearly moral, for it links families together in love and unity; and it is clearly theologically sound, for it teaches what family and marriage really is for Judaism, a mutually empowering partnership, and what Shabbat is: a time for rest and rediscovery of individual in community.

Finally, what do I mean by neutral observances? I mean mitsvot that do not satisfy my criteria, but equally cannot be said to contradict them. As an example, consider covering the head in the Synagogue. I cannot think of any clear reason to do or not to do it. As a result, as it is embedded in Jewish history, I will do it as a symbol of identity. But I will certainly not condemn another Jew who finds it meaningless. And I will often go bareheaded without any qualm of conscience. There are many more things to worry about!

CARTOONS AND ISLAM *Vol. 16, No. 4 - March/April 2006*

Muslims have been offended by the publication of cartoons in a Danish newspaper, reproduced in Norway, that they feel to be an insult to the Prophet Muhammad and to Islam. As a result, Muslims throughout the world have demonstrated to show their anger, and, in some Islamic states, have burned the Danish and Norwegian embassies. They have carried placards that call for violence against Westerners, and death to those who demean Islam.

In most western democracies, there are laws to protect identifiable minority groups against incitement to hatred and violence. In Canada, for example, we have recently seen the province of Saskatchewan prosecute David Ahenekew under such Hate Legislation for making public statements of hatred against Jews and inviting violence against them. It is clear that any minority group is clearly able to defend its interests by invoking the law and protecting itself against defamation in the courts. It is not made easy to do so intentionally so as to protect also the right of freedom of speech. But an attempt is made honestly to balance free speech in a democracy and the right of minorities to be protected against incitement to hatred that could lead to violence against them.

If, therefore, the Muslim community feels that a cartoon defames Muhammad and Islam they have the undoubted right to proceed through the courts to defend themselves; the experience of Jews shows that they will receive a sympathetic hearing.

Their turning to demonstration in the streets instead is disturbing. Carrying banners demanding the beheading of non-Muslims is chillingly reminiscent of the acts of terrorists beheading their victims in Iraq. It is designed to pressure Western democracies to confer on the Islamic community a privileged status of immunity from criticism that would be regarded in most western democracies as fair comment. No religious group is, or should be, so immune. Religious leaders, like political leaders, are open to criticism, and they either respond through the courts or take their lumps. That is the nature of democracy, which is founded on reasonable freedom of speech.

Of course, any fair-minded person sympathizes with the sense of hurt of Muslims who see their faith seemingly demeaned. They are not used to the freedoms of western democracies, which they see as licenced and moral anarchy. However, by migrating to western Europe and the Americas, Muslims are implicitly accepting the rules of democracy, and must abide by them; that is the other side of the coin of economic advantage that the refugee must pay.

It is true that some, not all, Westerners, suffer from advanced Islamaphobia: it is certainly true that few Westerners have much knowledge of Islam as a religion. Nowadays fewer and fewer know much about Christianity or Judaism either. We live in an increasingly secular society, for both good and ill. That is the reality we have to live with.

It is also true that we live in democracies that have become less and less deferential to authority, religious or political; less and less respectful of leaders. The icons of the past are increasingly challenged. In the main, that is good. Vigorous criticism of those we choose to lead us is healthy and ensures honesty and integrity in leadership.

If the Muslim world and the world of western democracies are to live together peacefully, there needs to be a growth of mutual understanding based on real knowledge. That will produce a dialogue that will lead to the evolution of moral and spiritual values that can lead to a consensus that will enrich the future for us all.

We must first stop demonizing each other. The west is not Sodom and Gomorah heading to hell at breakneck speed: it is experimenting with new value systems based on liberal humanism rather than the former absolute values of religion, and in many ways is morally superior to what went before. Islam is not a medieval tyranny that leads inevitably to terrorism: it is trying to relate to a new universe of democracy and human values. Neither side can compromise its deepest values, nor need it or should it. But that is not the point. Neither can dictate to the other, and what will come to be will be an evolution from their dialogue.

What is certain is that the world needs more, not less, democracy, and perhaps also more spirituality and moral sensitivity and less absolutist religious claims: perhaps in short more humility and respect for each other's humanness. So, maybe Danish cartoonists should exercise more sensitivity and restraint for the moment; and our Islamic fellow citizens exercise more restraint, full stop. And for both, human rights extend both ways.

Understanding Synagogue Services

Vol. 16, No. 5 - May/June 2006

The problem that we have about our Services is that many Jews do not know the structure of the Synagogue Services, how they are choreographed and are constructed. And our Prayer Books are not all that user-friendly either and do not make it clear how the prayers are woven together into an overriding pattern. Far too often it seems that the Service is jut one prayer after another without meaning and structure.

In fact, the Services are very carefully choreographed. There is a pattern that links the prayers together. A basic knowledge brings that pattern clearly to view and enables the worshipper to get an overall picture.

The *Shabbat* morning Service is divided into clearly demarcated parts, with a form of the *Kaddish* dividing those parts.

1) The preliminary Service includes the morning blessings and some Psalms. This is often abbreviated in many Synagogues.

2) The morning Service begins with the *Barkhu*, which calls the *minyan* together to pray.

3) Then comes the *Shema*, with its blessings before and after.

4) The *Amidah* follows, the "standing" prayer, which on *Shabbat* contains seven blessings. The first three and the last three are the same as on all morning Services, the intermediate thirteen blessings coalesced into one for *Shabbat*.

5) The Torah Service follows.

6) After the Torah Service and the return of the *Sefer* to the *Aron*, comes the *Musaf* Service, ending with *Ein Keloheinu*.

7) The concluding prayers are basically the *Aleinu* and the Mourners' *Kaddish*.

After the Service it has become customary to add final songs such as the *Shir ha Kavod* and *Adon Olam*. As these are not an essential part of the Service as such, the *tallit* may be removed before they are sung.

The Service for Shabbat morning is quite long, even in our Synagogue where we shorten things somewhat. We aim to go for no longer than two hours.

Traditionally, if people enter the Synagogue late, they try to catch up with everyone starting from the beginning. I would suggest that this is not a good idea, involving as it does such a speed of praying as to reduce the whole exercise to meaninglessness. It is better to choose one or two of the prayers and concentrate on them before joining the rest of the community where they are. If the Torah Service has started already, go straight there, as the core of the Service is the reading of the Torah.

During the silent *Amidah* there is a temptation to give up and just sit down when others start to. More constructive is to use the silence for personal prayer or meditation. At no time try to compete by gabbling prayer in Hebrew or English just because it is there.

While the leader of prayer has to keep everyone together and will probably read much faster than you may be comfortable with, remember that he or she is more familiar with the prayers than you and is more fluent in Hebrew. Do not try to compete. Again, choose some of the prayers to read slowly, to try to understand and meditate about; you can always join the community at any time you want. A little with sincerity is always better than a lot without understanding.

There are many differing customs about bowing and bending the knee during the prayer. If it comes naturally to you to do so, by all means go ahead and *shokel*. Traditionally, one bows and bends the knee at the beginning and end of the first paragraph of the *Amidah*, rises on the toes for the *Kedushah*, and bows and bends again at the beginning and end of *Modim ahahnu*. Do not overdo it!

When the Torah scroll is paraded through the congregation, it is traditional to show respect for the Torah. Ashkenazim kiss the *sefer* with their *tsitsit*, Sefardim bow: the back should not be turned to the *sefer* at any time. I have always been uncomfortable at the appearance of idolatry here, and confine myself to a respectful bow.

There are many customs involved in the *Shabbat* morning Service. Do not get confused and try not to panic that you don't know them all. The important thing is to be comfortable and to have the courage to get out of the Service as much as you can. The more you understand, the more you will give to your fellow members in the Service. But the Service should never be seen as an obstacle course or an excuse for one-upmanship.

A final word about wearing the *tallit*. Do not regard it as a scarf. It is intended to be worn with the four *tsitsit* at the four corners, which you can only do by spreading it over the shoulders and flipping up the edges so that the four *tsitsit* are in the right place, two at the front, two at the back.

I look forward to seeing you at the *Shabbat* morning Service!

THE LEO BAECK COLLEGE *Vol. 16, No. 6 - July/August 2006*

In July, the Leo Baeck College in London will celebrate its 50th Anniversary. To mark the occasion, it convened an international conference, and invited its Rabbinic graduates from all over the world, their families, and numerous academics and scholars who have been associated with the College over the years, to come together to share guest lectures and study sessions and renew friendships from student days.

Rabbi Leo Baeck (1873–1956) was one of the greatest Rabbis of the first half of the 20th century. Early in his career he wrote *The Essence of Judaism* in which he developed a philosophy of theology of Judaism that links the rationalism of the 19th century with the later thought of Buber and Rosenzweig that has moulded modern Judaism.

When the Nazis came to power, Baeck became the acknowledged leader of German Jewry, representing the Jewish community to the government. Despite many invitations from communities elsewhere, he refused to leave Germany and continued to maintain Jewish life in Germany for as long as possible. Finally, in 1942, he was arrested and sent to Theresienstadt, the "model" concentration camp. There, without access to any materials, he led Services and study groups, and served the Jewish community as pastor and Rabbi. On his release, he decided to spend the rest of his life, half the year in the US and half in Britain. He continued to study and write and was a role model to Jews all over the world as Rabbi, scholar, teacher and committed Jew.

When he died, his colleagues and pupils determined to found a Rabbinical Seminary in his memory, to preserve and rebuild Judaism in Europe. Many of them had left Nazi Germany before the war and reestablished their own lives in Britain, some serving British Synagogues.

The Leo Baeck College opened its doors in September, 1956. For some years the College functioned in the attic of the West London Synagogue and in various Rabbinic homes. I well remember studying in that draughty attic wrapped in thick woollies and trying to turn pages while wearing gloves; I'm not sure whether our breath in the frozen atmosphere was a different shape when we were reading English or Hebrew!

Later, we shared with the children of the Synagogue Hebrew School using some new classrooms that the Synagogue had built. At least they were heated. So we learned and studied: Bible, with both traditional and modern commentaries; Talmud and Responsa; Rabbinic Codes; Midrash; History; Jewish philosophy and theology; Pedagogics; Homiletics; Comparative Religion; Modern Hebrew Literature; Biblical archaeology; practical Rabbinics; Liturgy and hazzanut. And after five years we came to the end of this phase of study. We were examined in all subjects and required to prepare two theses. Mine were a comparative study of Rabbinic semihah and Christian ordination in the first two centuries; and an analysis of Rabbinic interpretation of Bible as illustrated in Tractates Berahow and Shabbat of the Talmud.

The final examination was a four-hour oral that included (i) a defence of the two theses; (ii) an oral examination in halakhah; (iii) reading and translating and commenting on a passage of Talmud that we had not studied in the course (my passage was from *Tractate Gittin*). Then we were let loose on the unsuspecting community with the title *Rabbenu u morenu*, Rabbi and teacher, and the right granted by our teachers, and now colleagues, to teach Judaism and make decisions in *halakhic* matters for Jewish communities.

The details of curriculum and examinations have changed since. But the course remains a rigorous one, based on the assumption that a Rabbi must be a scholar and able to function in both a modern and a traditional sphere. When I compare my training there with my *yeshivah* experience, I am still impressed by the College. Nowadays, too, it has become a totally post graduate course.

No one ever enquired as to our personal approach to Judaism. So long as we were capable scholars, our Jewish decisions were respected. So, while most graduates have gone to Reform communities, many have gone elsewhere — to Conservative and Reconstructionist, even Orthodox congregations. As the training is based on high academic standards, few I think would be happy in an Orthodox context, which denies, for example, modern Biblical scholarship.

The College has seen its role in three special ways: to provide Rabbis for English-speaking Jews all over the world; to help to re-establish Jewish life in Europe; and give to Jews in the former Soviet Union both a possibility of Jewish life, and especially a modern and non-Orthodox form of Judaism more in tune with their needs. For the first time, there are now Reform and Conservative Synagogues in Russia and the Ukraine. Its students have come from Britain and the Commonwealth; from Europe, from Russia; from the USA; and from Israel. And, to give it credit, the Leo Baeck College has always ordained women and gays and lesbians.

Now there are 150 Rabbis ordained by the College, and the College has a high reputation throughout the Jewish world. On its 50th anniversary, I wish my alma mater well, *ad meah ve esrim* and beyond. And I would suggest that if any member is looking for a Jewish recipient for their *tsedakah*, don't forget the Leo Baeck College as a possibility.

THE LEO BAECK COLLEGE II *Vol. 17, No. 1 - Sept/October 2006*

First and foremost, I want to thank the Board of Trustees who helped me to attend the 50th Anniversary Conference of the Leo Baeck College. Their generosity enabled me to renew old friendships and make new ones, and to refresh myself with some learning in various directions. Over the next few *Bulletins* I will raise some issues arising from the Conference of special relevance to our situation.

But I have to begin with some memories about the life and work of Rabbi Dr. Louis Jacobs who died on the *Shabbat* just before the Conference, and whose funeral was at the same time as the ordination of three new Rabbis on the Sunday afternoon of July 2nd. In the long list of names read out before the *Kaddish* at that Ordination Service, names of graduates and teachers, his dominated.

Louis Jacobs was one of the most outstanding Jewish scholars of our time, a profound thinker, a gifted teacher, a tolerant model of a modern cultured Jew at home in both the Rabbinic sources and in the intellectual currents of our time, a mentor for two generations of Rabbis.

He was born to working class parents in Manchester in 1920, educated in the *yeshivah* and at London University, where he earned a Ph.D. He was appointed Rabbi of the New West End Synagogue, probably the most prestigious Orthodox Congregation in London, and was also Senior Lecturer at Jews' College, the seminary for training modern Orthodox clergy, affiliated to London University. He was seen as the outstanding Rabbi in the United Synagogue, next in line to be Chief Rabbi and Head of Jews' College. He was one of the few Orthodox Rabbis to write and publish widely, with a following in the general community.

One of his books was *We Have Reason to Believe*, in which Louis questioned the fundamentalist view of Torah and reinterpreted the idea of Torah *min ha shamayim*. His acceptance of modern scholarship, which he blended with traditional faith, enabled an Orthodox Jew to retain both Orthodoxy and intellectual and moral integrity. Although he sent a copy to the then-Chief Rabbi, Israel Brodie, it was obviously not read. Anglo-Jewry was, and still is, marked by a near total lack of intellectual enquiry!

Someone, however, brought the book to Brodie's notice. The British United Synagogue is unlike the American United Synagogue in everything but name. In particular, the United Synagogue in London owns its constituent Synagogues and its Chief Rabbi has to give permission for any Synagogue to appoint a Rabbi. Rabbi Brodie cancelled Louis' licence to serve his congregation, and fired him from Jews' College. Fortunately Louis' community supported him and his right to intellectual freedom and formed a new Synagogue around him. Later, ironically, they bought Rabbi Brodie's own Synagogue.

Rabbi Jacobs joined the Conservative movement, and his Synagogue became the core of a small but vigorous Masorti movement in Britain. For nearly 40 years, Louis also taught in the Leo Baeck College, and continued to write. He became the outstanding Jewish scholar in Britain. His work is easily accessible to intelligent Jews everywhere because he writes clearly and puts philosophical and theological concepts in simple, though never simplistic, language of outstanding clarity.

But Louis taught, too, in the way he lived and the way he was. Totally observant and traditional in his own Jewish lifestyle, he was also warmly accepting of all Jews and the way that they expressed their own understanding of being Jewish, so long as they were honest and maintained their integrity. He preached in Reform Synagogues, while his own Synagogue was basically Orthodox. All ways of being Jewish were acceptable, he was a genuine pluralist. His scholarship was impeccably honest, and he was a warm and welcoming human being. We have lost a fine model of what a Rabbi should be, a true *mensch*.

A Vision for the Future *Vol. 17, No. 2 - Nov/Dec 2006*

An edited version of the Yom Kippur Afternoon Service.

Every member of our community, of whatever background, religious commitment or level of knowledge, has something to contribute to our community. Beneath all the disparate forms of Judaism in its long history and that it manifests today, there is a fundamental unity. That there are many Judaisms is I think true: that there is a basis for agreement despite that is also I think true. Some concepts underlie all forms of Judaism, and there are shared implications that flow from them. From this I want to suggest what a community that accepts both pluralism and also the possibility of fundamental unity would look like.

1. Jews are a people united by a Covenant with God, the terms of which are Torah. Jews understand themselves and their God through their historical experience. History is the stage on which God works out a plan for humankind, a drama in which Jews play a leading role.

2. Jews define religion as practicing justice, loving compassion, and walking humbly with God.

3. To avoid being trapped in the written text of the Hebrew Bible, Jews have created the idea of an oral tradition that dialogues continually with the written text, and enables it to speak to ongoing change. That oral text is the Rabbinic tradition of *Talmud* and *Responsa* and *Midrash*, which encompasses *halakhah*, law, *aggadah*, theology and ethics.

4. Living Torah includes all of human life. Noble ideals are fine, but it is the actual doing that counts. This includes living morally; having certain beliefs about the world as it is and as it could and should be; doing certain ritual acts that mark the passing of time and enfold continuing change into the eternal. In short, the discipline of living so as to fill life with infinite possibility, so as to the sensitize us to the other dimensions of reality.

5. Judaism demands study. Unless we know what we have to do we cannot do it.

These are the foundations of all and any form of Judaism.

Every one of us brings our own experience and insight to the way we understand Judaism. Especially important to us is — or should be — the contribution to our religious life of the arts and the sciences. We have to strive to integrate human experience into a whole that inspires and satisfies the heart, the mind and the conscience.

The autonomous freedom of the individual mind and conscience cannot be constrained by the group. Any community must be founded on compromise. Unless we willingly constrain our personal freedom, we cannot form community. And without community our personal freedom is ultimately meaningless. We need each other. So we function in two worlds: the private domain and the public domain. As *Midrash* reminds us: Everyone must have two pieces of paper in their pockets. On one is written: for my sake the world was created; on the other: I am but dust and ashes.

So, bearing this in mind, what do I see our Jewish community looking like?

The core will be worship on all Sabbaths and Festivals, and daily if possible, both in the Synagogue and in the home. Such worship should reflect both the old and the new, tradition and innovation, Hebrew and English. It should be open to the influence of the liturgical creativity and spiritual insights of all Judaisms, yet not trapped in any. There can be no compromise with gender equality: our prayer must reflect the spirituality of both men and women, for the good of both women and men.

The calendar of Sabbaths and Festivals will be maintained in its essentials. There is no reason to maintain the additional days observed historically in the Diaspora, and there may be debate about some of the lesser special occasions. Purim, for example — but the calendar should remain.

There are areas of Jewish thought and practice that are open to question in the light of modern scholarship. Fundamentalism is totally unacceptable, intellectually and morally. Such areas would include, for instance: the status of non-Jewish partners in the Synagogue; the definition of *kashrut* for a modern Jew concerned with ecology and the morality of our relations with other life forms, but also disturbed by the corruptions of *kashrut* among some Orthodox Jews; cremation — which has nothing whatever to do with burning a body; and many others.

Our communal decision-making must be in conformity with modern integrity and also with the integrity of Jewish sources. This entails the centrality in Synagogue life of education, which is primarily adult education, for, however well we educate our children, if they enter an adult community for whom Jewish sources are unknown, they will not be able to live their knowledge. Jewish knowledge without Jewish living is an absurdity. And the core of our educational program must be Hebrew, for without it, Judaism is a closed world. Hebrew is the entrance to Judaism. Basic literacy and the ability to tackle *Tanach*, *Siddur* and *Talmud*, is a sine qua non of being a Jew.

My vision is, of course, of our community as a religious community. We may, and probably should, struggle with religious ideas. Judaism is never closed but always growing and changing. But to replace Judaism as religious struggle with Judaism as secular culture makes no sense. A Synagogue must remain a Synagogue and not become a golf club for Jews. The willingness of Jews in history to accept martyrdom was a *kiddush HaShem*, for the sake of God, not to preserve gefilte fish recipes. We will struggle with what we can mean by the word "God," but it would be a negation of our history to abandon it. Without Judaism, the Jewish people would end their history not with a bang but with a whimper.

This, then, is a Rabbi's vision for our future.

THE JEWISH LIFE CYCLE - MARRIAGE

Based on comments made at a 25th anniversary celebration. Vol. 17, No. 3 - January/February 2007

Jewish tradition sees marriage as built into Creation. Immediately after creating Adam, God sees that it is not good that Adam should be alone, and goes on to create Eve as Adam's partner. The Hebrew term that is used is *ezer ke negdo*. Literally it means "a helper corresponding to him," and Rabbinic interpretation makes clear what it is taken to mean. *Ezer* is someone who helps; *negdo* means opposite to him, corresponding to him, completing him; and *ke* means like, as. The phrase therefore means "someone who is a helper who completes him." I interpret the Rabbinic interpretation as an empowering partner, without whom both are incomplete in their humanness. When I define marriage as a mutually empowering partnership of love, I am reading Torah correctly.

Of course we are human and often fall short of the ideal. But it is an ideal that we still cling to, flawed as we are in our humanity. We know that we are not intended to be alone; alone, we are incomplete. No one can exist without others; we are mutually interdependent. And this is especially so in the special relationship that is marriage. Partners who share their lives in mutually empowering love guaranteeing each other's personhood and identity, and give meaning to the struggles of life.

This is a romantic view of marriage, yet it is practical and realistic as well. Without loving and caring for others we are lonely, and life is nasty, brutish and short. The relationship of partners in marriage is, at its best, the closest we can know of the relationship of God the Creator to life, Her Creation.

When we fall in love and commit ourselves to someone, we begin the journey that is eternal. Over the years that we go through life together we discover a deeper dimension in each other: we discover ourselves, each other, what we are and what we continually are becoming together. We retain our own personality, but in the ongoing dialogue with our partner we change, as do they. The wonders of exploring and the delights of discovery enrich each of us and both of us. The times of adversity are softened; the times of joy are heightened. And we walk together through days and years of mutual growing. There are times for me, there are times for you, and there are times for us. There are times to be together and times to be alone; there is never loneliness.

And however many years we are granted together, they are too few in this journey of delight. There will come a time when we are called on to pay the price of togetherness, the price which is the pain of being separated. Not one of us would not willingly pay that price; for the journey is so wonderful, in good times and in bad. Grasp each moment, never take each other for granted, never let a day go by without saying "I love you," in word and in deed. And, however many the years, keep fresh the wonderful days of youth when everything was young and filled with the miracle of love. And at the very end still see each other with those eyes of youth, and rediscover each moment, the transforming revelation of falling in love with each other yet again.

When God created the world, we are told that God saw the Creation and it was good. And when Creation was fulfilled in Adam and Eve and God brought them together in the partnership of marriage, then God saw that it was very good. So it has been in every generation since, and so will it be to the end of time as partners say to each other *Hare mekudeshet/mekudash li*, "See, you have become very special to me, and my beloved is mine and I am my beloved's."

THE JEWISH LIFE CYCLE II - THOUGHTS ON DEATH
In memory of Mike and Abe. Vol. 17, No. 4 - March/April 2007

No human being can avoid death. All of us have experienced the death of someone we have loved. We have wept and mourned that death and the loss of human companionship and love that it meant for us. Truly no man is an island: all human pain and suffering is our pain and suffering.

When we meet death, we find some measure of comfort in five ways in which we interact with each other.

We are supported by family and friends. They, too, have known death, and remember how much they needed the support of others. And so they reach out to us with gestures of love and sympathy in our despair, for they, too, have been there. Our pain is lessened by their hands and their tears.

We find support, too, in our community. In the Jewish community we find our identity; we are rooted in a past that reaches into a future. We are embedded in generations who have mourned death and found ways to transcend their grief, ways that they hand on to us as we, too, pass through the shadow of death. They comfort us by their presence. They support us in so many practical ways.

And the tradition that speaks through the generation of shared faith and destiny of a folk, also speaks to us. Customs that guide us through mourning, ways of doing things that work because they have been tested through centuries, guide us through our own times of sorrow. It teaches us how to mourn so that we can come to healing, through the depths of despair to the beginnings of new hope. And it teaches us to face whatever we have to go through with courage. For it tells us that life is good, despite all that seems to deny that good and work against it. It tells us that life and love triumph over death. It tells us that at the end it is love that survives despite pain and sorrow.

We look also to memory. The ability to remember is what makes us human. And memory defeats death. It is not what we do that is important, it is what we are. We share love with each other. We create together a life that is filled with beauty, caring for each other, building together experiences that create memories that can never be lost. Nothing can ever take away those memories that we create: of friendship, of falling in love, of creating and moulding together the new life of children, of laughter and tears in good years and bad, of growing old together, of bring to fruition the promises and dreams of youth.

And we know, too, that human life, brief though it is, has infinite potential. Each of us in our lifetime is a spark cast into the infinity of time and space. Like a pebble in a pool, the ripples never end, and voices we have known whisper to us forever. What a wonderful thing is life! It is given to us to make what we can: and whatever we are able to do is miraculous. It abides for all time, even when we are physically gone.

When death strikes one we love, we mourn. Tears are the tribute we pay for the privilege of sharing the wonders of this life with someone else, and discovering with them the mystery and beauty of love. It is too soon gone and we must grieve what we have lost.

Yet we had those moments. And for that we must be grateful. We must celebrate what we had, whether we had it for many years or few.

Now we grieve but we shall come to celebrate. Tears will give way to smiles as we remember the joy of life shared as well as the pain that must also bring. We must accept the gift of life in its entirety, both tragedy and triumph. But we are willing to pay the price for living and loving which is the ultimate loss in death, because the living is so wonderful it makes the pain bearable.

As the Psalmist says, Even when I walk through the valley of the shadow of death I fear no ill, because You are with me. Yes, we have to walk through the shadow and it is deeply dark; yet we do walk through. Now there is the stark absence of the presence of one we have loved so much, and that is a wound that will never be healed. But there is also at the end the presence of memory held in love. And that is a blessing that nothing can ever take from us.

THE WANDERING JEWS - OUR BIG FAT
28,000 KM CRUISE. *Vol. 17, No. 6 - July/August 2007*

We have been on cruises before, and thoroughly enjoyed ourselves. But this was something a little different: a long, long, Mediterranean/North Africa cruise, 56 days long, visiting 31 ports and inevitably producing thought and reflection that transcends a mere holiday.

We started from Fort Lauderdale, Florida, and headed to the West Indies (St. Barts, Dominica and Barbados). From there we crossed the Atlantic to Cape Verde. Once arrived in African waters, we called in at Gambia and Senegal (where Patricia bought a djembe drum that she is anxious to play); sailed north to the Canary Islands and

Madeira (where the wine comes from, m'dear?); back to the African coast of Morocco ("I came to Casablanca for the waters!" — it rained!); Cadiz, Spain and through the Strait of Gibraltar, where we had a visit with the Barbary Apes; into the Mediterranean. We then went along the north of the Mediterranean, calling at Barcelona, Marseilles and Monaco, to Italy. Sailing down the west coast of Italy, we passed Sicily (with wonderful views of two active volcanos, Stromboli and Etna) to Dubrovnik in Croatia. Then came Corfu and Greece, including beautiful Santorini where, a few days before, the cruise ship *Sea Diamond* had sunk with the loss of two lives. On to Turkey and back to Athens. Patricia had to pinch herself to make sure she wasn't dreaming she was on the Acropolis. Then we sailed back along the southern coasts of the Mediterranean, calling at Malta, Tunis and Ceuta (a small Spanish enclave in Morocco), and so back past Gibraltar. Then, calling at the Azores islands on the way to Bermuda and New York and back to Fort Lauderdale.

We tried to make contact with Jewish communities during the trip, but we were constrained by the ship's schedule and the fact that the shore excursions arranged by the ship were not directed to Jewish interests. We did manage to visit the Synagogue in Livorno in northern Italy and persuade the caretaker to open the building and let us see a really beautiful modern Synagogue replacing the 17th century building destroyed in the War; much of the contents, however, including a wonderfully decorated wooden Ark, were taken from the 17th century Synagogue. And in the old walled town in Dubrovnik (a world heritage site) we found the Medieval Synagogue in a little alleyway. Unfortunately, we got there outside the hours when the community had the Synagogue open, and found only a little locked door. We had to be content with a photograph of a postcard showing the interior. The Synagogue in Ceuta was being repaired, and our bus passed the Great Synagogue in Casablanca at great speed along the main road. Likewise, our bus in New York turned into Central Park just as we reached Temple Emanuel, the world's largest Synagogue.

On board the ship there was a Cantor from New York who led *Shabbat* evening Services and a *Seder* for *Pesah*. A member of the ship's orchestra was Jewish and he played saxophone at the *seder*. The ship also provided *matsot* throughout *Pesah* and wonderful *kiddushim* for *Shabbat*. On cruises that include the times of Jewish Festivals, the Cruise Lines ensure the presence of a Rabbi or Cantor, on other cruises it is up to knowledgeable passengers to lead Services. So if you take a cruise, do support all the Jewish activities that are available, and if they are not, try to help ensure their provision yourself. The Cantor had a good voice (he was given an "encore" at the talent show), but was direly lacking in liturgical know-how. To misquote Dr. Johnson, It was not so important that it was done badly but that it was done at all!

Look for a presentation, probably to the senior's group, in the fall!

Reflections About the Future
of Our Community Vol. 18, No. 1 - September/October 2007

As I leave the pulpit of Agudas Israel and retire to the back benches as an ordinary member, I want to look forward and share with you some thoughts about the future of our community.

1. I wish all the best to Cantor Schwartz and hope that all our members will make every effort to get to know him and support him in his work for the congregation. He will need all our help in working together to ensure our healthy survival into the future. Above all, I urge our members to be aware always that the path of the religious leader is often a lonely one, and even the clergy who give guidance and support to members in their times of need, also need tender loving care if they are to be able to function at their best: even the clergy are human!

2. Our community has declined in numbers and we are demanding more from an ever-smaller pool of resources. Leadership is becoming older and in danger of burn-out. We need to have very clear priorities and to concentrate on what is essential, aware that, unfortunately, some of our programming may have to be sacrificed to ensure the continued viability of our core programs.

3. That non-negotiable core must be the *Shabbat* and Festival Services and religious education, for both children and adults. Everything else is negotiable. We are a Synagogue, a religious congregation, not a Jewish social club: we exist to maintain Judaism!

4. The time may have come when we may have to consider coming together once again in a Kallah to examine carefully that religious future. My long-term questioning of our affiliation with the United Synagogue is not a personal whim; it is carefully thought about in terms of our specific community and its needs. All sorts of factors have to be considered very seriously and as part of our planning for long-term survival as a Synagogue. We can no longer duck the issue and hope that benign neglect will see us through; an English attachment to muddling through somehow, a Micawberish hope that something will turn up, just will not do.

5. In our serious thought, all options should be available to us. To be honest, if Agudas Israel were a brand new community of Jews looking to organize itself and place itself in the North American Jewish scene, I would suggest that the option of affiliating with the Reconstructionist movement is well worth considering!

6. Commitment to Judaism derives from study and knowledge of Jewish sources related to specific experience. It must be a matter of total integrity: we cannot and must not say we are something which involves us in responsibility for subsequent action that we have no intention of taking. We must say and do what

Rabbi Pavey ✡ 201

we really are and really believe we ought to say and do. Honesty is all: hypocrisy is the unacceptable face of religion. Let us not play for the supposed sake of the children, and be pre-modern Jews in the Synagogue and fully modern humanists in our daily lives.

7. Every aspect of Judaism must be part of our Synagogue. By that I mean that those of our members who want to be Jews find a real Jewish home, whether they are "secular" or religious, want to daven, want to experiment with ritual life, want to study, want to engage in social action, or want to explore their connection with Israel (hopefully, they will be all these!) There are many ways to be Jewish. To impose only one-size-fits-all derived from *halakhah* excludes most Jews today.

8. Over my 40 years as a Rabbi I have gained a great deal of experience and knowledge, and, more important, thought about that experience and knowledge, both academically and practically. And I have come to the realization that time is not on our side and do-nothing policies so as not to rock the boat are a sure recipe for disaster. I would urge that the need for serious thought and discussion and hard decision-making is now upon us and cannot be postponed much longer. We may need to slay a few sacred cows! The Jewish community is in serious decline everywhere, Judaism is in serious danger of becoming an irrelevance. We must act. *V'im lo achshav eimatai*? If not now, when?

Congregation Agudas Israel Mourns Rabbi Roger Pavey May 5, 1939-October 21, 2009 Eulogy by Heather Fenyes

Vol. 20, No. 2 - November/December 2009

Roger, you were a gentle man. In a world that models the successful male as tough and aggressive, you showed your true strength with quiet determination and gentle persistence.

Your passion for Judaism and this community was remarkable. You were ordained as a Reform Rabbi, but never let that stop you from leading a Conservative community. You welcomed and encouraged debate and always abided by the rules of the Rabbinical Assembly. I know there were things you wished were different, but for the sake of *Shalom bayit*, peace in the family, you always acquiesced, and then went on to lead with intention and meaning.

You encouraged your congregants to always grow and learn. Your quiet leadership loudly empowered us to lead — and therefore choose our own destiny. I believe you did this by design.

You made a huge impression on the community outside Congregation Agudas Israel. You created relationships with other religious leaders that brought dialogue, mutual respect and understanding to people in the three major religions in our city — Christianity, Judaism and Islam. The relationships that you created will endure for years to come. You asked for moderation, tolerance and open-mindedness, and gave it unconditionally in return.

You had no patience for racism or intolerance. You always saw the best in people. You rarely criticized, even when we made mistakes. I remember years ago feeling nervous when I led a service that you attended. I made mistakes and later, full of guilt, I apologized to you. I still remember you said, "Heather, I would never judge you for your mistakes, I'm proud of your accomplishments." You always made me feel more learned and knowledgeable than I know I am.

Just before *Rosh Hashannah*, I visited you in the hospital to read you the speech I was giving to the community. Your eyes welled up and you told me, "I wish I had written that." I can't imagine greater praise.

That you were brilliant was obvious. But you balanced this need for intellectual pursuit with an equally large belief in our collective responsibility for *tikkun olam* — repairing our world. Your need for social justice, and simple goodness outshone your extraordinary mind.

Roger, you loved this community. A few days ago, I sat with you and Patricia as a young student nurse asked you to participate in a questionnaire. She asked, "What gives you strength" and you answered, "My wife, my boys and my community." You told her that the gifts of friendship, song, prayer and food that you have been given during your stay in the hospital were beyond your imagination, and comforting beyond your expectations.

Roger, you were blessed to love and be loved by two remarkable women. Your first wife was Miriam. Together you had two sons, Daniel and Jonathan. After Miriam's tragic death, you met and fell in love with Patricia. The two of you were married in 1991. Your love for Miriam never diminished, nor shadowed the extraordinary relationship you had with Patricia. Just last Sunday you reminded me of your wish to order ten new Reform *siddurim* — five in Miriam's memory, and five in Patricia's honour. Over these past months of difficult times, I have been privileged to watch you and Patricia interact. You fit together perfectly. Your deep friendship, love and profound mutual respect were a palpable force in the room. The thing we talked about most in our visits over these past weeks was your great love for Patricia. You were focused on renewing your marriage vows before your family, and community. I know Patricia feels empty from the huge piece of her life and heart that you fill. But I also know that the kind of relationship you shared is dimensionless and will accompany Patricia the rest of her days.

When you first came to Saskatoon, I was one of your Shabbat singers. You encouraged some of us to help because singing was never your greater calling. I'm certainly not a singer, but you always made me feel like my voice enhanced services when in fact, it was your *kavannah* that compelled us to prayer, and G-d.

When you moved here 21 years ago, my Mom became one of your first friends. Twenty years later, I too have lost a dear friend.

Your congregation will always bear the mark of your leadership, your spirit and your goodness, and we, your friends, will carry your memory with us forever.

My Roger by Patricia Pavey

Vol. 20, No. 3 - January/February 2010

I don't know how I'd have got through the past few months had it not been for members of Congregation Agudas Israel. You cared for both Roger and me through his illness and have been there for me since his death. In hospital, the visits and e-mails showed him how much he was respected and loved in the community. He was very touched and humbled by these and the special Rosh Hoshanah service put on in the multi-faith room at RUH.

Roger Pavey was a quiet man. He didn't care for "small talk" and this made him a bit difficult to get to know. Ask him about politics, cricket, Judaism or other religions, though, and you'd have his company for hours. His mind was encyclopaedic.

He was only too pleased to help put this crazy world right. His was a mission of *Tikkun Olam*. He was passionate about human rights, gender equality, education and equal health care for all. He was honest to a fault.

Roger was fond of cats and teddy bears! And I'll bet not many of you knew that your Rabbi liked to cook! He was most creative. Where else have you seen a pizza piled high with broccoli and baked beans?

I first met Roger when I served on a multi-faith committee which was struck to look at racism in Saskatoon. We found we had similar backgrounds, both having grown up in working-class families in the West Midlands of England. Over the years, through diverse paths, we both grew away from our childhood homes, took higher education and ended up in — of all places — Saskatoon!

The rest, as they say, is history.

I have recently begun sorting through his book collection. Roger's organizational methods left much to be desired by a librarian like me, and I have found several sermons, lectures and talks folded up and used as bookmarks. I am collecting them and perhaps will get them printed some time in the future. The man I loved so much lives on in his words!

"May the beauty of his life shine for ever and may my life bring honour to his memory."*

*(From Forms of Prayer, Movement for Reform Judaism's 2008 prayer book)

CPSIA information can be obtained at www.ICGtesting.com
Printed in the USA
LVOW04s2257180115

423369LV00002B/6/P